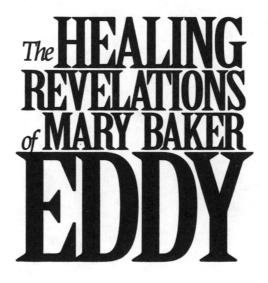

The HEALING
REVELATIONS
of MARY BAKER
EDDY

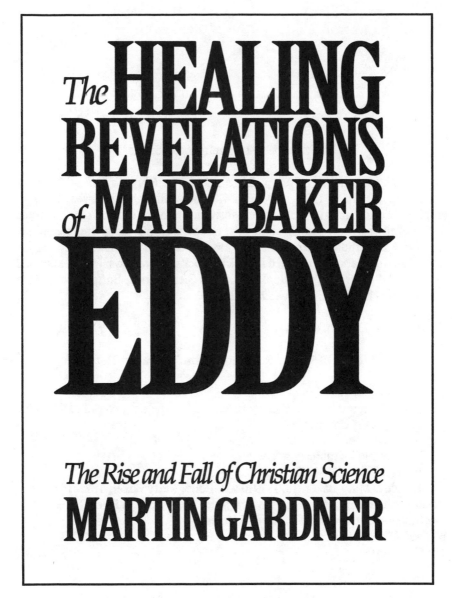

The HEALING
REVELATIONS
of MARY BAKER
EDDY

The Rise and Fall of Christian Science
MARTIN GARDNER

Prometheus Books • Buffalo, New York

Published 1993 by Prometheus Books

97 96 95 94 93   5 4 3 2 1

Library of Congress Cataloging-in-Publication Data

Gardner, Martin, 1914–
    The healing revelations of Mary Baker Eddy : the rise and fall of Christian Science / Martin Gardner.
        p.   cm.
    Includes bibliographical references.
    ISBN 0-87975-838-4 (alk. paper)
    1. Eddy, Mary Baker, 1821–1910. 2. Eddy, Mary Baker, 1821–1910. Science and health, with key to the Scriptures. 3. Christian Science—Doctrines—Controversial literature. I. Title.
BX6955.G29   1993
289.5′2—dc20   93-25142
                                                                              CIP

Printed in the United States of America on acid-free paper.

It is related that a father plunged his infant babe, only a few hours old, into the water for several minutes, and repeated this operation daily, until the child could remain under water twenty minutes, moving and playing without harm, like a fish. Parents should remember this, and learn how to develop their children properly on dry land.

—*Science and Health with Key to the Scriptures*, pp. 556–57

If mathematics should present a thousand different examples of one rule, the proving of one example would authenticate all the others. A simple statement of Christian Science, if demonstrated by healing, contains the proof of all here said of Christian Science. If one of the statements in this book is true, every one must be true, for not one departs from the stated system and rule. You can prove for yourself, dear reader, the Science of healing, and so ascertain if the author has given you the correct interpretation of Scripture.

—Ibid., pp. 546–47

Contents

7

8   THE HEALING REVELATIONS OF MARY BAKER EDDY

Introduction

That I should write an entire book about Mary Baker Eddy and her "discovery," as she liked to say of Christian Science, surprised even me. Here's how it came about.

From an antiques shop several years ago I acquired a book defending New Thought by the once-renowned poet Ella Wheeler Wilcox. I knew nothing about Ella, not even what she looked like, but her connection with the New Thought movement intrigued me. I started researching her life and was amazed to learn that she ended her career as a passionate believer in spiritualism and reincarnation. I was also astonished by the extent to which today's New Age fantasies were so thoroughly aired a hundred years ago by New Thought leaders, and by the many ways in which Shirley MacLaine resembles Ella: talented, attractive, and enormously gullible. Miss MacLaine's trance channelers have missed a great opportunity—persuading Shirley that she's a reincarnation of Mrs. Wilcox.

My research on Ella, which resulted in this book's final chapter, led me to Phineas Quimby, the whimsical "father" of both New Thought and Christian Science. I intended to write only one essay about Mrs. Eddy and her church, but after reading for the first time *Science and Health* and other writings by Mrs. Eddy, and some two dozen books about her and the history of Christian Science, my single chapter grew to several, and finally expanded into this book. It was not easy to stop writing!

Having myself been a Protestant fundamentalist for a brief period of youthful ignorance and confusion, I know what it's like to be a true believer. I have never ceased to be fascinated by the ease with which strong, charismatic personalities—Moses, Jesus, Saint Paul, Mohammed, Joseph Smith, Ellen White, Mary Baker Eddy—can fabricate a set of beliefs that seem outrageous to outsiders, yet will win the allegiance of millions.

Although converts are occasionally drawn into a cult by reading a book, it seldom happens that believers will abandon a cult because of anything they see in print. Indeed, vigorous attacks on a set of closed, self-sealing convictions often have the opposite effect. In his autobiography Benjamin Franklin attributes his conversion to what then was called deism to reading a book lambasting deism. I have no illusions about this volume altering the opinions of a single Christian Scientist. At most it may in some small way discourage new converts and help prod the church into moving a bit faster away from its extreme opposition to drugs and medical science. No one, John Dewey once wrote, ever gives up a religion because of arguments. They have to outgrow it.

In a curious way, I must confess, I admire true believers more than I do lukewarm or even unbelieving persons who remain loyal to a church out of force of habit, or to preserve social or political status. I dislike hypocrisy almost as much as did Jesus. You may recall that he once called the religious leaders of his day hypocrites who resembled whited sepulchers, white and clean on the outside, but with decaying corpses within. He was even down on public prayer. When you pray, he said, shut yourself up in a closet where only God can hear you.

Is it not incredible that Paul Tillich who believed neither in a personal God nor an afterlife (the two doctrines nearest the heart of Christianity) could become one of the world's most respected Protestant theologians? I am amazed and amused by the fancy footwork of Hans Kung and other Catholic thinkers, who long ago abandoned all distinctively Catholic dogmas for views indistinguishable from liberal Protestantism, to stay within their church.

I am equally astonished by the skill with which such "feel good" ministers as Norman Vincent Peale and Robert Schuller can hold the admiration of multitudes by preaching a vague, nondoctrinal Christianity without letting anyone know exactly what they believe about such doctrines as, say, the Virgin Birth or the bodily resurrection of Jesus. I prefer being entertained by Billy Graham or Jimmy Swaggart to being bored by the sermons of ultra liberals who carefully conceal their private beliefs. My religious novel, *The Flight of Peter Fromm,* is essentially a blast at this kind of hypocrisy.

And so it is that I have a sneaking admiration for successful cult leaders and their devoted followers. The leaders may be half-crazy and their doctrines unadulterated balderdash, but at least they have the courage to believe and proclaim, with all their heart and mind, the doctrines of their faith. Mary Baker Eddy never doubted for a moment that God had called upon her to restore a Christianity she believed had been forgotten for almost two thousand years—a faith destined to dominate the world. This obviously will not happen. The church is now in serious decline. Will my attack accelerate this tumble?

It will not. In spite of dwindling wealth and membership—most Christian Science congregations now consist mainly of elderly women—the true believers, with their confident smiles and radiations of cheer, will surely be with us for another century or more. Like old soldiers, religious movements may slowly fade, but they seldom expire. Even Zoroastrianism is alive and kicking in India and Iran. I wouldn't be surprised to learn that hidden away somewhere in Greece or Italy a small, secret band of pagans are still making blood sacrifices to Zeus.

Martin Gardner

1

Childhood, Marriages, and Spiritualism

Mary Baker Eddy (1821–1910) was born on a farm in Bow, New Hampshire, a few miles south of Concord. The house burned down in 1910, the year Mrs. Eddy died, and the site is now a vacant field.

James F. Lord, a Boston Christian Scientist who bought the old farm, decided that the site needed a permanent memorial. In 1918 he bought from the New England Granite Works, of Concord, the largest hunk of granite ever quarried in New England. A flat car carried it to a crossing, then a specially designed truck took it over dirt roads to the site of Mrs. Eddy's homestead. There it was mounted on a concrete slab and carved into an exact replica of the Great Pyramid of Egypt.

The pyramid's square base was eleven feet on the side. It stood about eight feet high and weighed forty tons. The four sloping sides faced directly north, south, east, and west to symbolize the universality of Christian Science, and its apex pointed upward to God.

Mrs. Eddy herself, in *Christian Healing,* had likened Christian Science to the Great Pyramid:

The only immortal superstructure is built on Truth; her modest tower rises slowly, but it stands and is the miracle of the hour, though it may seem to the age like the great pyramid of Egypt—a miracle in stone. (p. 11)

Each face of the granite monument bore a bronze tablet. On the south side the tablet read: "Mary Baker Eddy, discoverer of Christian Science." This was followed, in Mrs. Eddy's handwriting, by a quotation from a letter to her cousin Rufus Baker: ". . . This Baker homestead. Around the memory thereof clusters the golden days of my childhood. Mary Baker Eddy."

The tablet on the east side carried a quotation from Isaiah 28:16:

Therefore thus saith the Lord God, Behold, I lay in Zion for a foundation a stone, a tried stone, a precious corner stone, a sure foundation: he that believeth shall not make haste.

On the pyramid's north face the tablet quoted from Mrs. Eddy's book *No and Yes* (p. 38):

This truth is the rock which the builders rejected, but "the same is become the head of the corner." This is the chief corner-stone, the basis and support of creation, the interpreter of one God, the infinity and unity of good.

The west tablet bore the Latin motto that appears beneath the pyramid on the green side of our dollar bill: Novus Ordo Seclorum (The New Order of the Ages).

Mr. Lord gave the farm to Mother Church in 1927. In 1962 a strange thing happened: the pyramid was blasted to smithereens by a charge of dynamite. I have not been able to learn who destroyed it or why. Rick Broussard, a newspaper man in Concord who supplied me with valuable clippings and a postcard photograph of the pyramid, tells me that the explosion was heard for miles. A local farmer, who liked to sit on the pyramid while grazing his cows, kept a chunk of the monument to place in the rock border of his flower bed. I would be pleased to hear from anyone who can shed light on who ordered the monument's obliteration, or who can tell me what happened to its bronze plates.

Mary's parents were devout Congregationalists. Her father, a quarrelsome man with a quick temper, held stern Calvinist views about hell and predestination. As a child Mary was frail and nervous. As an adult she was shorter than medium height and so thin that she seldom weighed more than a hundred pounds. She had reddish-brown hair and large, deep-set gray-blue eyes so dark that in later years they were often described as black.

It has been speculated that her constant quarrels with her father, who feared her damnation because she would not go along with his fundamentalist doctrines, contributed to what were called her constant "fits." Neighbors considered them temper tantrums designed to get her way. A family doctor described them as "hysteria mixed with bad temper." The attacks were far from mild. Mary would scream and writhe on the floor, and at times go into a cataleptic state that would last for hours. Rocking her in a cradle seemed to pacify her, and sometimes she would be given a shot of morphine.

The "fits" persisted throughout Mary's adult life, though with less frequency. Sibyl Wilbur, in *The Life of Mary Baker Eddy* (1907), the first church-authorized biography, tells of one such occasion when Mrs. Eddy was thirty-five. An eyewitness gave this account:

> She was all alone in her home and I heard her bell ringing. I went in and found her lying rigid with foam on her lips. I brought her around with cold water. She motioned to her medicine chest, and

I gave her what she wanted. Then I sat with her till she got better. (pp. 59–60)

There are many reports of young Mary's psychic powers. She cured the ills of friends. Her hand on a brother's leg wound caused it to heal rapidly. In games of hide-the-thimble she always went directly to the thimble. She claimed she could give orders to her dog Ben merely by thinking, and the dog would obey. Among neighbors her clairvoyant powers were legendary. She was often asked to locate lost or stolen objects. She tried, but failed, to find the body of a drowned boy. She "saw" a spot near Lynn, Massachusetts, where she said Captain Kidd had buried a treasure. Efforts were made to dig for it, but no treasure was found. It was said that she once caused a hungry zoo lion to stop roaring and lie down so peacefully that Mary reached into the cage and patted its head. Her most peculiar physiological trait was a total lack of a sense of smell. It explained why throughout her life she never used perfume.

As a child Mary heard voices. In her autobiography *Retrospection and Introspection,* in the chapter titled "Voices Not Our Own," she tells of one such episode:

Many peculiar circumstances and events connected with my childhood throng the chambers of memory.

For some twelve months, when I was about eight years old, I repeatedly heard a voice, calling me distinctly by name, three times, in an ascending scale. I thought this was my mother's voice, and sometimes went to her, beseeching her to tell me what she wanted. Her answer was always: "Nothing, child! What do you mean?" Then I would say: "Mother, who *did* call me? I heard somebody call *Mary,* three times!" This continued until I grew discouraged, and my mother was perplexed and anxious.

One day, when my cousin, Mehitable Huntoon, was visiting us, and I sat in a little chair by her side, in the same room with grandmother,—the call again came, so loud that Mehitable heard it, though I had ceased to notice it. Greatly surprised, my cousin turned to me and said, "Your mother is calling you!" but I answered not, till again the same call was thrice repeated. Mehitable then said sharply, "Why don't you go? your mother is calling you!" I then left the room, went to my mother, and once more asked her if she had summoned me? She answered as always before. Then I earnestly declared my cousin had heard the voice, and said that mother wanted me. Accordingly she returned with me to grandmother's room, and led my cousin into an adjoining apartment. The door was ajar, and I listened with bated breath. Mother told Mehitable all about this mysterious voice, and asked if she really did hear Mary's name pronounced in audible tones. My cousin answered quickly, and emphasized her affirmation.

That night, before going to rest, my mother read to me the Scriptural narrative of little Samuel, and bade me, when the voice called again, to reply as he did, "Speak, Lord; for thy servant heareth." The voice came; but I was afraid, and did not answer. Afterward I wept and prayed that God would forgive me, resolving to do, next time, as my mother had bidden me. When the call came again I did answer, in the words of Samuel, but never again to the material senses was that mysterious call audibly repeated. (pp. 16–18)

Adam Dickey, in *Memoirs of Mary Baker Eddy* (we shall have more to say about this suppressed book in a later chapter), recalls Mrs. Eddy telling him something about this incident she said she had never before revealed. After she had answered the "voice" in the words of Samuel, "Speak, Lord, for thy servant heareth," she said to Dickey:

. . . in a voice filled with awe, that when she made the reply a most unusual phenomenon took place. Her body was lifted entirely from the bed on which she lay, to a height it seemed to her, of about one foot. Then it was laid gently back on the bed. This was repeated three times. As a child she was afraid to tell the circumstances to anybody, but she pondered it deeply in her heart and thought of it many years afterward when she was demonstrating the nothingness of matter and that the claim of the human body was a myth. (Springer, p. 23)

Did Mrs. Eddy in her old age actually remember it this way? Or did she lie to Dickey, then her personal secretary, to bolster her image as some sort of saint? She must have known that the Catholic church had declared many a person a saint on the basis of miraculous levitations. Thomas Aquinas, for example, a heavy man, was believed to have once been levitated while praying.

Too nervous to attend grade school, Mary was taught at home by her parents and siblings. Here is how she described her early studies in her autobiography:

My father was taught that my brain was too large for my body and so kept me much out of school, but I gained book-knowledge with far less labor than is usually requisite. At ten years of age I was as familiar with Lindley Murray's Grammar as I was with the Westminster Catechism; and the latter I had to repeat every Sunday. My favorite studies were Natural Philosophy, Logic, and Moral Science. To my brother Albert I was indebted for lessons in the ancient tongues, Hebrew, Greek, and Latin. My brother studied Hebrew during his college vacations. After my discovery of Christian Science, most of the knowledge I had gleaned from schoolbooks vanished like a dream. (p. 19)

In 1843, at age twenty-two, Mary married George Washington Glover of Charleston, South Carolina. Fifteen years her senior, he was a former mason who had become a wealthy building contractor. His service in the militia earned him the honorary title of "Major." In her autobiography, Mrs. Eddy apologized for having once mistakenly referred to him as a colonel. Mary was so ill on their wedding day that "Wash," as she called him, had to carry her down a stairway for the ceremony, then afterwards carry her back up again. Six months after the marriage, Wash died of yellow fever.

Mary's only child, named George Glover after his father, was born a few months after the father's death. Her curious relationship with the boy was strained from the start, and seldom cordial in later years. Most historians agree that Mary, showing little affection for the child, willingly gave him to Mahala Sanborn, a family nurse who later married but kept the boy. Years later in her autobiography, Mrs. Eddy claimed that the boy had been taken from her. Here is her totally untrustworthy account:

> A few months before my father's second marriage to Mrs. Elizabeth Patterson Duncan, sister of Lieutenant Governor George W. Patterson, of New York—my little son, about four years of age, was sent away from me, and put under the care of our family nurse, who had married, and resided in the northern part of New Hampshire. I had no training for self-support, and my health was regarded as precarious. The night before my child was taken from me, I knelt by his side throughout the dark hours, hoping for a vision of relief from this trial. The following lines are taken from my poem, "Mother's Darling," written after this separation:
>
> > Thy smile through tears, as sunshine o'er the sea,
> >   Awoke new beauty in the surge's roll!
> > Oh, life is dead, bereft of all, with thee,—
> >   Star of my earthly hope, babe of my soul.
>
> The family to whose care my son was committed very soon removed to what was then regarded as the Far West, thus depriving me of the opportunity of having my son classically educated.
>   . . . My dominant thought in marrying again was to get back my child. The disappointment which followed was terrible. His step-father was envious; and although George was a tender-hearted and manly boy, he hated him as much as I loved him. A plot was consummated for keeping my son and myself apart; and after his

removal to the West, I never saw him again until he had reached
the age of thirty-four and came to visit me in Boston. (pp. 26–27)

Charles Braden, in *Christian Science Today* (1958), summed it up
ironically: "She who became 'Mother' to thousands was never really
mother to her own child."

In 1853 Mary married Daniel Patterson, a tall, handsome, black-
bearded dentist who practiced homeopathy on the side. At that time
homeopathy was the nation's most fashionable alternative medicine. Mary
was fascinated by it because it openly implied a mysterious spiritual
foundation. It relied entirely on drugs obtained by taking a natural
substance and diluting it until the dosage often contained nothing
whatever of the original substance. The more "attenuated" the dose,
the greater was believed to be its potency. Clearly, any healing power
of a nonexistent substance must come from a spiritual force unknown
to science. At that time orthodox medicine, or "allopathy" as the homeopaths called it, was in such a primitive state that many of its drugs
were actually harmful. Because a homeopathic dose obviously could
do no harm, the placebo effect took over, cures abounded, and homeopathy flourished.

For the rest of her life Mary constantly relied on homeopathic
doctors, and often alluded to homeopathy in her writings. There was
a period as a young woman during which she gave homeopathic remedies
to patients. Here, for instance, is a passage from chapter 6 of *Science
and Health:*

A case of dropsy, given up by the faculty, fell into my hands. It was
a terrible case. Tapping had been employed, and yet, as she lay in
her bed, the patient looked like a barrel. I prescribed the fourth
attenuation of *Argentum nitratum* with occasional doses of a high
attenuation of *Sulphuris*. She improved perceptibly. Believing then
somewhat in the ordinary theories of medical practice, and learning

that her former physician had prescribed these remedies, I began to fear an aggravation of symptoms from their prolonged use, and told the patient so; but she was unwilling to give up the medicine while she was recovering. It then occurred to me to give her unmedicated pellets and watch the result. I did so, and she continued to gain. Finally she said that she would give up her medicine for one day, and risk the effects. After trying this, she informed me that she could get along two days without globules; but on the third day she again suffered, and was relieved by taking them. She went on in this way, taking the unmedicated pellets—and receiving occasional visits from me—but employing no other means, and she was cured. (p. 156)

In her book *Christian Healing* (a printing of a sermon) Mrs. Eddy again recalls how she cured a woman of dropsy by giving her placebos:

The pharmacy of homeopathy is reducing the one hundredth part of a grain of medicine two thousand times, shaking the preparation thirty times at every attenuation. There is a moral to this medicine; the higher natures are reached soonest by the higher attenuations, until the fact is found out they have taken no medicine, and then the so-called drug loses its power. We have attenuated a grain of aconite until it was no longer aconite, then dropped into a tumblerful of water a single drop of this harmless solution, and administering one tea-spoonful of this water at intervals of half an hour have cured the incipient stage of fever. The highest attenuation we ever attained was to leave the drug out of the question, using only the sugar of milk; and with this original dose we cured an inveterate case of dropsy. After these experiments you cannot be surprised that we resigned the imaginary medicine altogether, and honestly employed Mind as the only curative Principle. (p. 13)

Mrs. Eddy's point is clear. It is belief in drugs, not the drugs themselves, that allows one's mind, a part of God, to heal. In later years Mrs. Eddy completely stopped giving homeopathic remedies to

patients, though she always regarded homeopathy as superior to allopathy, and when she sought medical advice, preferred homeopaths to
allopaths. She was also fond of referring to common substances by
their homeopathic names. "I use no drugs whatever," she once wrote
in the *Christian Science Journal,* "not even cofea (coffee), thea (tea),
capsicum (red pepper); although every day, and especially at dinner,
I indulge in homeopathic doses of natrium muriaticum (common salt)."
(The parentheses are hers.)

The passage quoted above in *Science and Health* about the woman
with dropsy is followed by these paragraphs:

> Metaphysics, as taught in Christian Science, is the next stately step
> beyond homeopathy. In metaphysics, matter disappears from the
> remedy entirely, and Mind takes its rightful and supreme place.
> Homeopathy takes mental symptoms largely into consideration in its
> diagnosis of disease. Christian Science deals wholly with the mental
> cause in judging and destroying disease. It succeeds where homeopathy
> fails, solely because its one recognized Principle of healing is Mind,
> and the whole force of the mental element is employed through the
> Science of Mind, which never shares its rights with inanimate matter.
>
> Christian Science exterminates the drug, and rests on Mind alone
> as the curative Principle, acknowledging that the divine Mind has all
> power. Homeopathy mentalizes a drug with such repetition of thought-
> attenuations, that the drug becomes more like the human mind than
> the substratum of this so-called mind, which we call matter; and the
> drug's power of action is proportionately increased. (pp. 156–57)

Similar remarks occur elsewhere in *Science and Health.* Here is
a passage from chapter 12:

> Homeopathy furnishes the evidence to the senses, that symptoms, which
> might be produced by a certain drug, are removed by using the same
> drug which might cause the symptoms. This confirms my theory that

faith in the drug is the sole factor in the cure. The effect, which mortal mind produoeo through one belief, it removes through an opposite belief, but it uses the same medicine in both cases. (p. 370)

In the years 1866 to 1870, though you won't learn much about them in authorized biographies of Mrs. Eddy, she dabbled in spiritualism. During these years she was very poor, wandering from one boarding house to another, most of the houses run by spiritualists. Christian Science historians like to compare this period with the years that Jesus spent in the wilderness. It is a poor comparison because there is no record that Jesus, while in the wilderness, channeled voices from the dead.

That Mrs. Eddy both believed in spiritualism and practiced mediumship there is no longer the slightest doubt. During her séances rappings occurred, and spirits of the departed came and went. While in trance, Mrs. Eddy's voice would change to the voice of the person behind the veil. Mrs. Richard Hazeltine, a spiritualist who lived in Lynn, signed an affidavit in which she described one of Mrs. Eddy's séances in 1866:

My husband, Richard Hazeltine, and I went to the circle at Mrs. Clark's and saw Mrs. Glover pass into the trance state, and heard her communicate by word of mouth messages received from the spirit world, or what she said and we believed were messages from the spirit world. I cannot forget certain peculiar features of these sittings of Mrs. Glover's. Mrs. Glover told us, as we were gathered there, that, because of her superior spiritual quality, and because of the purity of her life, she could only be controlled in the spirit world by one of the Apostles and by Jesus Christ. When she went into the trance state and gave her communications to members of the circle, these communications were said by Mrs. Glover to come, through her as a medium, from the spirit of one of the Apostles or of Jesus Christ. (Milmine, p. 111)

When Mrs. Eddy began her healing practice, using the methods of her mentor Phineas Quimby, she placed an advertisement in Boston's leading spiritualist journal, *Banner of Light*. It appeared in issues of June 20, 27, and July 4, 1868, and again the following year on December 4 and 11. Here is how the first ad read:

> ANY PERSON desiring to learn how to heal the sick can receive of the undersigned instruction that will enable them to commence healing on a *principle of science* with a success far beyond any of the present modes. No medicine, electricity, physiology or hygiene required for unparalleled success in the most difficult cases. No pay is required unless this skill is obtained. Address, MRS. MARY B. GLOVER, Amesbury, Mass., Box 61.

Mrs. Sarah Crosby, of Albion, Maine, was for a time a good friend of Mrs. Eddy. She recalled an occasion when Mrs. Eddy suddenly closed her eyes, shivered, went into a trance, and began to jabber in a deep masculine voice. The voice claimed to come from Sarah's dead brother, Albert Baker. Amazingly, the voice warned Mrs. Crosby not to trust Mrs. Eddy because she might exploit Mrs. Crosby for her (Mrs. Eddy's) ambitions! There were other occasions when Baker's voice came through Mrs. Eddy's lips. Sometimes it would tell Mrs. Crosby to look under a certain chair cushion where she would find a message from her brother, written by Mrs. Eddy while her hand was under the brother's control. Here is one of the messages reproduced in *The Life of Mary Baker G. Eddy and the History of Christian Science*, Mrs. Milmine's biography of Mrs. Eddy:

> Sarah dear Be ye calm in reliance on self, amid all the changes of natural yearnings, of too keen a sense of earth joys, of too great a struggle between the material and spiritual. Be calm or you will rend your mortal and your experience which is needed for your spiritual

progress lost, till taken up without the proper sphere and your spirit trials more severe.

This is why all things are working for good to those who suffer and they must look not upon the things which are seen but upon those which do not appear. P. Quimby of Portland has the spiritual truth of diseases. You must imbibe it to be healed. Go to him again and lean on no material or spiritual medium. In that path of truth I first found you. Dear one, I am at present no aid to you although you think I am, but your spirit will not at present bear this quickening or twill leave the body; hence I leave you till you ripen into a condition to meet me. You will miss me at first, but afterwards grow more tranquil because of it, which is important that you may live for yourself and children. Love and care for poor sister a great suffering lies before her. (p. 67)

Sibyl Wilbur, in her authorized hagiography of Mrs. Eddy, had the audacity to call these trances and automatic writings an "admirable though harmless hoax" designed by Mrs. Eddy to convince Mrs. Crosby that her belief in spiritualism was nonsense! Mrs. Crosby was furious when she read this. She fired off the following letter to the *Waterville Morning Sentinel* (Maine) (February 16, 1907):

At the time mentioned . . . I knew nothing whatever of spiritualism, I had never seen, or sought to know anything about it; and I have no reason to suppose that Mrs. Patterson had. When she commenced to go into those trances I did not in the least understand what it meant until the power that controlled her, explained the condition and purpose of it. Her messages to me were and are prima faci[e] evidence that they never came from her own consciousness.

However much she may since have acted the part of the charlatan . . . I shall defend her from such aspersions at the time when her ambition for money and power had not been kindled; when she was a devoted and humble follower of Dr. P. P. Quimby . . . aspiring only to follow in the footsteps of her teacher in humility of spirit. I am sure she was too honest then, too much of a lady to use the identity of an honored brother whose memory I think she revered, to attempt to practise a wicked fraud upon one who trusted her, for no purpose except to deceive.

My intimacy with her for years warrants this defence. That she was far from saintship no one knows better than I. (Springer, pp. 125-26)

If Mrs. Patterson (Eddy) only pretended to channel messages from Mrs. Crosby's dead brother, it was a joke that obviously failed. Instead of shaking a faith in spiritualism, which Mrs. Crosby denied she had at the time, it converted her to spiritualism! As Fleta Springer concludes in her unauthorized biography, *According to the Flesh* (1930), "The joke was repeated too often to remain a joke, and certainly it provided no laughter at the time."

In her later years Mrs. Eddy frequently denied she had ever believed in spiritualism. "I never could believe in spiritualism," she says in her chapter on the subject in *Science and Health*. In chapter 4 of *Miscellaneous Writings,* she answered a question this way:

Am I a spiritualist?

I am not, and never was. I understand the impossibility of inter-communion between the so-called dead and living. There have always attended my life phenomena of an uncommon order, which spiritualists have miscalled mediumship; but I clearly understand that no human agencies were employed—that the divine Mind reveals itself to humanity through spiritual law. (p. 95)

Mrs. Eddy lied. In addition to the previous quotations from persons who witnessed her séances, Mrs. Milmine, in her biography, gives other sworn affidavits. Mary Bartlett, for example, recalled how Mrs. Eddy had come to the door of her grandmother's house saying that her spirit controls had directed her there to find lodgings. The grandmother, a devoted spiritualist, took her in and they held many séances in which Mrs. Eddy went into trances and channeled communications from the dead. When Mrs. Eddy denied her former belief in spiritualism, she probably did not anticipate how thoroughly her life would be examined.*

The marriage to Dr. Patterson lasted twenty years, but turned into a stormy, miserable relationship. Mrs. Patterson was so frequently in bed, suffering from what she repeatedly called "spinal inflammations," that Dr. Patterson often had to carry her up and down stairs for meals. Finally, unable to bear living any longer with his wife, Dr. Patterson left her. In 1873 Mrs. Patterson obtained a divorce on grounds of desertion, but the real cause, she maintained (see chapter 17 of *First Church of Christ, Scientist, and Miscellany*), was adultery. In a letter to the *Boston Post* (March 7, 1883), she put it this way:

> I was taken to Dr. Quimby, and partially restored. I returned home, hoping once more to make that home happy, but only returned to a new agony—to find my husband had eloped with a married woman from one of the wealthy families of that city, leaving no trace save his last letter to us, wherein he wrote "I hope some time to be worthy of so good a wife." (Dakin, p. 64)

All this could be true, but to this day no historian has found any documentation of Dr. Patterson's adultery and elopement aside from Mrs. Eddy's letter. The dapper dentist died in a poorhouse in Saco, Maine, in 1896, at a time when his former wife was rapidly becoming a millionaire. He was buried in Potter's Field.

---

*The best Robert Peel can do to counter the evidence for Mrs. Eddy's spiritualist phase, in the first volume of his hagiography *Mary Baker Eddy: The Years of Discovery*, is to write: "Investigation has shown that a Mrs. Eddy and a Mrs. Glover, wholly unconnected with Mrs. Patterson, did apparently operate [as a medium] in one or another of those cities in the 'fifties and 'sixties" (p. 133).

In 1877, at age fifty-six, Mary married again—this time to Asa Gilbert Eddy, a small, mild, blue-eyed, affable gentleman ten or eleven years her junior. Mr. Eddy is on record as saying he had no inkling they would marry until Mrs. Eddy suddenly proposed. On the marriage license each gave an age of forty, although he was then forty-five and she was fifty-six.

Asa was a former professional weaver who made his own pants and worked for a sewing machine company in East Boston. His parents were ardent spiritualists, and Asa himself accepted the same faith as a youth. After a brief period as one of Mary's students, he embraced her views with such enthusiasm that he became the first authorized Christian Science practitioner.

In 1882, six years after their marriage, Asa Eddy became seriously ill. Dr. Rufus K. Noyes, a highly respected mainline physician, diagnosed the ailment as a valvular disease of the heart, now in an acute stage, and said that Mr. Eddy was near death. Mrs. Eddy flatly refused to believe it. She was then obsessed by the notion that her enemies were trying to destroy her and Christian Science by practicing "Malicious Animal Magnetism" against her and her husband.

Her husband's illness, Mrs. Eddy was firmly convinced, was a counterfeit form of arsenic poisoning generated from a distance by her enemies. Her docile husband readily agreed. To get a second opinion she called in "Doctor" C. J. Eastman. He was a quack homeopath who did not even have a degree in homeopathy. He had been arrested several times for performing illegal abortions, and soon would serve five years in prison. But Mrs. Eddy still trusted any homeopath more than any allopath. Eastman assured her that her husband was indeed suffering from simulated arsenic poisoning.

When Asa Eddy finally died in 1882, Mrs. Eddy was so convinced of her crazy theory about the cause of death that she ordered Dr. Noyes to perform an autopsy. This he did, finding no trace of anything resembling arsenic poisoning. He even showed her Mr. Eddy's defective heart, but Mrs. Eddy's opinion was so set that she refused to believe it was a damaged heart that killed her husband. We will have more to say about all this in chapter 6.

Mrs. Eddy invited her son, George Glover, to her husband's funeral, but he refused to come. She published a poem titled "Meeting of My Departed Mother and Husband" that imagined how the pair would converse in heaven. It was later discovered that she had written the poem much earlier, about the death of her first husband. Because it had not been published, she was able to revise it slightly so that it applied to her third husband.

In her declining years, bereft of a husband and lonely, Mrs. Eddy legally adopted as her son a forty-one-year-old homeopathic physician named Ebenezer Foster. Mrs. Augusta Stetson, then one of Mrs. Eddy's close associates, later called Dr. Foster a "young puppy" because he so adored Mrs. Eddy and obeyed her every whim.

Benny, as Mrs. Eddy called him, became Mrs. Eddy's publisher. Her books were then selling well even though the church membership then numbered only a few thousand. Eventually Benny was accused of falsifying account books and having an affair with a married woman. Mrs. Eddy blamed both scandals on Malicious Animal Magnetism, and booted him out of the church. Like Dr. Patterson, he faded into obscurity. In 1909, when Milmine published her biography, she reported, "Dr. Foster traveled in the West and in Alaska for a time, then settled down at his old home at Waterbury Center, Vermont, where he now lives."

I am sure that the date and place of Benny's death are recorded somewhere in the voluminous literature on the history of Christian Science, but I was unable to find this information in any of the major biographies of Mrs. Eddy. Dr. Foster was hired and fired the way one would hire and fire an incompetent servant. Bliss Knapp, in *The Destiny of the Mother Church* (1991), says that Dr. Foster rejoined the Methodist church. We shall encounter him again in chapter 5 as the plaintiff in a murder case, the most bizarre court trial in the history of Christian Science.

2

Mrs. Eddy's Debt to Quimby

The central idea of Christian Science, that Divine Mind is the sole reality, is an old one. It is found in the philosophy of ancient thinkers such as Plotinus and other Neoplatonists; in Eastern religions such as Hinduism, which view the material universe as *maya* or illusion; and of course in the writings of idealists such as Bishop Berkeley, who called matter a "stupid, thoughtless somewhat," incapable of existing without being perceived. That matter is in some sense unreal was also a theme in New England's transcendentalist movement led by Ralph Waldo Emerson, Henry David Thoreau, Bronson Alcott, and Margaret Fuller.

Christian Science, however, is much more than just another form of metaphysical idealism. It also embraces the notion that sin, sickness, and death, being illusions created by false belief, can be conquered by a person's divine mind, an eternal part of God, if it learns to accept completely the nonexistence of all matter with its attendant illusions of evil. Mrs. Eddy's reliance on the awesome power of divine mind to heal, all historians outside of the Christian Science church agree, sprang from the teachings of an uneducated, sincere but simple-minded

31

New England quack doctor named Phineas Parkhurst Quimby (1802–1866). The story of how his wild views led to the founding of Christian Science is complex, controversial, and fascinating.

Born in London, New Hampshire, the son of a village blacksmith, Quimby began his curious career as a clockmaker and repairer. In the mid-1830s, he developed a passionate interest in mesmerism. His great success in healing individuals by what is now called hypnotism, combined with his claim that he possessed clairvoyant powers to detect ailments, turned him into one of the nation's earliest and most famous "mind healers." All medical doctors, Quimby convinced himself, were money-grubbing humbugs. Almost every bodily ill, he believed, is the result of "wrong thinking," easily banished by teaching a patient how to think correctly.

"All sickness is in the mind," Quimby wrote. Inside each of us, he taught, is a higher self, a spark of God that he liked to call "the mind of Christ." Once this higher self can be induced to give up false beliefs in illness and pain, true thoughts will flood in and ailments will evaporate like morning dew. "The truth," he declared, "is the cure."

In the early stages of his career, Quimby exploited the widespread belief that when a person is mesmerized, an invisible electromagnetic field flows from the mesmerist's hands or eyes into the body of the ailing subject. Accordingly, Quimby would dip his hands in water to strengthen electrical contact points, then place one wet hand on the patient's bare belly and the other on the patient's head. Patients would usually say they felt a strong tingling go through their body. Because Quimby liked to rub the head, female patients, who far outnumbered men, would get their hair badly rumpled. They considered the cure worth it. Often their body would warm during the healing and they would break into perspiration.

When Mrs. Eddy began her practice of healing, she followed Quimby's technique of head rubbing. One of her early pupils, Richard Kennedy, had this to say in *McClure's* magazine (May 1907): "I went to

Lynn to practice with Mrs. Eddy. Our partnership was only in practice, not in her teaching. The mode was operating upon the head by giving vigorous rubbing."

If a patient complained of pain at a spot other than the head, Quimby would rub that spot with his free wet hand. A frequent dodge was to transfer the pain to an extremity where it could be more easily massaged. A pain in the abdomen, for example, might be shifted to a shoulder or to the fingers or toes.

As years went by, Quimby became convinced it was a patient's faith, not mesmerism, that did the healing. Even body manipulations, he decided, were unnecessary, though he occasionally used them because patients believed they helped. His eventual technique was simply to talk quietly to the patient, explaining that God did not wish anyone to be ill, and that their pain would go away if they strongly believed it would. His authoritative voice and his penetrating "magnetic" eyes had a lot to do with bolstering a patient's faith.

Quimby was far from the first to heal by touching and stroking. Such practices go back to ancient cultures and forward to today's faith healers, both Christian and psychic. Here, for instance, is a passage from Plato's dialogue *Charmides* that could have been written today by a Christian Scientist, or by any doctor familiar with psychosomatic ills (in Quimby's day they were called "functional" ills) and the enormous power of placebos. Socrates begins by recalling the words of a Thracian physician:

> This Thracian told me that in these notions of theirs, which I was just now mentioning, the Greek physicians are quite right as far as they go; but Zamolxis, he added, our king, who is also a god, says further, "that as you ought not to attempt to cure the eyes without the head, or the head without the body, so neither ought you to attempt to cure the body without the soul; and this," he said, "is the reason why the cure of many diseases is unknown to the physicians

of Hellas, because they are ignorant of the whole, which ought to be studied also; for the part can never be well unless the whole is well." For all good and evil, whether in the body or in human nature, originates, as he declared, in the soul, and overflows from thence, as if from the head into the eyes. And therefore if the head and body are to be well, you must begin by curing the soul; that is the first thing. And the cure, my dear youth, has to be effected by the use of certain charms, and these charms are fair words; and by them temperance is implanted in the soul, and where temperance is, there health is speedily imparted, not only to the head, but to the whole body. And he who taught me the cure and the charm at the same time added a special direction. "Let no one," he said, "persuade you to cure the head, until he has first given you his soul to be cured by the charm. For this," he said, "is the great error of our day in the treatment of the human body, that physicians separate the soul from the body." (*The Dialogues of Plato,* vol. 1 [New York: Random House, 1937], pp. 6–7)

The Middle Ages and Renaissance swarmed with Christian faith healers. Even kings were thought to have the ability to heal by the "king's touch." A typical and famous healer of seventeenth-century England was the Irish Anglican Valentine Greatrakes. We know from the gospels that Jesus, like the Jews of his time, believed that bodily ills, both physical and mental, were not God-intended. They were caused by Satan and his devils. Like other Christian healers, from Jesus to Oral Roberts, Greatrakes based his healing on this belief. His cures, which required touching and stroking, like Quimby's stroking in his early years, would force pains to migrate to extremities such as fingers, toes, nose, ears, and so on. A patient would feel the pain moving outwardly until it finally broke free. Hundreds of eminent and learned people, including chemist Robert Boyle and philosopher Ralph Cudworth, were convinced of Greatrakes's paranormal powers. Like all Christian faith healers, Greatrakes insisted it was not he, but the Holy Spirit, who did the healing.

America's first world-famous faith healer was Alexander Dowie, the evangelist who founded Zion City, Illinois, a religious community north of Chicago that was noted for its persuasion that the earth is flat. Hundreds of American evangelists, most of them in the Pentecostal tradition, followed in Dowie's footsteps. Occasionally a healer would get in trouble with postal authorities by mailing out items such as handkerchiefs that had been blessed and vitalized to give a healing power. In recent decades Oral Roberts has carried this practice to its loftiest heights. Of course, when followers receive a healing item blessed by Oral or his son, or both, they are expected to send love donations to cover the huge expenses of Oral's ministry.

When mesmerism flourished, the fancied electromagnetic field became for a while the most popular "scientific" explanation for mind cures. Even today psychic healers invoke mysterious energy fields and vibrations unknown to physicists to account for their seemingly miraculous cures. As we shall see, Mary Baker Eddy was never able to break completely away from mesmerism, although instead of seeing it as a beneficent force she regarded it as just the opposite.

Quimby was a small man with white hair and beard, and a kindly, charismatic personality. He was not a charlatan. He claimed success in banishing cancer, tuberculosis, smallpox, heart and lung diseases, diphtheria—you name it, he could cure it. His seeming ability to heal without the aid of drugs or surgery became the basis for hundreds of mind healers and sects, with varied names, that sprouted throughout the land in the last decades of the nineteenth century. Most were short-lived. Christian Science was by far the most successful and lasting, with Kansas City's Unity Christianity running a close second. We will consider Unity in chapter 14.

Throughout her entire life Mrs. Eddy was periodically bedridden with what she called "spinal inflammation." To what extent these ills were psychosomatic will probably never be known. In 1862, when she was forty-one and still married to Dr. Patterson, she became seriously crippled by spinal pain and deeply depressed. Quimby's great fame as a mind curer had reached her. When he refused to come see her, she made the trip to his office in Portland, Maine, where he was busy treating some five hundred patients each year. Mrs. Eddy described her amazing cure in Portland's *Evening Courier* (November 7, 1862). It is such a remarkable letter that it deserves quoting in its entirety:

> When our Shakespeare decided that "there were more things in this world than were dreamed of in your philosophy," I cannot say of a verity that he had a foreknowledge of P. P. Quimby. And when the school Platonic anatomised the soul and divided it into halves to be reunited by elementary attractions, and heathen philosophers averred that old Chaos in sullen silence brooded o'er the earth until her inimitable form was hatched from the egg of night, I would not at present decide whether the fallacy was found in their premises or conclusions, never having dated my existence before the flood. When the startled alchemist discovered, as he supposed, an universal solvent, or the philosopher's stone, and the more daring Archimedes invented a lever wherewithal to pry up the universe, I cannot say that in either the principle obtained in nature or in art, or that it worked well, having never tried it. But, when by a falling apple, an immutable law was discovered, we gave it the crown of science, which is incontrovertible and capable of demonstration; hence that was wisdom and truth. When from the evidence of the senses, my reason takes cognizance of truth, although it may appear in quite a miraculous view, I must acknowledge that as science which is truth uninvestigated. Hence the following demonstration:
>
> Three weeks since I quitted my nurse and sick room *en route* for Portland. The belief of my recovery had died out of the hearts of those who were most anxious for it. With this mental and physical depression I first visited P. P. Quimby; and in less than one week from that time I ascended by a stairway of one hundred and eighty-two steps to the dome of the City Hall, and am improving *ad infinitum*. To the most subtle reasoning, such a proof, coupled too, as

it is with numberless similar ones, demonstrates his power to heal. Now for a brief analysis of this power.

Is it spiritualism? Listen to the words of wisdom. "Believe in God, believe also in me; or believe me for the very work's sake." Now, then, his works are but the result of superior wisdom, which can demonstrate a science not understood; hence it were a doubtful proceeding not to believe him for the work's sake. Well, then, he denies that his power to heal the sick is borrowed from the spirits of this or another world; and let us take the Scriptures for proof. "A kingdom divided against itself cannot stand." How, then, can he receive the friendly aid of the disenthralled spirit, while he rejects the faith of the solemn mystic who crosses the threshold of the dark unknown to conjure up from the vasty deep the awestruck spirit of some invisible squaw?

Again, is it by animal magnetism that he heals the sick? Let us examine. I have employed electro-magnetism and animal magnetism, and for a brief interval have felt relief, from the equilibrium which I fancied was restored to an exhausted system or by a diffusion of concentrated action. But in no instance did I get rid of a return of all my ailments, because I had not been helped out of the error in which opinions involved us. My operator believed in disease, independent of the mind; hence I could not be wiser than my master. But now I can see dimly at first, and only as trees walking, the great principle which underlies Dr. Quimby's faith and works; and just in proportion to my right perception of truth is my recovery. This truth which he opposes to the error of giving intelligence to matter and placing pain where it never placed itself, if received understandingly, changes the currents of the system to their normal action; and the mechanism of the body goes on undisturbed. That this is a science capable of demonstration, becomes clear to the minds of those patients who reason upon the process of their cure. The truth which he establishes in the patient cures him (although he may be wholly unconscious thereof); and the body, which is full of light, is no longer in disease. At present I am too much in error to elucidate the truth, and can touch only the keynote for the master hand to wake the harmony. May it be in essays, instead of notes! say I. After all, this is a very spiritual doctrine; but the eternal years of God are with it, and it must stand firm as the rock of ages. And to many a poor sufferer may it be found, as by me, "the shadow of a great rock in a weary land." (Milmine, pp. 58–59).

Mary and Quimby became good friends. She visited him again in 1864, and spent several months going through his papers, studying his healing methods and his metaphysical opinions. She idolized him. When Quimby died in 1866, she wrote a tribute to him in verse that ran in the *Lynn Reporter* (February 14, 1866). Throughout her long life Mrs. Eddy fancied herself a poet. She was always sending poems to newspapers and magazines, and eventually two books of her verse were published. Her poems are without merit, almost as bad as her unedited prose, except for a rare occasional line. Dozens of anthologies of religious verse have been published since her death. I have yet to see one of her poems included in such a collection.

Mrs. Eddy's tribute to Quimby had the marvelous title, "Lines On the Death of Dr. P. P. Quimby, Who Healed With the Truth that Christ Taught in Contradistinction to All Isms."

> Did sackcloth clothe the sun and day grow night,
>   All matter mourn the hour with dewy eyes,
> When Truth, receding from our mortal sight,
>   Had paid to error her last sacrifice?
>
> Can we forget the power that gave us life?
>   Shall we forget the wisdom of its way?
> Then ask me not amid this mortal strife—
>   This keenest pang of animated clay—
>
> To mourn him less; to mourn him more were just
>   If to his memory 'twere a tribute given

For every solemn, sacred, earnest trust
    Delivered to us ere he rose to heaven.

Heaven but the happiness of that calm soul,
    Growing in stature to the throne of God;
Rest should reward him who hath made us whole,
    Seeking, though tremblers, where his footsteps trod.

(Milmine, p. 70)

For many years Mrs. Eddy was Quimby's adoring disciple. One of her lectures in Maine was titled "On P. P. Quimby's spiritual science of healing disease as opposed to deism or Rochester-rapping Spiritualism." Her sister Abigail, who often helped Mrs. Eddy out financially, considered Quimby a fraud. It led to a rift between the two sisters that was never healed. Mrs. Eddy's other sister, Martha, and a brother, Albert, also had no use for Quimby or for Christian Science.

Quimby died at his home in Belfast, Maine, in 1866 when he was sixty-four. Just before he passed on, attended by a homeopathic doctor, he made a remark to his son George that reminds one of W. C. Fields's proposal for his epitaph: "I would rather be in Philadelphia." Said Quimby: "I do not dread the change any more than if I were going on a trip to Philadelphia."

About two weeks after Quimby died, Mary Baker Eddy had a terrible fall on an icy sidewalk in Lynn. It crippled her in a way that she likened to her bedridden state before Quimby had cured her. In an 1871 letter to a prospective student named W. W. Wright, of Lynn, she described her injury and its cure:

I have demonstrated upon myself in an injury occasioned by a fall, that it did for me what surgeons could not do. Dr. Cushing of this city pronounced my injury incurable and that I could not survive three days because of it, when on the third day I rose [like Jesus] from my bed and to the utter confusion of all I commenced my usual avocations and notwithstanding displacements, etc., I regained the natural position and functions of the body. How far my students can demonstrate in such extreme cases depends on the progress they have made in this science. (Milmine, p. 83)

Quimby was no longer available to cure her, but she managed to do the job without his help. The Dr. Cushing referred to was Alvin Cushing, a homeopathic physician. "Displacements" refers to displacements of spinal bones.

Many years later, in *Miscellaneous Writings,* Mary recalled that her cure had been precipitated by randomly consulting the Bible, a practice in which she often indulged. On the third day, she writes, she opened her Bible to Matthew 9:2, which tells how Jesus healed a man of palsy. "As I read, the healing Truth dawned upon my sense; and the result was that I rose, dressed myself, and ever after was in better health than I had before enjoyed" (p. 24).

In her autobiography she tells it this way:

It was in Massachusetts, in the year 1866, that I discovered the Science of Divine Metaphysical Healing, which I afterwards named Christian Science. The discovery came to pass in this way. During twenty years prior to my discovery I had been trying to trace all physical effects to a mental cause; and in the latter part of 1866 I gained the Scientific certainty that all causation was Mind, and every effect a mental phenomenon.

My immediate recovery from the effects of an injury, caused by an accident, an injury that neither medicine nor surgery could reach, was the falling apple that led me to the discovery how to be well myself, and how to make others so.

Even to the physician who attended me, and rejoiced in my recovery, I could not then explain the *modus* of my relief. I could only assure him that the divine Spirit had wrought the miracle—a miracle which later I found to be in perfect Scientific accord with divine law. (p. 32)

Mrs. Eddy's claim that Dr. Cushing told her that her spinal problem was incurable and that she had but three days to live was another of her fibs. On January 2, 1907, the *Union* of Springfield, Massachusetts, published a long, notarized affidavit by Dr. Cushing in which he stoutly denied having told Mrs. Eddy any such things. The statement was reprinted in a series of fourteen sensational articles about Mrs. Eddy that ran in *McClure's* magazine in 1907 and 1908. Before giving this affidavit, let me digress with some remarks about this series, which aroused enormous excitement when it appeared. The articles were revised and expanded in 1909 as a book titled *The Life of Mary Baker G. Eddy and the History of Christian Science* by Georgine Milmine. It was the first major attack on Mrs. Eddy, and the primary source for all later unauthorized biographies, including these chapters.

The church was amazingly successful in suppressing sales. The book quickly went out of print and its plates were destroyed. Not until more than sixty years later, in 1971, was a reprint edition published. This, too, is now a scarce item, with copies available in only a few large libraries.

Although the series and the book bore the byline of Mrs. Milmine, the wife of a Rochester, New York, newspaperman, the series actually was a joint effort of research and writing by many hands. A young Willa Cather, then chief editor of *McClure's,* supervised the project and did most of the editing and much of the actual writing. She became so fascinated by Mrs. Eddy's neurotic behavior and strange opinions that when she became a famous novelist, she modeled several of her characters on Mrs. Eddy, most notably Mrs. Cutler in her novel *My Antonia.*

The *McClure's* series got off to an embarrassing start. A supposed photograph of Mrs. Eddy, printed in the December 1906 issue that announced the series, was actually a photo of one of Mrs. Eddy's friends! Mrs. Eddy, then eighty-six, made a brief reply to the early installments.

(The reply is reprinted in *The First Church of Christ, Scientist, and Miscellany,* chapter 17.) As the series continued, however, the material proved to be so overwhelming and accurate that she remained silent.

Now back to Dr. Cushing. Here is the full text of his remarkable statement as given in Mrs. Milmine's biography:

> Alvin M. Cushing, being duly sworn, deposes and says: I am seventy-seven years of age, and reside in the City of Springfield in the Commonwealth of Massachusetts. I am a medical doctor of the homeopathic school and have practised medicine for fifty years last past. On July 13 in the year 1865 I commenced the practice of my profession in the City of Lynn, in said Commonwealth, and, while there, kept a careful and accurate record, in detail, of my various cases, my attendance upon and my treatment of them. One of my cases of which I made and have such a record is that of Mrs. Mary M. Patterson, then the wife of one Daniel Patterson, a dentist, and now Mrs. Mary G. Eddy, of Concord, New Hampshire.
>
> On February 1, 1866, I was called to the residence of Samuel M. Bubier, who was a shoe manufacturer and later was mayor of Lynn, to attend said Mrs. Patterson, who had fallen upon the icy sidewalk in front of Mr. Bubier's factory and had injured her head by the fall. I found her very nervous, partially unconscious, semi-hysterical, complaining by word and action of severe pain in the back of her head and neck. This was early in the evening, and I gave her medicine every fifteen minutes until she was more quiet, then left her with Mrs. Bubier for a little time, ordering the medicine to be given every half hour until my return. I made a second visit later and left Mrs. Patterson at midnight, with directions to give the medicine every half hour or hour as seemed necessary, when awake, but not disturb her if asleep.
>
> In the morning Mrs. Bubier told me my orders had been carried out and said Mrs. Patterson had slept some. I found her quite rational but complaining of severe pain, almost spasmodic on moving. She declared that she was going to her home in Swampscott whether we consented or not. On account of the severe pain and nervousness,

I gave her one-eighth of a grain of morphine, not as a curative remedy, but as an expedient to lessen the pain on removing. As soon as I could, I procured a long sleigh with robes and blankets, and two men from a nearby stable. On my return, to my surprise found her sound asleep. We placed her in the sleigh and carried her to her home in Swampscott, without a moan. At her home the two men undertook to carry her upstairs, and she was so sound asleep and limp she "doubled up like a jack-knife," so I placed myself on the stairs on my hands and feet and they laid her on my back, and in that way we carried her upstairs and placed her in bed. She slept till nearly two o'clock in the afternoon; so long I began to fear there had been some mistake in the dose.

Said Mrs. Patterson proved to be a very interesting patient, and one of the most sensitive to the effects of medicine that I ever saw, which accounted for the effects of the small dose of morphine. Probably one-sixteenth of a grain would have put her sound asleep. Each day that I visited her, I dissolved a small portion of a highly attenuated remedy in one-half a glass of water and ordered a teaspoonful given every two hours, usually giving one dose while there. She told me she could feel each dose to the tips of her fingers and toes, and gave me much credit for my ability to select a remedy.

I visited her twice on February first, twice on the second, once on the third, and once on the fifth, and on the thirteenth day of the same month my bill was paid. During my visits to her she spoke to me of a Dr. Quimby of Portland, Maine, who had treated her for some severe illness with remarkable success. She did not tell what his method was, but I inferred it was not the usual method of either school of medicine.

There was, to my knowledge, no other physician in attendance upon Mrs. Patterson during this illness from the day of the accident, February 1, 1866, to my final visit on February 13th, and when I left her on the 13th day of February, she seemed to have recovered from the disturbance caused by the accident and to be, practically, in her normal condition. I did not at any time declare, or believe, that there was no hope for Mrs. Patterson's recovery, or that she was in a critical condition, and did not at any time say, or believe, that she had but three or any other limited number of days to live. Mrs. Patterson did not suggest, or say, or pretend, or in any way whatever intimate, that on the third, or any other day, of her said illness, she had miraculously recovered or been healed, or that, discovering or perceiving the truth of the power employed by Christ to heal the sick, she had, by it, been restored to health. As I have stated, on the third and subsequent days of her said illness, resulting from her said fall on the ice, I attended Mrs. Patterson and gave her medicine; and on the 10th day of the following August, I was again called to see her, this time at the home of a Mrs. Clark, on Sumner Street, in said City of Lynn. I found Mrs. Patterson suffering from a bad cough and prescribed for her. I made three more professional calls upon Mrs. Patterson and treated her for this cough in the said month of August, and with that, ended my professional relations with her.

I think I never met Mrs. Patterson after August 31, 1866, but saw her often during the next few years and heard that she claimed to have discovered a new method of curing disease.

Each of the said visits upon Mrs. Patterson, together with my treatment, the symptoms and the progress of the case, were recorded in my own hand in my record book at the time, and the said book, with the said entries made in February and August, 1866, is now in my possession.

I have, of course, no personal feeling in this matter. In response to many requests for a statement, I make this affidavit because I am assured it is wanted to perpetuate the testimony that can now be obtained, and be used only for a good purpose. I regard it as a duty which I owe to posterity to make public this particular episode in the life of Mary Baker G. Eddy. (pp. 84–86)

Ten days after Mrs. Eddy's seemingly miraculous cure, which she said was so complete that "ever after" she was in better health than before, Mrs. Eddy began failing again. Quimby was dead, but Julius Dresser had long been his closest disciple. Mrs. Eddy begged him for help in the following letter:

> Sir: I enclose some lines of mine in memory of our much-loved friend, which perhaps *you* will not think overwrought in meaning: others *must* of course.
>
> I am constantly wishing that *you* would step forward into the place he has vacated. I believe you would do a vast amount of good, and are more capable of occupying his place than any other I know of.
>
> Two weeks ago I fell on the sidewalk, and struck my back on the ice, and was taken up for dead, came to consciousness amid a storm of vapours from cologne, chloroform, ether, camphor, etc., but to find myself the helpless cripple I was before I saw Dr. Quimby.
>
> The physician attending said I had taken the last step I ever should, but in two days I got out of my bed *alone* and *will* walk; but yet I confess I am frightened, and out of that nervous heat my friends are forming, spite of me, the terrible spinal affection from which I have suffered so long and hopelessly. . . . Now can't *you* help me? I believe you can. I write this with this feeling: I think that I could help another in my condition if they had not placed their intelligence in matter. This I have not done, and yet I am slowly failing. Won't you write me if you will undertake for me if I can get to you? (Milmine, pp. 69–70)

Mrs. Eddy and Dresser had first met when both had been patients at the Granite State Water Cure Hospital, run by Dr. William T. Vail, a quack physician in Hill, New Hampshire. Dresser declined seeing Mrs. Eddy. He soon became a leader of the New Thought movement (the topic of chapter 14) and an implacable foe of Mrs. Eddy. He regarded her as a lying thief who had stolen all her basic ideas about mental healing from his beloved Quimby.

For the rest of her life, after the tumble on the ice, Mrs. Eddy was perpetually falling ill, having an abrupt recovery through practicing Christian Science, only to fall ill again. To relieve her bouts of intense pain, especially in her elder years, she took morphine. This was not to banish the pain, you understand, because from her point of view the pain was not real. It was to aid her in getting rid of her false belief that produced the dreadful illusion of pain. In *Science and Health,* here is how she justified the use of morphine:

> If from an injury or from any cause, a Christian Scientist were seized with pain so violent that he could not treat himself mentally—and the Scientists had failed to relieve him—the sufferer could call a surgeon, who would give him a hypodermic injection, then, when the belief of pain was lulled, he could handle his own case mentally. Thus it is that we "prove all things; [and] hold fast that which is good." (p. 464)

We will have more to say about Mrs. Eddy's morphine habit in chapter 7.

Mrs. Eddy labored long and hard to minimize her obvious debt to Quimby, often by outrageous lying. In a chapter on Quimby in her autobiography she speaks of her 1862 visit to see the "distinguished mesmerist, Mr. P. P. Quimby, whose method of treatment was by manipulations and water. . . . I gave him some of my own writings, which remained among his papers, and have been spoken of, by persons unfamiliar with the facts, as his own" (p. 44).

Mrs. Eddy goes on to say that she offered to pay Quimby's son to publish his father's writings, "but he declines to publish them, for this would silence the insinuation that Mr. Quimby originated my system of healing" (p. 44). Christian Science, she insists, differs from Quimbyism mainly by having a spiritual base whereas Quimbyism had only a material base. "He believed in matter, and employed it as the visible agent of his cure" (p. 45).

It was, of course, necessary for Mrs. Eddy to play down her debt to Quimby because she claimed that Christian Science was solely her own discovery, or more accurately, had been revealed to her by God in 1866 after Quimby's death. Not only did she refuse to acknowledge her debt to Quimby, she had the audacity to claim that passages in Quimby's papers, so similar to her own, were actually written by her and given to Quimby! Instead of being taught by Quimby, she came to believe, unless she consciously lied, that *she* had been the teacher and poor Quimby had been the pupil!

Quimby's son refused to allow his father's papers to be printed, but in 1921 they were gathered into a volume by Horatio W. Dresser, Julius Dresser's son, and published by Crowell in 1921 as *The Quimby Manuscripts*. Ervin Seale, a prominent leader of New Thought, wrote the book's introduction.

No one can go through *The Quimby Manuscripts* without realizing how much Mrs. Eddy took from Quimby. When she wrote that Quimby had no spiritual basis for his healing, she must have known that this was false. Quimby was a deeply religious man. He constantly called his method of healing a science, believing (as did Mrs. Eddy) that it was the same science used by Jesus in his healings. In the next chapter we shall learn that he even used the term "Christian Science." When Mrs. Eddy left Quimby in 1864 she took with her a manuscript by Quimby titled *Questions and Answers*. Huge chunks of it were incorporated in Mrs. Eddy's pamphlet *The Science of Man,* which she published herself in 1870. With numerous alterations it was eventually added to *Science and Health* as the chapter titled "Recapitulation." Even after all the changes one can still see how much of it was taken from Quimby's paper.

One of Quimby's most enthusiastic disciples was Warren F. Evans, a former Swedenborgian. It is instructive to look into two of his books that were published before *Science and Health: The Mental Cure* (1869) and *Mental Medicine* (1872). His later books were *Soul and Body* (1875), *The Divine Law of Cure* (1881), *The Primitive Mind Cure* (1885), and

Esoteric Christianity (1886). These books were basic to the rise of New Thought, a movement we will consider in our final chapter. To what extent his books influenced Mrs. Eddy is not known, but they reveal clearly how strongly Quimby's ideas had percolated into the minds of mental healers before Mrs. Eddy's *Science and Health* was published in 1875.

Fleta Springer, in her unauthorized biography of Mrs. Eddy, *According to the Flesh* (1930), closes a chapter with these perceptive paragraphs:

> It is this writer's belief that Mrs. Eddy's denial of Quimby delivered a wound to her emotional body from which she did not recover, and from which she suffered all the days of her life.
>
> If this be thought fantastic, it should be remembered that Mrs. Eddy was the victim of fantasies. She had been truly grateful to Quimby, and now she must extend her doctrine of evil very far indeed to include the kindly figure of her benefactor. She believed in the law of retribution. She believed in demons. She had sat in spiritualistic seances and heard the voices of the dead. The ghost of Phineas P. Quimby haunted her all her life.
>
> In a pamphlet published by the Christian Science Parent Church in 1929, there appears the following extract from the diary kept by Calvin Frye. It is dated April 14, 1897, and reads:
>
> This morning she told me the mental threat urged upon her was "you have got to confess, that is, go tell that you got it from Quimby or you will be damned."

It is true that even Mrs. Eddy's enemies, in their effort to show the inferiority and the irrationality of her mental processes, have held that she really did progress by stages to the literal belief that she had received nothing of her theory from Quimby. But her healing at Quimby's hands and her adoption of his doctrines, were the turning point in her life. The details of that experience were part of her deeply emotional memory. She may have forgotten and rationalized away many other episodes and relationships of her life, but she never forgot or succeeded in rationalizing to herself the fact that she had repudiated the man from whom she had received the ideas and the impetus upon which she had built her success. (pp. 323–24)

3

Matter, Sickness, and Pain

It is not a coincidence that 1866, the year Quimby died, was the very year Mrs. Eddy finally decided was the year God had revealed to her the mighty truth of Christian Science, a truth that had not been given to mankind since the time of Christ. She was then fifty-four. Here is how she opened chapter 6 in early editions of *Science and Health* (the paragraph is slightly altered in the current edition):

> In the year 1866, I discovered the Science of Metaphysical Healing, and named it Christian Science. God had been graciously fitting me, during many years, for the reception of a final revelation of the absolute Principle of Scientific Mind-healing. No human pen or tongue taught me the science contained in this book and neither tongue nor pen can overthrow it.

In the book's first edition (1875) she gave an earlier date. "We made our first discovery that science mentally applied would heal the sick, in 1864, and since then have tested it on ourselves and hundreds of others and never found it fail. . . ." In a letter to the *Boston Post* (March 7, 1883) she gave a still earlier date: "We made our first experiments in mental healing about 1853, when we were convinced that mind had a science, which, if understood, would heal all disease."

Why did she finally settle on 1866? The answer seems clear: She was trying desperately to deny her great debt to Quimby. What better way than to assert she had discovered Christian Science shortly *after* Quimby's death? Mrs. Eddy never ceased to believe she had been chosen by God to establish on earth a new religion superior to the grim doctrines she had been taught as a child, and which she believed had misunderstood and perverted the true teachings of Jesus for almost two thousand years. "Healing, as I teach it, has not been practiced since the days of Christ," she wrote in *The Unity of Good* (p. 9).

Norman Beasley, in *The Cross and the Crown,* a believer's history of Christian Science, reports an interview in which Mrs. Eddy tells of her constant practice of consulting the Bible by opening it at random. One day, after praying for a special message from God, she opened the Holy Book and saw the words "Now, go, write it in a book." She was condensing Isaiah 30:80, which reads: "Now go, write it before them in a table, and note it in a book, that it may be for the time to come for ever and ever."

In *Science and Health* (chapter 6) she compares her discovery of Christian Science to the Copernican revolution. Our senses tell us the earth is at rest, with the heavens going around it. The Copernican revolution reversed that belief. In a similar way, Mrs. Eddy writes, Christian Science reverses the role of mind and matter. Our senses tell us that matter is real and mind is the operation of a physical brain. For Mrs. Eddy, it is the other way around. Only immortal Mind is real, and matter is an illusion fabricated by what Mrs. Eddy called "mortal mind." This is a mind that really doesn't exist because it is made of unreal matter. Kant, by the way, had earlier characterized his metaphysics, in which Mind is made central, to a Copernican revolution in the history of philosophy. That could have been where Mrs. Eddy found the metaphor.

If matter is an illusion, then our body, including our brain, must also be illusory. "Man is not matter," Mrs. Eddy writes in *Science and Health*, "he is not made up of brain, blood, bones, and other material elements . . . man is made in the image and likeness of God" (p. 475).

But do we not *see* a material world, out there, not made by us? We only think we see such a world. Images of material things are produced on our retinas by our mortal mind, itself an illusion. Mrs. Eddy was fond of the word "illusion," and uses it many times in her writings. "The whole function of material sight is an illusion, a lie," she wrote in her chapter "There is no Matter," in *Unity of Good* (p. 34). Over and over again in *Science and Health,* more than a thousand times, Mrs. Eddy harps on the unreality of matter. Sounds, tactile sensations, smells, and tastes are similar illusions. All the qualities we confer on matter are phantoms of mortal mind, a mind which in turn does not exist. To quote once more from *Unity of Good:*

> Mortal mind says, "I taste; and this is sweet, this is sour." Let mortal mind change, and say that sour is sweet, and *so* it would be. If every mortal mind believed sweet to be sour, it would be so; for the qualities of matter are but qualities of mortal mind. Change the mind, and the quality changes. Destroy the belief, and the quality disappears.
>
> The so-called material senses are found, upon examination, to be mortally mental, instead of material. Reduced to its proper denomination, matter is mortal mind; yet, strictly speaking, there is no mortal mind, for Mind is immortal, and is not matter, but Spirit. (p. 35)

Here is how Mrs. Eddy expressed this idea in the first chapter of *Rudimental Divine Science:*

The sweet sounds and glories of earth and sky, assuming manifold forms and colors,—are they not tangible and material?

As Mind they are real, but not as matter. All beauty and goodness are in and of Mind, emanating from God; but when we change the nature of beauty and goodness from Mind to matter, the beauty is marred, through a false conception, and, to the material senses, evil takes the place of good.

Has not the truth in Christian Science met a response from Prof. S. P. Langley, the young American astronomer? He says that "color is in *us,*" not "in the rose"; and he adds that this is not "any metaphysical subtlety," but a fact "almost universally accepted, within the *last few years,* by physicists." (p. 6)

Of course the *sensation* of colors and smells are in the mind, not on the rose. Far from being the discovery of recent physicists, this had been made clear by Locke, Berkeley, Hume, and other English empiricists of that period, and even much earlier by the ancient Greek Skeptics. Berkeley is often accused of denying the reality of the outside world. He did no such thing. For Berkeley the world is as independent of our minds as it is for the most hard-nosed realist. He simply redefined matter as an aspect of the mind of God. As he once said, he never doubted that fire is hot and ice is cold. By denying that matter exists even in a spiritual Berkeleyan sense, Mrs. Eddy adopted a language so extreme that outside the circle of her believers, it is almost impossible to adopt it without producing confusion.

It is, of course, trivially true that if God is the sole reality, then matter can be considered in some sense "unreal." As Mrs. Eddy herself said in the passage quoted above, "as Mind," our sensations of the outside world are "real." Were she alive today she might point out that, according to physicists, the ultimate particles of matter are simply quantized aspects of mathematically defined fields. These fields are not made of anything. They simply exist as pure mathematical constructs, and hence can be thought of as geometrical projections from the Mind of God. It is not that Mrs. Eddy can be proved wrong in assuming that the physical universe is in the Mind of God, but that she adopted a way of speaking about the universe that causes unnecessary confusion. It's as if someone announced that the only color in the world is purple, and all other colors are "unreal." It then becomes necessary to explain why certain purple objects appear to be blue, green, and other non-purple colors. In brief, you can't escape from the reality of sin, sickness, pain, and matter by the verbal trick of redefining them as dreams. "Sin, sickness, and death are error," Mrs. Eddy said in her sermon, *Christian Healing* (p. 17). "They are not Truth, and therefore are not TRUE."

Was Mrs. Eddy a pantheist? It depends on how the word is defined. She was certainly a pantheist in the usual meaning of the word: a person who believes that everything is part of an Eternal Mind. But Mrs. Eddy liked to use words in Pickwickian ways. To her a pantheist is a materialist who believes in the reality of matter, then identifies matter with God. Nevertheless, when pinned down, Mrs. Eddy recognized that there is a sense in which God is transcendent and wholly unknowable. We must, however, model God in some way. The best way is to use the metaphor of "person" even though we cannot know how the analogy applies. This, of course, is a familiar theme in theology; that God is "personal" in a way we cannot comprehend was constantly stressed, not only by Judaic-Christian thinkers, but also by theologians of other world faiths. Here is how Mrs. Eddy puts it in *Miscellaneous Writings* (chapter 3):

Do I believe in a personal God?

I believe in God as the Supreme Being. I know not what the person of omnipotence and omnipresence is, or what the infinite includes; therefore, I worship that of which I can conceive, first, as a loving Father and Mother; then, as thought ascends the scale of being to diviner consciousness, God becomes to me, as to the apostle who declared it, "God is Love"—divine Principle—which I worship; and "after the manner of my fathers, so worship I God." (p. 96)

In *Science and Health,* Mrs. Eddy uses a variety of terms for God. In the glossary of that book she defines God as follows: "God. The great I AM; the all-knowing, all-seeing, all-acting, all-wise, all-loving, and eternal; Principle; Mind; Soul; Spirit; Life; Truth; Love; all substance; intelligence." Her most unusual synonym for God, which she got from Quimby, is Principle. One can worship and pray to a personal God, but it is not easy to worship and pray to a Principle. Why did Mrs. Eddy so often use the term? I think it was to make her theology sound scientific, like invoking the principle of inertia or the principle of cohesion, and all the other principles of physics and chemistry that she heard about and dimly understood.

Mrs. Eddy firmly believed that Christian Science was not only a science, but it was as demonstrable as a valid syllogism or such mathematical statements as three times three is nine. She liked to call the cures of Christian Science "demonstrations," like experimental demonstrations in scientific laboratories. "In fifty years," she wrote in a letter, "aye less, Christian Science will be the dominant religion of the world."

More than a century has gone by, and this has not happened, but Christian Science did become one of the three great organized religions to spring up in America from the minds of women. The other two were Shakerism, founded by Ann Lee, and the Seventh-day Adventist church of Mrs. Ellen G. White. That such faiths, winning the allegiances of millions of disciples, could spring from the minds of semi-literate women is one of the awesome marvels in the annals of American religions.

The most often repeated (and accurate) quip about Christian Science, made by its detractors, is that it is neither Christian nor science. Moreover, Mrs. Eddy was not the first to use the term. As early as 1854 a minister named William Adams titled his book *The Elements of Christian Science.* Quimby himself used the term in an 1863 paper, although he preferred to call his theology "Christ Science."

Mrs. Eddy always thought of the healing power of God as a form of genuine science, not as something supernatural. It was simply the application of divine laws as objective and real as the law of gravity. These were the same laws used by Jesus in healing the sick and raising the dead. "Jesus of Nazareth," she wrote in *Science and Health,* "was the most scientific man that ever trod the globe" (p. 313). In an 1897 lecture she declared that "Christian Science is not only the acme of Science but the Crown of Christianity" (*Miscellaneous Writings,* p. 252).

For Mrs. Eddy, Christian Science relies not on matter and its laws, which are not real, but on the divine laws of God, which alone are truly real. Sin, sickness, and death—three nouns that Mrs. Eddy links together hundreds of times in her writings—simply do not exist, just as black does not exist as a color but is only our term for the absence of color. "Sickness is a dream from which the patient needs to be awakened," she once wrote. Death, too, is an illusion caused by humanity's false belief in matter. True, our bodies (which are unreal) may cease to function, but our immortal minds will continue to exist on some higher plane.

In her sermon *Christian Healing* Mrs. Eddy argues that "so-called death" is "produced by belief alone." To prove it, she cites a case in England where some unnamed Oxford students killed a "felon" by making him think he was bleeding to death. "Had they changed the felon's belief that he was bleeding to death, removed the bandage from his eyes, and he had seen that a vein had not been opened, he would have resuscitated." As usual, Mrs. Eddy provides no documentation for this startling incident.

Christian Scientists do not like to think about death. It is seldom mentioned in the *Christian Science Monitor,* and obituaries of even famous people seldom appear in that excellent newspaper. To this day the church has no burial service. Neither does it have marriage or baptismal services. It does have a communion service, but it is not to commemorate the Last Supper. Christian Scientists do not look upon the blood atonement as an actual historical event, but as a metaphor for "at-one-ment" of a human soul with God. The church's communion service honors the meal that the risen Jesus prepared for his disciples on the shore of the Sea of Galilee. It is observed by kneeling in silent prayer. For a while Mother Church, in Boston, celebrated this kind of communion, but Mrs. Eddy abolished it by Article 18 of her *Church Manual.* Branch churches observe the ceremony on the second Sunday of January and July. There are no special Easter services in Mother Church, as decreed by Article 17, Section 2, of the *Church Manual.* Mrs. Eddy did not believe in the bodily death and resurrection of Jesus. Having completely mastered the divine laws of Christian Science, he simply never died.

Christian Scientists make no effort to save sinners from hell because neither sin nor hell exist. Birthday celebrations are frowned upon because they remind us of what Mrs. Eddy, in chapter 8 of *Science and Health,* calls an error of thinking:

> The error of thinking that we are growing old, and the benefits of destroying that illusion, are illustrated in a sketch from the history of an English woman, published in the London medical magazine called The Lancet.
>
> Disappointed in love in her early years, she became insane and lost all account of time. Believing that she was still living in the same hour which parted her from her lover, taking no note of years, she stood daily before the window watching for her lover's coming. In this mental state she remained young. Having no consciousness of time, she literally grew no older. Some American travellers saw her when she was seventy-four, and supposed her to be a young woman. She had no care-lined face, no wrinkles nor gray hair, but youth sat gently on cheek and brow. Asked to guess her age, those unacquainted with her history conjectured that she must be under twenty.
>
> This instance of youth preserved furnishes a useful hint, upon

which a Franklin might work with more certainty than when he coaxed the enamoured lightning from the clouds. Years had not made her old, because she had taken no cognizance of passing time nor thought of herself as growing old. The bodily results of her belief that she was young manifested the influence of such a belief. She could not age while believing herself young, for the mental state governed the physical. (p. 245)

"Never record ages," Mrs. Eddy adds. "Chronological data are no part of the vast forever. Time-tables of birth and death are so many conspiracies against manhood and womanhood" (p. 246). She recalls a woman of eighty-five who had a return of sight, and a woman of ninety who grew a new set of teeth.

In certain Hindu religions the entire material world is called *maya,* or illusion. So it was for Mrs. Eddy. She liked to distinguish between the eternal mind, which is God, and our "mortal minds," which generate the illusion of matter. In *Science and Health* (chapter 11) she reminds her readers that doctors treat mental patients for hallucinations even though they know the hallucinations are not real. "Ought we not, then, to approve any cure, which is effected by making the disease appear to be—what it really is—an illusion?" (p. 348).

Mrs. Eddy occasionally coined neologisms. One of her crudest was "chemicalization" (*Science and Health,* p. 401). This is a process that occurs when sin, sickness, and death are seen to be illusions. It is a curious term because the body, which alone can experience a chemical change, is regarded by Mrs. Eddy as nonexistent. She chose the term, I suspect, because she wanted to make her system sound scientific, even though she neither knew nor cared a rap about chemistry or any other science.

"You say a boil is painful," Mrs. Eddy writes in *Science and Health,* "but that is impossible, for matter without mind is not painful. The boil simply manifests, through inflammation and swelling, a belief in pain, and this belief is called a boil" (p. 153).

It is, of course, obvious that a boil, in itself, cannot feel pain. Over and over again Mrs. Eddy reminds her readers that matter cannot feel, see, hear, taste, or smell. The feeling of pain obviously is a sensation in our mind. But to do away with pain by redefining it as a false belief and calling it unreal certainly doesn't make the sensation of pain unreal. Mrs. Eddy's dodge of eliminating something by redefining it gave rise to an anonymous, often quoted limerick:

> There was a faith healer named Neil,
> Who said, "Although pain isn't real,
>   If I sit on a pin,
>   and it punctures my skin,
> I dislike what I fancy I feel."

In all fairness I must add that no Christian Scientist need object to the limerick's truth. Believers readily agree that although pain isn't real, our mortal mind, in its error, experiences the sensation of pain. A toothache does not reside in matter, because matter doesn't exist. The pain is a state of mind. It seems real, but will vanish when our false belief in its reality vanishes. If one is overweight, Mrs. Eddy once said, the excess fat is an illusion that arises from an "adipose belief" (*Miscellaneous Writings*, p. 47). Get rid of the false belief and the fat will go away. There is, in brief, nothing really the matter with anybody because there really isn't any matter.

Although pain isn't real, you can be sure that the most devout Christian Scientist will leap out of the way of a car just as quickly as Mrs. Eddy would have jumped out of the way of a running horse. She looked forward to a future millennium in which the entire world would become Christian Scientists. When that day dawns, sin, sickness, pain, and death will be no more. Even terrible accidents that kill and maim will also disappear because they, too, are illusions springing from humanity's false beliefs. Until this millennium comes, however, we have to make compromises. Mrs. Eddy gave her followers permission to let surgeons take care of broken bones because we have not yet reached the wonderful epoch when bones no longer will be broken. Here is what she says about this in *Science and Health:*

> Until the advancing age admits the efficacy and supremacy of Mind, it is better for Christian Scientists to leave surgery and the adjustment of broken bones and dislocations to the fingers of a surgeon, while the mental healer confines himself chiefly to mental reconstruction and to the prevention of inflammation. Christian Science is always the most skilful surgeon, but surgery is the branch of its healing which will be last acknowledged. However, it is but just to say that the author has already in her possession well-authenticated records of the cure, by herself and her students through mental surgery alone, of broken bones, dislocated joints, and spinal vertebrae. . . . In Science, no breakage nor dislocation can really occur. You say that accidents, injuries, and disease kill man, but this is not true. The life of man is Mind. The material body manifests only what mortal mind believes, whether it be a broken bone, disease, or sin. (pp. 401–402)

Today Christian Scientists seldom hesitate to see a surgeon if they break an arm, leg, or hip. They go to dentists to have cavities filled, teeth pulled, and bridges made. They wear glasses and wigs. If they develop a serious disease, they may go both to a Christian Science practitioner and to a medical doctor. Although there is a small hard core of Christian Scientists who prefer to die, or let their spouses and children die, rather than seek medical help, increasingly the rank and file practice Christian Science more as an odd way of talking than an odd way of behaving.

"Liberal" Christian Scientists, as contrasted with fundamentalists who take every sentence in *Science and Health* as divinely inspired, must be dismayed by the small amount of wiggle room Mrs. Eddy allowed. Here are some passages on sickness from the current authorized edition of *Science and Health:*

A child may have worms if you say so, or any other malady, timorously held in the beliefs concerning his body. (pp. 413–14)

* * *

A thorough perusal of the author's publications heals sickness. If patients sometimes seem worse while reading this book, the change may either arise from the alarm of the physician, or it may mark the crisis of the disease. Perseverance in the perusal of this book has generally completely healed such cases. (p. 446)

* * *

The author never knew a patient who did not recover when the belief of the disease had gone. (p. 377)

* * *

The less mind there is manifested in matter the better. When the unthinking lobster loses its claw, the claw grows again. If the Science of Life were understood, it would be found that the senses of Mind are never lost and that matter has no sensation. Then the human limb would be replaced as readily as the lobster's claw,—not with an artificial limb, but with the genuine one. (p. 489)

Are contagious diseases spread by microbes? No, they are spread by false beliefs. On page 154 of *Science and Health* Mrs. Eddy tells of a man who was falsely told that the bed he slept in was a bed on which a cholera patient had died. The man at once caught cholera and died. "The fact was, that he had not caught the cholera by material contact," but because he believed he would catch it. That the mind can influence the body in many ways is, of course, a truism, but for Mrs. Eddy, the mind is the cause of *every* disease.

When you burn a finger, you might suppose that heat, arising from the motions of molecules, burned it. Not so. When you say "*I* have burned my finger," Mrs. Eddy writes in *Science and Health,* "This is an exact statement, more exact than you suppose; for mortal mind, and not matter, burns it" (p. 161).

> Experiments have favored the fact that Mind governs the body, not in one instance, but in every instance. The indestructible faculties of Spirit exist without the conditions of matter and also without the false beliefs of a so-called material existence. Working out the rules of Science in practice, the author has restored health in cases of both acute and chronic disease in their severest forms. Secretions have been changed, the structure has been renewed, shortened limbs have been elongated, ankylosed joints have been made supple, and carious bones have been restored to healthy conditions. I have restored what is called the lost substance of lungs, and healthy organizations have been established where disease was organic. Christian Science heals organic disease as surely as it heals what is called functional, for it requires only a fuller understanding of the divine Principle of Christian Science to demonstrate the higher rule. (p. 162)

Did Mrs. Eddy actually elongate a shortened limb? It is possible that she believed she did. I am more inclined to think she lied.

Even animals can be persuaded to get sick by giving them false beliefs:

> Every medical method has its advocates. The preference of mortal mind for a certain method creates a demand for that method, and the body then seems to require such treatment. You can even educate a healthy horse so far in physiology that he will take cold without his blanket, whereas the wild animal, left to his instincts, sniffs the wind with delight. The epizoötic is a humanly evolved ailment, which a wild horse might never have. (*Science and Health*, p. 179)

A man swallows poison by mistake and neither he nor his doctor know it is poison. Yet the person dies. How can this be? Was it because the poison actually poisoned him? Not at all. Here is Mrs. Eddy's incredible explanation:

> In such cases a few persons believe the potion swallowed by the patient to be harmless, but the vast majority of mankind, though they know nothing of this particular case and this special person, believe the arsenic, the strychnine, or whatever the drug used, to be poisonous, for it is set down as a poison by mortal mind. Consequently, the result is controlled by the majority of opinions, not by the infinitesimal minority of opinions in the sick-chamber. (*Science and Health*, pp. 177–78).

It is a well established fact that certain body and mental ailments are genetic and inherited. Mrs. Eddy flatly denied this. "The [Christian] Scientist knows that there can be no hereditary disease, since matter is not intelligent and cannot transmit good or evil intelligence to man, and God, the only Mind, does not produce pain in matter" (*Science and Health*, pp. 412–13).

Not only are all bodily ills illusions arising from false belief, but even such cravings as thirst arise from belief. "You say or think, because you have partaken of salt fish, that you must be thirsty, and you are thirsty accordingly, while the opposite belief would produce the opposite result" (*Science and Health*, p. 385).

As I said before, Mrs. Eddy reminds her readers repeatedly that matter cannot see, feel, hear, taste, or smell. Obviously these are sensations in the mind; they arise from the body's contacts, through the senses, with a material world. For Mrs. Eddy, there is no such world. Matter is an illusion. Since it doesn't exist, naturally it cannot have any properties or cause any sensations.

You might suppose, in your ignorance of Christian Science, that a blacksmith's arm muscles were produced by exercising them. Wrong again! It was the blacksmith's belief that his muscles would enlarge that enlarged them.

Because the muscles of the blacksmith's arm are strongly developed, it does not follow that exercise has produced this result or that a less used arm must be weak. If matter were the cause of action, and if muscles without volition of mortal mind, could lift the hammer and strike the anvil, it might be thought true that hammering would enlarge the muscles. The trip-hammer is not increased in size by exercise. Why not, since muscles are as material as wood and iron? Because nobody believes that mind is producing such a result on the hammer.

Muscles are not self-acting. If mind does not move them, they are motionless. Hence the great fact that Mind alone enlarges and empowers man through its mandate,—by reason of its demand for and supply of power. Not because of muscular exercise, but by reason of the blacksmith's faith in exercise, his arm becomes stronger. (*Science and Health,* pp. 198–99)

Mrs. Eddy's belief in the power of Mind to control the unreal body was so extreme, and her credulity so monumental, that she could write in *Science and Health:*

It is related that a father plunged his infant babe, only a few hours old, into the water for several minutes, and repeated this operation daily, until the child could remain under water twenty minutes, moving and playing without harm, like a fish. Parents should remember this, and learn how to develop their children properly on dry land. (pp. 556–57)

The Christian Science church has refused to modify *Science and Health* in any way since Mrs. Eddy died. Surely it must find it embarrassing to allow this preposterous passage to remain in the sacred text.

Why do so many drugs seem to heal? In Mrs. Eddy's view they heal because so many people believe they will. Although Mrs. Eddy does not use the term, which did not become current until after her death, she firmly believed in PK, or psychokinesis. She not only believed that practitioners could heal at a distance—a practice still followed today—but that "malicious animal magnetism" could produce injuries at a distance. (We will devote chapter 5 to this witchcraft.) In themselves, drugs for Mrs. Eddy had no power to heal. Here is one of her funniest nonsequiturs:

> If drugs are part of God's creation, which (according to the narrative in Genesis) He pronounced *good,* then drugs cannot be poisonous. If He could create drugs intrinsically bad, then they should never be used. If He creates drugs at all and designs them for medical use, why did Jesus not employ them and recommend them for the treatment of disease? Matter is not self-creative, for it is unintelligent. Erring mortal mind confers the power which the drug seems to possess. (*Science and Health,* p. 157)

Unlike any other sacred text, *Science and Health* closes with a "Fruitage" chapter devoted to a hundred pages of testimonies from persons who were miraculously healed by Christian Science of almost every major ailment known. As I said earlier, Mrs. Eddy considered these healings to be scientific "demonstrations." Writers of the letters are identified only by their initials and the city where they lived, making it impossible even at the time for any skeptic to verify the accuracy of a diagnosis or its cure. Cancer, tuberculosis, hernias, heart and lung diseases, blindness, deafness, Bright's disease, and many other terrible ills vanish quickly when patients are made to overcome their false beliefs that their ailments are real.

There has never in the history of medicine been a single authenticated case of a cataract dissolving. A cataract is an irreversible clouding of the eye lens. It would be like seeing a fried egg unfry itself. Yet on page 608 of *Science and Health,* a man in Liverpool, England, claims that his cataracts completely vanished while he was reading *Sci-*

ence and Health! Of course there is no supporting evidence, such as an affidavit from an eye doctor saying the man had cataracts to begin with, or that they later disappeared. Assuming the man gave an honest testimony, he may have had incipient cataracts that did not develop further, and he imagined his vision had improved.

It is a scandal that to this day Christian Scientists, like faith-healing evangelists and psychic healers, make no effort to document their miracles in ways that can be verified. Many ills go away by themselves. Many are psychosomatic, responding to faith in any sort of healer whether he be mainstream doctor, a psychic, or a quack. No one today denies the powerful effect of mental attitudes on the body. Moreover, many believers, eager to advance a strong belief, will unconsciously exaggerate or even lie about a cure. Records of failures, including deaths of persons who sought a Christian Science cure rather than seek orthodox medical aid, are never publicized by the church and only rarely are reported in the news. The church, like faith-healing televangelists, makes little or no effort to follow up years later on a supposed cure.

One of the most publicized cases of a tragic failure occurred in 1888. It involved a Mrs. Abby Corner, of West Medford, Massachusetts, who practiced what was then called "metaphysical obstetrics," as taught by Mrs. Eddy herself. Mrs. Corner took it upon herself to handle, without medical help, the birth of her daughter's child. Both mother and child died. Mrs. Corner was arrested for manslaughter, and the press had a field day with the story. Church officials insisted that Mrs. Corner had never attended Mrs. Eddy's lectures on obstetrics. They branded her a "quack." It soon turned out that she had indeed taken the obstetrics course in Mrs. Eddy's "college." Charles Troube, then secretary of the Christian Science Association, resigned over what he said was an attempt by his superiors to alter Mrs. Corner's records. More than thirty other members of the association also resigned, leaving the Boston church with only about 160 members. Mrs. Corner was eventually acquitted on the grounds that the daughter and child died from causes that would have been fatal even if experienced obstetricians had been present.

For a time Mrs. Eddy turned her course in obstetrics over to Ebenezer (Benny) Foster, the homeopathic physician she later adopted as a son. Homeopathic doctors are not trained in obstetrics, so this did little to improve the course. In 1902 Mrs. Eddy declared that "Obstetrics is not Science," and dropped the course altogether from her college. Few Christian Scientists today risk giving birth to children without medical aid.

In his book *The Faith and Works of Christian Science* (1909) Dr. Stephen Paget cited sixty-eight cases of needless suffering, brutality, and death that resulted when Christian Scientists refused medical attention from doctors. Dr. Paget sums them up as follows:

> These short notes, put here as I got them, give but a faint sense of the ill working of Christian Science. It would be easy to collect hundreds more. Of course, to see the full iniquity of these cases, the reader should be a doctor. But everybody, doctor or not, can feel the cruelty, born of fear of pain, in some of these Scientists—the downright madness threatening not a few of them, and the appalling self-will. They bully dying women, and let babies die in pain; let cases of paralysis tumble about and hurt themselves; rob the epileptic of their bromide, the syphilitic of their iodide, the angina cases of their amyl nitrite, the heart cases of their digitalis; let appendicitis go on to septic peritonitis, gastric ulcer to perforation of the stomach, nephritis to uraemic convulsions, and strangulated hernia to the *miserere mei* of gangrene; watch, day after day, while a man or a woman bleeds to death; compel them who should be kept still to take exercise; and withhold from all cases of cancer all hope of cure. To these works of the Devil they bring their one gift, willful and complete ignorance; and their "nursing" would be a farce, if it were not a tragedy. Such is the way of Christian Science, face to face, as she loves to be, with bad cases of organic disease. . . .

In a rage, Common-sense cries, "For God's sake leave the children alone. It doesn't matter with grown-up people; they can believe what they like about Good and Evil, and germs, and things. But the children; they take their children to these services. Why can't they leave the children out of it?" . . . The corner stone of her church is not Jesus Christ but her own vanity. She is cruel to babies and young children; she is worse than close-fisted over her money; she despises Christianity, and is at open war with experience and common sense. . . . We examine her testimonials, and find them worthless. We are told that she is Christ come again, and we can see that she is not. We listen to her philosophical talk, and observe that she is illiterate, and ignorant of the rudiments of logic. We admit, and are glad, that she has enabled thousands of nervous persons to leave off worrying, and has cured many "functional disorders"; but she has done that, not by revelation, but by suggestion. The healed, whom she incessantly advertises, are but few, compared with them that are whole, . . . and a thousand brave and quiet lives, the unnamed legion of good non-Scientists. They bear, not deny, pain; they confess, not confuse, the reality of sin; they face, not outface, death. (Snowden, pp. 243–44)

Obviously the greatest tragedy that can happen to Christian Scientists occurs when they die of a curable disease after postponing a consultation with a medical doctor. A more subtle kind of tragedy afflicts believers who, after not being healed by faith, assume that the failure is a defect in themselves. If an evangelist calls you on stage and assures you that your cataracts have been dissipated, and you find later they were not, you may believe that the fault was not with the evangelist but with yourself for lacking sufficient faith in God's healing power. Roman Catholics who visit healing shrines such as Lourdes and return unhealed often blame themselves for lack of faith. If Christian Science fails to effect a cure, patients may conclude, on the basis of Mrs. Eddy's clear teachings, that it was because they were unable to let go of their false belief that they were ill.

In recent decades, as the influence of Christian Science wanes, the media have been less timid about publicizing cases of child abuse by Christian Science parents, and local courts are developing the courage to take stricter action. The most publicized of recent tragedies involved David and Ginger Twitchell, of Boston, the home of Mother Church. In 1990 they were sentenced to ten years probation for involuntary manslaughter. Their twelve-year-old son Robyn had died four years earlier from a bowel obstruction that could easily have been removed. Instead, the Twitchells called only a Christian Science practitioner. The Twitchells were ordered to take their three surviving children to a doctor for regular checkups.*

This was by no means the first case of such court action. I have only scant data, but I find in my files a clipping from the *New York Times* (November 17, 1967) saying that in 1967 Mrs. Dorothy Sheridan, a Christian Scientist in Barnstable, Massachusetts, was convicted of involuntary manslaughter when she refused medical help for Lisa, her seven-year-old daughter who died from lung disease. In the January-February 1990 issue of *In Health* Dr. Edward Dolnick had an article titled "Murder by Faith." It details the sad case of Amy Hermanson, a child who died of diabetes after being refused medical aid by her Christian Science parents. I am told that since 1980 there have been seven prosecutions of Christian Science parents for similar child deaths, with five convictions.

Although Mrs. Eddy paid for vaccinations of her grandchildren, and even recommended vaccinations to her followers, many devout Chris-

---

*Details on the Twitchell case can be found in Tamar Lewin's article, "When It's One Absolute Against Another," in the *New York Times* (May 29, 1988); Stephanie Schorow's Associated Press release, "Christian Science Couple Gets Probation in Death of Their Son" (July 7, 1990); Alex Beam, "Christian Scientists Uneasy as Beliefs Go On Trial," *The Boston Globe* (May 2, 1988); Mark Starr, "Prayer in the Courtroom," *Newsweek* (April 30, 1990); A. L. Sanders, "Convicted of Relying on Prayer," *Time* (July 16, 1990); and "Twitchells Found Guilty," *Christian Century* (July 15, 1990).

tian Scientists still oppose vaccinations. As late as 1985 two unimmunized students at the church's Principia College in Elsah, Illinois, died during a measles outbreak. In 1972, at the Daycroft School in Greenwich, Connecticut, most of the students were Christian Scientists who refused immunization for polio. When a rare outbreak of polio occurred at the school, eleven students came down with the disease, and four of them became partially paralyzed. There was no danger of the outbreak spreading beyond the school because other children in the city had been given polio shots.*

For decades the Christian Science church has managed to persuade legislatures in forty-three states, including Massachusetts, Florida, and California, to pass laws exempting parents from child abuse when they practice religious healing without seeking medical help. Now that media attention to such deaths is growing, and courts are becoming braver, there is a chance that at least some of these abominable laws may be repealed.

---

*See Jonathan Randell, "The Price Paid by Believers," *The New York Times* (October 29, 1972).

4

Heaven and the Second Coming

Plato's opinion that each of us has a nonmaterial "soul" inside our material brain, or the view that our bodies will be reconstituted after death, were anathema to Mrs. Eddy. We think we have bodies, but that's an illusion of mortal mind. Only our eternal soul, part of the Mind of God, is real. It is immortal because God is immortal.

When Jesus called Lazarus from the tomb, Mrs. Eddy explains in *Science and Health*, he did not resurrect a dead body.

> Jesus restored Lazarus by the understanding that Lazarus had never died. . . . Had Jesus believed that Lazarus had lived or died in his body, the Master would have stood on the same plane of belief as those who buried the body, and he could not have resuscitated it. (p. 75)

Note that Mrs. Eddy refers to Jesus as resuscitating a dead body. This may seem like a contradiction until you understand that she means that Jesus resuscitated the *illusion* of a dead body, a body which did not exist. Matter, you will recall, is nothingness. Dead bodies are as unreal as stones and stars. Because our bodies are not real, we only seem to die. Did Mrs. Eddy imagine that she herself, who had so thoroughly overcome false beliefs, might escape death? Probably not. Nevertheless, she never took out any form of life insurance. In an interview near the end of her life she said she had no need of such insurance because "God insures my life." It is possible she half-believed she was immortal.

Although heaven, for Mrs. Eddy, is not a place in the sense of being somewhere in our space and time, it is a state on some higher level of being in which we retain our identities. We will recognize loved ones who have gone on before. "Mortals waken from the dream of death with bodies unseen by those who think that they bury the body" (*Science and Health*, p. 429).

There is no way, Mrs. Eddy taught, that we can communicate with those who have passed on because they are in an entirely different region of God's eternal Mind. There is, however, one exception. Just before dying we may have what in today's New Age terminology is an NDE, or Near-Death Experience, in which we catch a momentary glimpse of those awaiting us on the other shore:

> There is one possible moment, when those living on the earth and those called dead, can commune together, and that is the moment previous to the transition,—the moment when the link between their opposite beliefs is being sundered. In the vestibule through which we pass from one dream to another dream, or when we awake from earth's sleep to the grand verities of Life, the departing may hear the glad welcome of those who have gone before. The ones departing may whisper this vision, name the face that smiles on them and the hand which beckons them, as one at Niagara, with eyes open only to that wonder, forgets all else and breathes aloud his rapture. (*Science and Health*, pp. 75–76)

Science and Health repeatedly says that death, like sin and sickness, is an illusion that will be removed from Earth at some far distant millennial age when everybody has become a Christian Scientist and all false beliefs have been removed. It is easy to understand why so many of Mrs. Eddy's more devout followers did not expect her to die. When she finally did, was it because she and the rest of humanity had not fully overcome their error of supposing death to be real? There are grounds in *Science and Health* for just such an opinion.

> Much yet remains to be said and done before all mankind is saved and all the mental microbes of sin and all diseased thought-germs are exterminated.
>   If you or I should appear to die, we should not be dead. The seeming decease, caused by a majority of human beliefs that man must die, or produced by mental assassins, does not in the least disprove Christian Science; rather does it evidence the truth of its basic proposition that mortal thoughts in belief rule the materiality miscalled life in the body or in matter. But the forever fact remains paramount that Life, Truth, and Love save from sin, disease, and death. "When this corruptible shall have put on incorruption, and this mortal shall have put on immortality [divine Science], then shall be brought to pass the saying that is written, Death is swallowed up in victory" (St. Paul). (p. 164)

Exactly what happens to a person's immortal soul after he or she seems to die? Mrs. Eddy is extremely vague in answering this question. She denies that a soul inhabits a body because the body, being made of matter, is not real. A corpse "deserted by thought, is cold and decays," she wrote in *Science and Health* (p. 429). The coldness and decay are, of course, illusions of mortal mind. In her book's glossary "heaven" is not defined as a place, but as "Harmony; the reign of Spirit; government by Divine Principle; spirituality; bliss; the atmosphere of Soul." One gathers from Mrs. Eddy's obscure remarks about life after death that the soul, being immortal, passes on to a higher realm about which we know nothing. "Mortals waken from the dream of death with bodies unseen by those who think that they bury the body" (*Science and Health,* p. 429). Presumably she means that after death we receive a spiritual body such as the one Saint Paul said would replace our old one. For Mrs. Eddy there is no replacement of a *material* body, though perhaps she went along with Paul in thinking the immortal soul would be given a spiritual body.

In *Science and Health* there are hints that we may have existed before we were born: "If we live after death and are immortal, we must have lived before birth, for if Life ever had any beginning, it must also have an ending, even according to the calculations of natural science" (p. 429). Exactly in what manner we existed before birth is not clear. At any rate, there is no suggestion of a previous life on earth, or a reincarnation in another earth body. Mrs. Eddy had a low opinion of theosophy and Eastern religions that assume reincarnation. This did not prevent a few Christian Science leaders from combining their faith with reincarnation. For some instances, see Altman K. Swihart's *Since Mrs. Eddy* (1931). This book deals mainly with the rebellions of Annie C. Bill in England and Augusta E. Stetson in New York City, both of whom we shall meet in later chapters.

Although *Science and Health* has no references to Mary Baker Eddy raising the dead, there are documents by her close associates that say she claimed to have raised the dead on at least three occasions. Sue Harper Mims, in her essay "An Intimate Portrait of Our Leader's Final Class" (in *We Knew Mary Baker Eddy,* Second Series, published by the church in 1950), recalls Mrs. Eddy telling a class that on three occasions she had raised the dead. "I could not help thinking of Jesus," Mims writes, "first raising the little maid, then the young man, then Lazarus."

Mrs. Eddy provided details of only one instance. After a child died and the doctor had left, the mother sent for Mrs. Eddy. Mrs. Eddy asked to be alone with the corpse. She took the lifeless body in her arms. According to Mims, when the mother returned, the child ran across the floor to meet her. Irving C. Tomlinson repeats the story in *Twelve Years with Mary Baker Eddy* (1945, p. 57).

There are said to be other accounts of Mrs. Eddy reviving dead bodies—accounts given in documents owned by Mother Church but not published for obvious reasons. Adam Dickey, in *Memoirs of Mary Baker Eddy* (1925), describes an occasion on which Mrs. Eddy seemed to bring back to life her loyal servant Calvin Frye. Frye had passed out from some sort of seizure, and appeared to be either dead or dying.

> Never shall I forget the picture that was before us in that small bedroom, the light shining on the half-scared faces of the workers, and our Leader's intense determination to keep Mr. Frye with her. I had heard of similar occasions when rumors had reached the workers in the field that at different times our Leader had restored prominent students to life after experiences of this kind, but of this incident I was an eye-witness and from the very first my attention was not diverted for one second from what was going on, and I am simply relating this event exactly as it occurred. (p. 40)

Although Mrs. Eddy never claimed in her own writings that she had ever revived a corpse, some of her claims of instant healings are almost as miraculous. They put to shame the healings described in the "Fruitage" section of *Science and Health* or the testimonies you can hear at Wednesday night meetings of the faithful. Mrs. Eddy often wrote about her cures in the days before she retired from the practice. A footnote in *Pulpit and Press* reads:

> Note:—About 1868, the author of Science and Health healed Mr. Whittier with one visit, at his home in Amesbury, of incipient pulmonary consumption.—M. B. Eddy. (p. 54)

I have not checked biographies of John Greenleaf Whittier to see if the poet ever corroborated this claim. And what, by the way, is "incipient pulmonary tuberculosis"? Maybe it just means a bad cold that improved the next day. As Mrs. Eddy later remembered, she found Whittier coughing by a fire, his cheeks flushed. Before she left, he seemed better. "I thank you Mary for your call," he said at the door, "it has done me much good, come again."

A section in Mrs. Eddy's *Miscellaneous Writings* is headed "Letters from Those Healed by Reading *Science and Health with Key to the Scriptures.*" It includes the following polite letter from Henry Wadsworth Longfellow:

> Having so many occupations and interruptions, I have not found time to read "Science and Health with Key to the Scriptures" sufficiently, but will not on that account delay thanking you for its excellence. (p. 454)

Did Longfellow ever read it, I wonder? If so, just what illness did it heal?

In *The First Church of Christ, Scientist, and Miscellany* we find:

> After my discovery of Christian Science, I healed consumption in its last stages, a case which the M.D.'s, by verdict of the stethoscope and the schools, declared incurable because the lungs were mostly consumed. I healed malignant diphtheria and carious bones that could be dented by the finger, saving the limbs when the surgeon's instruments were lying on the table ready for their amputation. I have healed at one visit a cancer that had eaten the flesh of the neck and exposed the jugular vein so that it stood out like a cord. I have physically restored sight to the blind, hearing to the deaf, speech to the dumb, and have made the lame walk. (p. 105)

The statement about the exposed jugular vein is a bit much. Did this really happen? I strongly doubt it. Either Mrs. Eddy lied or she remembered it wrong. Naturally we are not told the name of the man or woman who was cured so quickly, the time or place of the cure, or the name of any doctor who diagnosed the person before or after.

But back to our main topic. Here is a passage about heaven from chapter 14 of *The First Church of Christ, Scientist, and Miscellany:*

> Is heaven spiritual?
> Heaven is spiritual. Heaven is harmony,—infinite, boundless bliss. The dying or the departed enter heaven in proportion to their progress, in proportion to their fitness to partake of the quality and the quantity of heaven. One individual may first awaken from his dream of life in matter with a sense of music; another with that of relief from fear or suffering, and still another with a bitter sense of lost opportunities and remorse. Heaven is the reign of divine Science. (p. 267)

When Mrs. Eddy denies that heaven is a "place," presumably she means, as suggested earlier, a place outside our space and time. That we persist as individuals after the illusion of dying, in some sort of spiritual state with our memories intact, is not only affirmed, but Mrs. Eddy speaks elsewhere (in *Science and Health*) of a kind of purgatory—she calls it a period of "probation"—during which we continue to make progress toward conquering our illusions:

> If the change called *death* destroyed the belief in sin, sickness, and death, happiness would be won at the moment of dissolution, and be forever permanent; but this is not so. Perfection is gained only by perfection. They who are unrighteous shall be unrighteous still, until in divine Science Christ, Truth, removes all ignorance and sin.
> The sin and error which possess us at the instant of death do not cease at that moment, but endure until the death of these errors.

To be wholly spiritual, man must be sinless, and he becomes thus only when he reaches perfection. (p. 290)

In her pamphlet *No and Yes* Mrs. Eddy puts it this way:

Surely the probation of mortals must go on after the change called death, that they may learn the definition of immortal being; or else their present mistakes would extinguish human existence. How long this false sense remains after the transition called death, no mortal knoweth; but this is sure, that the mists of error, sooner or later, will melt in the fervent heat of suffering, mortality will burst the barriers of sense, and man be found perfect and eternal. Of his intermediate conditions—the purifying processes and terrible revolutions necessary to effect this end—I am ignorant. (pp. 27–28)

What happens to those who, after death, never succeed in conquering their illusions? Here we encounter one of the many contradictions in Mrs. Eddy's writings. She constantly speaks of every soul as immortal. But in the following passage from *Miscellaneous Writings* she says that after death those who refuse to move toward perfection will experience a "second death" and be annihilated!

Man's probation after death is the necessity of his immortality; for good dies not and evil is self-destructive, therefore evil must be mortal and self-destroyed. If man should not progress after death, but should remain in error, he would be inevitably self-annihilated. Those upon whom "the second death hath no power" are those who progress here and hereafter out of evil, their mortal element, and into good that is immortal; thus laying off the material beliefs that war against Spirit, and putting on the spiritual elements in divine Science. (p. 2)

It is astonishing to find this doctrine of the annihilation of the wicked turning up in Mrs. Eddy's thinking. It is a doctrine common today to Seventh-day Adventism and Jehovah's Witnesses, as well as to many other fringe sects of the past, not to mention many distinguished theologians who have favored obliteration of the wicked as more humane than eternal burning in hell.

What about the prospects of a Second Coming of Jesus, as prophesied in the New Testament? Here we have a splendid example of how Mrs. Eddy, flourishing her thousands of biblical quotations, always *sounds* like a Christian, but actually reinterprets passages in perverse ways. The Second Coming, according to Mrs. Eddy, is none other than the arrival on earth of Christian Science! Because Christian Science was Mrs. Eddy's discovery, or so she claimed, we can only conclude that her work was the fulfillment of what Jesus predicted about his Second Coming. Mrs. Eddy clearly suggested this in *The First Church of Christ, Scientist, and Miscellany:*

> Thirty years ago (1866) Christian Science was discovered in America. Within those years it is estimated that Chicago has gained from a population of 238,000 to the number of 1,650,000 inhabitants.
>
> The statistics of mortality show that thirty years ago the death-rate was at its maximum. Since that time it has steadily decreased. It is authentically said that one expositor of Daniel's dates fixed the year 1866 or 1867 for the return of Christ—the return of the spiritual idea to the material earth or antipode of heaven. It is a marked coincidence that those dates were the first two years of my discovery of Christian Science. (p. 181)

Mrs. Eddy had second thoughts about the date of the Second Coming. In her *Message to the Mother Church, 1900,* she moved the date up to 1875:

> Again, that Christian Science is the Science of God is proven when, in the degree that you accept it, understand and practise it, you are

made better physically, morally, and spiritually. Some modern exegesis on the prophetic Scriptures cites 1875 as the year of the second coming of Christ. In that year the Christian Science textbook, "Science and Health with Key to the Scriptures," was first published. From that year the United States official statistics show the annual death-rate to have gradually diminished. Likewise the religious sentiment has increased; creeds and dogmas have been sifted, and a greater love of the Scriptures manifested. In 1895 it was estimated that during the past three years there had been more Bibles sold than in all the other 1893 years. Many of our best and most scholarly men and women, distinguished members of the bar and bench, press and pulpit, and those in all the walks of life, will tell you they never loved the Bible and appreciated its worth as they did after reading "Science and Health with Key to the Scriptures." This is my great reward for having suffered, lived, and learned, in a small degree, the Science of perfectibility through Christ, the Way, the Truth, and the Life. (pp. 6–7)

Whether 1866 or 1875, it is clear that Mrs. Eddy regarded the coming of Christian Science as the Second Coming of Christ. Egocentric though she was, there was a streak of modesty in her character. As far as I know, she never suggested that the true date of the Second Coming was 1821, the year she was born on a farm in Bow.

5

Malicious Animal Magnetism I

Mrs. Eddy never abandoned her youthful belief in the power of what Mesmer called "animal magnetism." To this term she prefixed the word "malicious," creating the phrase "Malicious Animal Magnetism," or MAM for short. To her dying day she firmly believed that MAM was a powerful malignant force which earlier ages called witchcraft, and which today is called malicious psychokinesis, or PK. By using this force, a person with evil motives could transmit vibes, over long distances, that would make hated persons ill or even kill them.

During the last half of her life, Mrs. Eddy developed clear symptoms of paranoia. Not only did she have delusions of grandeur about her role as God's chosen instrument for a new religious revelation that would conquer the world, she also believed she was under never-ending attacks by the MAM of her enemies. Her creeping old age, with its inevitable changes in her appearance and health, surely contributed to her delusions of persecution. As we have seen, she taught that Christian Science could forestall the ravages of old age. How, then, could she explain to her followers and to herself that she was forced to go to

83

dentists, to wear false teeth and spectacles, use a cane, and take morphine to relieve pain? In her confused mind these blights of aging could only be explained by the MAM of her detractors. MAM became her substitute for the personalized Satan of her father's theology. In the glossary of *Science and Health* she explicitly identifies MAM with the Red Dragon of the Apocalypse.

"Mother never has and cannot be mistaken in her diagnosis of MAM," Mrs. Eddy wrote in a letter. In her *Church Manual* (Article 11, Section 7) we find: "If the author of *Science and Health* shall bear witness to the offense of mental malpractice, it shall be considered a sufficient evidence thereof." In other words, if Mrs. Eddy decided someone was bombarding her with MAM, her decision about this was not to be questioned. In the second and third editions of *Science and Health* she demanded that law courts recognize the terrible crimes committed by MAM. Articles about MAM appeared regularly in the *Christian Science Journal*. In 1887 a department of the magazine was devoted entirely to it. When readers complained that their leader was obsessed with the topic, she replied (October 1885): "Those who deny my right or wisdom to expose its crimes are either participants in this evil, afraid of its supposed power, or ignorant of it."

In 1878 Mrs. Eddy sued Daniel Harrison Spofford, a former associate, for using MAM to inflict "great suffering of body and mind and spinal pains and neuralgia and a temporary suspension of mind" on Miss Lucretia Brown, age fifty, one of Mrs. Eddy's students. Lucretia lived in Ipswich, Massachusetts. A trial was held in, of all places, Salem, where it became known as the "Ipswich witchcraft trial." Edward J. Arens, a German cabinetmaker in Lynn who had become one of Mrs. Eddy's most devoted students, represented Miss Brown at the trial. A much amused judge dismissed the case.

Mrs. Eddy promptly formed a group of twelve students whose task it was to beam energy back to Spofford, in relays of two hours each, to counteract the MAM she was certain he was beaming toward her and her students. Quimby, by the way, often treated patients in absentia, as do Christian Science practitioners to this day. It was not the first time Mrs. Eddy had used students in this way. As we shall see shortly, she had used students earlier to combat the MAM of Richard Kennedy, another one-time associate. Spofford behaved like a gentleman. He never retaliated against Mrs. Eddy's venom. For the rest of his life he expressed gratitude toward her, and maintained that *Science and Health* was the "greatest book in the world outside the Bible."

In her writings Mrs. Eddy always played down her occasional use of morphine, and Christian Scientists studiously avoid mentioning it. However, there is no longer any doubt that it was a long-standing habit. Much of the evidence comes from a diary kept by a servant of Mrs. Eddy named Calvin Frye. Before quoting from the diary, we must answer the question, "Who was Frye?"

Frye was a large, taciturn, seemingly stupid man who became a student of Mrs. Eddy at the age of thirty-seven, and later joined her staff as her most trusted servant. He had married when he was twenty-eight, but his wife died less than a year later, leaving no children. Frye suffered from occasional cataleptic seizures similar to Mrs. Eddy's, perhaps inherited from his mother who died insane. Like Mrs. Eddy, he became convinced that his ills were caused by MAM.

One of the best of many unauthorized biographies of Mrs. Eddy is *According to the Flesh* (1930) by Fleta Campbell Springer. Here is her colorful description of Calvin Frye:

> Calvin Frye succeeded in becoming the most enigmatic figure in the history of the Christian Science Church. Whether his character was so simple as to be an enigma, or so complex that it was incomprehensible, no one will ever know. Soft-footed, silent, suave, he entered Mrs. Eddy's household in 1882, and soft-footed, silent, suave, he moved through the rooms of the vast mansion at Chestnut Hill on the day

of Mrs. Eddy's death. It was said that for twenty-five years Calvin Frye had never been outside the call of Mrs. Eddy's voice. Coachman, footman, secretary, bodyguard, and errandboy—no task and no position was too menial for him to assume. Dark powers have been attributed to him. It was said that he came to wield an evil, hypnotic control over Mrs. Eddy, that under his calm exterior he plotted to seize control of her fortune and her church. It has also been said that Mrs. Eddy held Calvin Frye under her hypnotic control. When two people exhibit the symptoms of being mutually hypnotized, we are certainly faced with the conclusion that each has hypnotized himself. But all these stories are out of the later years. (p. 294)

Now for a portion of Frye's diary:

Mr. Dickey last night told Mrs. Eddy that she shall not have any more morphine! She had for several days been suffering . . . but yesterday seemed normal and so having had hypodermic injections twice within a few days he believed she did not need it but that it was the old morphine habit reasserting itself and would not allow her to have it. (pp. 297–98)

Fleta Springer conjectures that Mrs. Eddy's lifelong dependence on morphine shots and tablets contributed to her frequent hysterical rages, her delusions, and her constant irrational accusations of MAM practiced by her friends. The habit has been amply confirmed by others. Springer quotes the following remarks by Mrs. Miranda Rice, which appeared in the *New York World* (October 30, 1906):

I was one of Mrs. Eddy's first converts and associates. I have treated her hundreds of times. Finally we could not support Mrs. Eddy's pretensions to evil powers. We resigned in a body. I was not able to subscribe to Mrs. Eddy's practices. When she received my resignation she came to my house and pounded on all three of the doors with a stone. She was wild. She sent me word she intended to have me arrested for deserting her.

I know that Mrs. Eddy was addicted to morphine in the seventies. She begged me to get some for her. She sent her husband Mr. Eddy for some, and when he failed to get it went herself and got it. She locked herself into her room and for two days excluded everyone. She was a slave to morphine. (p. 299)

Mrs. Eddy's adopted son, Ebenezer Foster, also spoke about his foster mother's morphine addiction in an interview in the *New York World* (March 12, 1907). Mrs. Eddy had accused him of falsifying her account books. Here is how Springer summarizes what he told the *World:*

Foster-Eddy charged that his account books had been stolen one by one and secretly falsified; that the story about the woman in his office was deliberately circulated to effect his downfall. He heard the story in his Boston office and within an hour was on his way to Pleasant View. The one thought in his mind was "to see Mother and vindicate myself." "At Pleasant View I hurried into my Mother's room and found her seated at her desk. At sight of me she sprang to her feet, shrieked for help and darted out of the room. Of course I followed, thinking that she had been seized by one of her mad attacks; but she fled before me, stumbling, falling, dragging herself along in terror. Through it all she never ceased to shriek 'Murder' at the top of her voice. Satisfied at last that I could not quiet her I left the house dazed, and took the next train back to Boston. Three weeks later I learned the truth. The plotters had convinced Mrs. Eddy that I was going to Pleasant View to kill her. In her weakness of mind, she had believed the lie, and my arrival had terrified her."

The story tells how he "again defeated Frye," and managed to see his mother and convince her of his innocence. "She put her trembling hands in mine and begged me never to leave her, never to desert her. 'You know how things are here,' she said, 'and I want you to promise that when you receive an order from me to go away, to do something in another city, do not obey it. Remember, my boy, that I shall have been forced to make the order; that I shall not mean it. Promise me my son.' " He gave her his promise, but it proved to be their last interview. The "conspirators" were too much for him.

Foster-Eddy had other stories to tell. He told of "periods of frenzy" that seized Mrs. Eddy when she "rushed around the room filling the house with her cries." In these paroxysms, he said, she was uncontrollable. "At dead of night on one occasion I was aroused by Frye's knocking at my door. 'Come quick,' said he; 'your mother is mad, she thinks that a tumor has suddenly grown on her chest. She is calling for you.' I do not know what arts had been practised upon the unfortunate woman that night, but I do know that I found poor Mrs. Eddy crouching under the bed clothes and clutching at her breast with both hands. In vain I made an examination and assured her that the tumor had vanished. 'No it is still there,' she would cry. 'I see it. It is there,' she would cry, 'I see it. It is there—there.' Morning dawned before I could quiet her."

He also told of a night when Calvin Frye obtained a morphine tablet from him (he had been using the tablets for his own neuralgia!) and, his curiosity aroused, he followed Frye to Mrs. Eddy's room where she lay screaming and hysterical, and saw Frye "force the tablet into her mouth and hold her firmly down among the pillows." (pp. 417-18)

As I said earlier, Spofford was not the first of Mrs. Eddy's associates whom she accused of harming her with MAM. Richard Kennedy, after taking lessons from Mrs. Eddy and even for a time sharing offices with her, set up his own private practice. Mrs. Eddy could not countenance any kind of competition. Kennedy continued to use Quimby's head-rubbing technique that he had learned from Mrs. Eddy before she discontinued the practice. The exact cause of her fury against him remains obscure, but it was not long until she was calling him the "chief of the Demonologists." Few Christian Scientists today are aware that in the first edition of *Science and Health,* in the chapter titled "Healing the Sick," Mrs. Eddy indulged in violent personal attacks on Kennedy. Here is a sample of her wrath:

> Rubbing the head he keeps his cases constantly on hand. . . . No enthusiasm or praise is as zealous or fulsome as this malpractitioner can elicit, while nothing is more relentless or unyielding than the prejudice he can arouse. . . . Manipulating the head, even to a thinness that would reveal the brains, can never heal the sick in science. . . . This secret trespasser on human rights manipulates the head to carry out, on a small scale, a sort of popery that takes away voluntary action instead of encouraging the science of self-control, and sets himself up for a doctor who is a base quack. (Springer, p. 210)

In this same incredible chapter Mrs. Eddy spoke of MAM as "Satan let loose," proving that "the peril of Salem witchcraft" is still abroad in the land. It is "More subtle than all the other beasts of the field, it coils itself about the sleeper, fastens its fang of innocence, and kills in the dark." It is a "weapon of revenge," a way to influence a juror, to convince patients they are getting well when they are in truth dying. It is a way of corrupting entire communities.

> In coming years the person or mind that hates his neighbor, will have no need to traverse his fields to destroy his flocks and herds, and spoil his vines; or to enter his house to demoralize his household; for the evil mind will do this through mesmerism; and not in *propria persona* be seen committing the deed. Unless this terrible hour be met and restrained by *Science,* mesmerism, that scourge of man, will leave nothing sacred when mind begins to act under direction of conscious power. . . . Stir the evil sensual mind, and worse than the deadly Upas are the plagues it emits. (Springer, pp. 211–12)

Not having been able to obtain access to the first edition of *Science and Health,* my quotations are taken from Fleta Springer's biography. She summarizes the notorious chapter 8 this way:

> And through all these amazing passages there runs the constantly recurring theme of "the student whose history had diverged into a dark channel of its own," and so revealed this scourge to her. His sole sin seems to have been that he had deserted her, and that his friends and patients were his friends and patients, and not hers.
> These passionate expressions of resentment against Kennedy are quite literally difficult to believe. But here we have followed implicitly the Leader's own admonition that she is to be found in her writings.
> The accusations in the first edition of *Science and Health* are only the beginning of the things she was to have to say of her enemies. It was as if she were moved by some inner compulsion to leave embedded in the body of her written work the record of the personal drama of her life. If her autobiography, *Retrospection and Introspection,* veers sharply from the personal record and seems to conceal rather than to reveal, the opposite is true of the writings proposed as text books and statements of her theory. For here she veers as sharply from the abstract and general to the personal and concrete. (p. 212)

The second edition of *Science and Health* had a chapter on "Demonology" as demented as chapter 8 of the first edition. Violent attacks on Kennedy continue, but now identical attacks are made on poor Spofford. Of Kennedy she writes:

> Among our very first students was the mesmerist aforesaid, who has followed the cause of metaphysical healing as a hound follows its prey, to hunt down every promising student if he cannot place them in his track and on his pursuit. Never but one of our students was a voluntary malpractitioner; he has made many others. . . . This malpractitioner tried his best to break down our health before he learned

the cause of our sufferings. It was difficult for us to credit the facts of his malice or to admit they lie within the pale of mortal thought. (Springer, p. 235)

Now for Spofford's bashing:

Behold! thou criminal mental marauder, that would blot out the sunshine of earth, that would sever friends, destroy virtue, put out Truth, and murder in secret the innocent befouling thy track with the trophies of thy guilt—I say, Behold the "cloud, no bigger than a man's hand," already rising in the horizon of Truth, to pour down upon thy guilty head the hailstones of doom. (Springer, p. 234)

Springer comments:

Her hatred and terror of Daniel Spofford were as great as her hatred and terror of Richard Kennedy had been, and her terror and hatred of Kennedy became even greater than before. The discovery that Mesmerism or Malicious Animal Magnetism could operate through mind alone threw a new and dreadful light upon Kennedy. He had wished her downfall. Nothing could stop him now. He would accomplish it. Secretly, subtly, he had corrupted Daniel Spofford's mind. No wonder Daniel Spofford had so often counseled her to leave off exposing Richard Kennedy's crimes. Under that gentle quiet exterior Daniel Spofford himself had hidden the soul of a fiend. (p. 235)

It is difficult to comprehend how such insults could flow from the pen of a woman who professed to follow the teachings of a man who urged his followers to love their enemies, and when injured, to turn the other cheek. There is not the slightest evidence that either Kennedy or Spofford did anything to injure Mrs. Eddy. Their only offense had been to set up independent healing practices. Mrs. Eddy's response was rage toward two students who had dared to leave her.

Spofford was excommunicated by Mrs. Eddy in 1878. She then began a series of lawsuits against students and others whom she said owed her cash. She sued Kennedy for back tuition. She sued Spofford on similar grounds. There were other suits against students who were behind in tuition payments. None of these court actions were successful.

*   *   *

It was in the fall of 1878 that the strangest, least understood, and funniest series of events occurred in the entire life of Mrs. Eddy. Rumors circulated around Boston that Arens and Mr. Eddy had tried to hire a man to murder Spofford! Suddenly Spofford vanished from the city. A Boston newspaper falsely reported that he had indeed been murdered, and that his body lay in Boston's morgue. Actually, Spofford had fled the city in fear of his life. On October 29, Arens and Mr. Eddy were arrested for conspiracy to murder, each held on a $3,000 bail until the trial in November. Peculiar witnesses testified to the conspiracy. One of them, George Collier, later admitted he had lied. Arens and Mr. Eddy pleaded not guilty. The case against them was dismissed before the pair were allowed to offer their defense. They were discharged in January 1879. To this day no one knows why the comic opera ended before Arens and Mr. Eddy had their day in court.

Again, although it is almost beyond belief, Mrs. Eddy gave an account of this absurd trial in the third edition (1881) of *Science and Health*. Kennedy is blamed once more for everything. In Mrs. Eddy's distorted mind it was he, the nation's "leading demonologist," who planned the whole evil episode:

> The purpose of the plotters was evidently to injure the reputation of metaphysical practice, and to embarrass us for money at a time when they hoped to cripple us in the circulation of our book. (p. 22)

*   *   *

The mental malpractitioners managed that entire plot; and if the leading demonologist can exercise the power over mind, and govern the conclusions and acts of people as he has boasted to us that he could do, he had ample motives for the exercise of his demonology from the fact that a civil suit was pending against him for the collection of a note of one thousand dollars, which suit Mr. Arens was jointly interested in. (p. 29)

It was not long after the trial until Mrs. Eddy became convinced that her former friend and student, Edward Arens, had suddenly turned into another evil mesmerist who was trying to destroy her, as she would later believe Mr. Eddy had been destroyed, by causing symptoms of arsenic poisoning. The real reason for her fury was that Arens, like Kennedy and Spofford, had left her to set up his own private practice. What was worse, he had written a pamphlet titled *Theology, or the Understanding of God as Applied to Healing the Sick*. In 1883 Mrs. Eddy sued him for plagiarizing material from *Science and Health*. Arens countered that he had taken only passages from papers by Quimby, which had not been copyrighted. Because *Science and Health* had been copyrighted, Arens lost the case. He was ordered to discontinue distributing his pamphlet.

By now Arens had joined Kennedy and Spofford as Mrs. Eddy's three archenemies bent on destroying her work by long-distance mesmerism. The third edition of *Science and Health* had an introduction by Mr. Eddy in which the plagiarism charges against Arens were raised. In Mr. Eddy's words:

. . . It would require ages and God's mercy to make the ignorant hypocrite who published that pamphlet originate its contents. His pratings are colored by his character, they cannot impart the hue of ethics, but leave his own impress on what he takes. He knows less of metaphysics than any decently honest man.

If simply writing at the commencement of a work, "I have made use of some thoughts of Emerson" gave one the right to walk over the author's copyrights and use page after page of his writings verbatim, publishing them as his own, any fool might aspire to authorship and any villain become the expounder of truth. (Springer, pp. 264–65)

In this third edition's "Demonology" chapter, Mrs. Eddy's attacks on Kennedy become still more strident:

The husband of a lady who was the patient of this malpractitioner poured out his grief to us and said: "Dr. K——— has destroyed the happiness of my home, ruined my wife, etc."; and after that, he finished with a double crime by destroying the health of that wronged husband so that he died. We say that he did these things because we have as much evidence of it as ever we had of the existence of any sin. The symptoms and circumstances of the cases, and the diagnosis of their diseases, proved the unmistakable fact. His career of crime surpasses anything that minds in general can accept at this period. We advised him to marry a young lady whose affection he had won, but he refused; subsequently she was wedded to a nice young man, and then he alienated her affections from her husband. (p. 6)

*   *   *

. . . The Nero of today, regaling himself through a mental method with the tortures of individuals, is repeating history and will fall upon his own sword, and it shall pierce him through. Let him remember this when, in the dark recesses of thought, he is robbing, committing adultery, and killing; when he is attempting to turn friend away from friend, ruthlessly stabbing the quivering heart when he is clipping the thread of life, and giving to the grave youth and its rainbow hues; when he is turning back the reviving sufferer to her bed of pain, clouding her first morning after years of night; and the Nemesis of that hour shall point to the tyrant's fate, who falls at length upon the sword of justice. (p. 38)

*   *   *

. . . Carefully veiling his character, through unsurpassed secretiveness, he wore the mask of innocence and youth. But he was young only in years; a marvelous plotter, dark and designing, he was constantly surprising us, and we half shut our eyes to avoid the pain of discovery, while we struggled with the gigantic evil of his character, but failed to destroy it. . . . When we discovered he was malpractising, and told him so, he avowed his intention to do whatever he chose with his mental power, spurning a Christian life, and exulting in the absence of moral restraint. . . . The habit of his misapplication of mental power grew on him until it became a secret passion of his to produce a state of mind destructive to health, happiness, or morals. . . . His mental malpractice has made him a moral leper that would be shunned as the most prolific cause of sickness and sin did the sick understand the cause of their relapses and protracted treatment, the husband the loss of his wife, and the mother the death of her child, etc. (p. 2)

Again, not having seen early editions of *Science and Health,* I quote from Springer's unauthorized biography. Mrs. Eddy's chapter on "Demonology," which ran in several editions before James Henry Wiggin (we will come to him in chapter 8) wisely removed all the libelous passages about Mrs. Eddy's archenemies. He also cut the chapter to its present length of seven pages, where it remains today in *Science and Health* under the title "Animal Magnetism Unmasked." It is a pale version of what it had once been. Here is how Springer described the earlier version:

It is certainly one of the most extraordinary chapters in the history of religious literature, and although it appeared in several editions it is doubtful if many Christian Scientists today believe its existence to be anything more than a myth. All references to it are carefully expunged from the later writings of the church, and references to it by outsiders are somehow felt to be an unwarranted attack upon Mrs. Eddy and the truth. No amount of explanation and no interpretation can drown the resounding and terrified voice of a Leader in that chapter. No denial of its personalities can convert that chapter into a parable. Her fear so pressed upon her that her words rush out hysterically, like the words of a frightened woman attempting to tell you in a single breath the details of some horrifying gossip. (pp. 265–66)

6

Malicious Animal Magnetism II

In 1887 Mrs. Eddy's son George Glover wrote that he and his wife and daughter were planning to visit her in Boston. Mrs. Eddy did not want them to come. Her letter to him on October 31, 1887, was published in the *New York World* (March 10, 1907) and reprinted in Mrs. Milmine's biography:

> Dear George: Yours received. I am surprised that you think of coming to visit me when I live in a schoolhouse and have no room that I can let even a boarder into.
>
> I use the whole of my rooms and am at work in them more or less all the time.
>
> Besides this I have all I can meet without receiving company. I must have quiet in my house, and it will not be pleasant for you in Boston. The Choates are doing all they can by falsehood, and public shames, such as advertising a college of her own within a few doors of mine when she is a disgraceful woman and known to be, I am going to give up my lease when this class is over, and cannot pay

your board nor give you a single dollar now. I am alone, and you never would come to me when I called for you, and now I cannot have you come.

I want quiet and Christian life alone with God, when I can find intervals for a little rest. You are not what I had hoped to find you, and I am changed. The world, the flesh and evil I am at war with, and if anyone comes to me it must be to help me and not to hinder me in this warfare. If you will stay away from me until I get through with my public labour then I will send for you and hope to then have a home to take you to.

As it now is, I have none, and you will injure me by coming to Boston at this time more than I have room to state in a letter. I asked you to come to me when my husband died and I so much needed someone to help me. You refused to come then in my great needs, and I then gave up ever thinking of you in that line. Now I have a clerk [Calvin Frye] who is a pure-minded Christian, and two girls to assist me in the college. These are all that I can have under this roof.

If you come after getting this letter I shall feel you have no regard for my interest or feelings, which I hope not to be obliged to feel.

Boston is the last place in the world for you or your family. When I retire from business and into private life, then I can receive you if you are reformed, but not otherwise. I say this to you, not to any one else. I would not injure you any more than myself. As ever sincerely,

M. B. G. Eddy. (pp. 454–55)

Mrs. Eddy always signed letters to her students and associates (before they fell from grace) with profuse expressions of love. Note that her letter to her son was signed "sincerely." As Mrs. Milmine remarks, just as Mrs. Eddy lacked a sense of smell, so she lacked any sense of maternity.

Glover came anyway, staying at a house in Chelsea. His mother was not pleased, and the rift between them widened. Mrs. Glover intensely disliked Mrs. Eddy. The feeling was mutual. No one in Glover's family became Christian Scientists.

Ten years earlier, when Mr. Eddy was still living and Mrs. Eddy was railing against Spofford for trying to kill her with MAM, Glover had visited his mother. On March 3, 1907, during his second visit to Boston, he was interviewed by the *New York World*. Even allowing for exaggeration by the newspaper, what he told them was truly astonishing. Here are excerpts from the interview as published in Springer's biography:

> Days passed before the desired information reached me. It came then, in the form of a telegram bearing mother's signature, and bidding me hurry to her in Boston, and mother and I met for the first time in thirty years.
>
> . . . I found her living with Dr. Eddy in a Boston boarding house, and in the midst of great trouble. She had launched Christian Science and things were not running smoothly. There had been a revolt of some sort among the people she called her "students," and two men—Daniel J. Spofford and Richard Kennedy—were leaders in the fight against her.
>
> Within a week of my arrival in Boston I learned many strange things. The strangest of these was that the rebellious students were employing black arts to harass and destroy my mother.
>
> The longer I remained with mother, the clearer this became. Pursued by the evil influence of the students, we moved from house to house never at rest and always apprehensive. It was a maddening puzzle to me. We would move to a new house and our fellow lodgers would be all smiles and friendliness. Then, in an hour, the inevitable change would come; all friendliness would vanish under the spell of black magic, and we would be ordered to go. But mother made it all clear to me. . . . She told me that the great secrets of Christian

Science when put to evil uses by designing men, were terrible in their power. She made me see that Daniel Spofford and Richard Kennedy in particular were using this mysterious power to crush and ruin and slay her.

. . . For some reason never explained to my satisfaction mother would not think of letting me return to my Western home. I had gone to her only prepared for a short visit, but she sternly silenced every suggestion of my departure.

There were imperative reasons why I should have been at home. My young wife was about to give birth to our first child, and my business affairs were also in need of attention. But mother would not permit me to leave her. So week after week and month after month, I stayed on in Boston moving from house to house, and learning to hate Spofford and Kennedy, the arch enemies of my mother's peace, with all my soul.

It was Kennedy that mother talked of most. He was a master hand at the black arts as mother pictured him daily to me, until at last I made up my mind to cut him short in his evil work. But I kept my plan to myself. One morning I slipped my revolver into my overcoat pocket and left our boarding-house, ostensibly for a stroll. It was a beautiful, clear morning, and the streets of old Boston never looked brighter or busier. But there was no brightness in my heart—nothing but a stern, fixed purpose to end Kennedy's devilish work and save my mother.

I had never seen this man, but I knew where he had offices, and I walked straight there. He was doing business as a healer, and his name, lettered on a brass plate, was on the door of his office. Every detail of that visit is as clear in my mind today as if it took place only a week ago.

The girl who admitted me asked if I was a patient, and I answered "yes." I remember distinctly that I laughed aloud as I made this reply. A great load of trouble seemed lifted from my heart. I felt that in another moment I would have Kennedy in my power, where black arts could not save him.

The unsuspecting girl led me straight to Kennedy's office on the second floor of the house, opened the door, bowed me into the room and hurried away. Kennedy was before me, seated at his desk.

He looked at me smilingly and asked:

"Are you in need of a treatment?"

Pulling out my revolver, I walked up to him, pressed the cold muzzle of the weapon to his head, and said:

"I have made up my mind that you are in need of a treatment."

Then while he shook like a jelly fish with terror, I gave him his one chance for life. I told him that my mother knew all of his black art tricks to ruin her, and that I had made up my mind to stop him or to kill him.

"You needn't tell me that you are not working your game of hypnotism to rob us of friends and to drive mother to madness," said I. "My one word to you is this: if we have to move from one other boarding-house I will search you out and shoot you like a mad dog."

I shall never forget how that man begged for his life at the end of my weapon and swore that the black art was false and that mother had deceived me.

"But it did the business alright," continued Glover. "We were not ordered out of another boarding-house that winter. Mother seemed very much surprised when I told her what I had done, but she did not scold me. Her spirits seemed to improve, and in a few days she consented to let me return home to my wife and the little son I had not yet seen." (pp. 260–62)

In 1881, when the third edition of *Science and Health* appeared, Mrs. Eddy's obsession with MAM so dominated her conversation and her Sunday sermons that eight of her oldest and most trusted disciples resigned from the church. They gave their reasons in the following letter:

We, the undersigned, while we acknowledge and appreciate the understanding of Truth imparted to us by our Teacher, Mrs. Mary

B. G. Eddy, led by Divine Intelligence to perceive with sorrow that departure from the straight and narrow road (which alone leads to growth of Christ-like virtues) made manifest by frequent ebullitions of temper, love of money, and the appearance of hypocrisy, *cannot* longer submit to such Leadership; therefore, without aught of hatred, revenge, or petty spite in our hearts, from a sense of duty alone, to her, the Cause, and ourselves, do most respectfully withdraw our names from the Christian Science Association and Church of Christ (Scientist).

> S. Louise Durant,
> Margaret J. Dunshee,
> Dorcas B. Rawson,
> Elizabeth G. Stuart,
> Jane L. Straw,
> Anna B. Newman,
> James C. Howard,
> Miranda R. Rice.

(Peel, *Mary Baker Eddy: The Years of Trial,* pp. 95–96)

Observe how superior and restrained was the attitude of the eight in contrast to the "hatred, revenge, or petty spite" displayed by Mrs. Eddy in her "Demonology" chapter. As might be expected, Mrs. Eddy denounced her followers as being under the influence of MAM, threatened them with expulsion (even though they had already resigned), and demanded they appear before her. They refused. A few days later two other top students, including the church's secretary, also resigned. They said they "could no longer entertain the subject of mesmerism which had lately been made uppermost in the meetings and in Mrs. Eddy's talks."

Mrs. Eddy took off for a vacation in Washington, D.C., to ride out the storm. The recovery was rapid. Early 1882 found her back in Boston, as energetic as ever, where she founded her Massachusetts Metaphysical College, with herself as the sole instructor. A bogus "college" operating from her home, it gave degrees of C.S.B. (Christian Science

Bachelor) and C.S.D. (Christian Science Doctor). The college lasted nine years. New disciples enrolled, and the movement resumed its steady growth.

By 1885 Mrs. Eddy was giving a course titled "Metaphysical Obstetrics." She gave herself the title of "Professor of Obstetrics, Metaphysics, and Christian Science." Of course Mrs. Eddy knew nothing about obstetrics. Her sole advice to practitioners was to persuade the mother that she was not really experiencing pain. The pain was just another illusion of mortal mind.

In 1888 Mrs. Abby Corner, a student of Mrs. Eddy's course in obstetrics, tried to put into practice what she had learned. When her daughter gave birth to a child, Mrs. Corner refused to let a physician be present while she herself served as "obstetrician." Both her daughter and the baby died. The tragedy generated a raft of bad publicity. Mrs. Corner was arrested and tried for involuntary manslaughter. The court acquitted her on grounds that the deaths had resulted from a massive hemorrhage that probably would have killed both mother and child even if a physician had been present.

From then on, the obstetrics course in Mrs. Eddy's "college" was taught by her student Ebenezer Foster, whom she later adopted as a son. Foster had a degree in homeopathy, which made him as qualified to teach obstetrics as if he had a degree in astronomy. "Dr. Foster," Mrs. Eddy announced, "will teach the anatomy and surgery of obstetrics, and I, its metaphysics." In 1902 the obstetrics course was dropped entirely. "Obstetrics is not Science," Mrs. Eddy declared, "and will not be taught."

After Mrs. Eddy returned to Boston from her vacation in Washington, D.C., she was struck another heavy blow. As was recounted in chapter 1, Mr. Eddy died of a heart attack. Mrs. Eddy insisted it was not his heart that failed, but that he had been killed by MAM. In a long letter to the *Boston Post* (June 5, 1882) she explained his death as follows:

My husband's death was caused by malicious mesmerism. Dr. C. J. Eastman, who attended the case after it had taken an alarming turn, declares the symptoms to be the same as those of arsenical poisoning. On the other hand, Dr. Rufus K. Noyes, late of the City Hospital, who held an autopsy over the body to-day, affirms that the corpse is free from all material poison, although Dr. Eastman still holds to his original belief. I know it was poison that killed him, not material poison, but mesmeric poison. My husband was in uniform health, and but seldom complained of any kind of ailment. During his brief illness, just preceding his death, his continual cry was, "Only relieve me of this continual suggestion, through the mind, of poison, and I will recover." It is well known that by constantly dwelling upon any subject in thought finally comes the poison of belief through the whole system. . . . I never saw a more self-possessed man than dear Dr. Eddy was. He said to Dr. Eastman, when he was finally called to attend him: "My case is nothing that I cannot attend to myself, although to me it acts the same as poison and seems to pervade my whole system just as that would."

This is not the first case known of where death has occurred from what appeared to be poison, and was so declared by the attending physician, but in which the body, on being thoroughly examined by an autopsy, was shown to possess no signs of material poison. There was such a case in New York. Every one at first declared poison to have been the cause of death, as the symptoms were all there; but an autopsy contradicted the belief, and it was shown that the victim had had no opportunity for procuring poison. I afterwards learned that she had been very active in advocating the merits of our college. Oh, isn't it terrible that this fiend of malpractice is in the land! The only remedy that is effectual in meeting this terrible power possessed by the evil-minded is to counteract it by the same method that I use in counteracting poison. They require the same remedy.

Circumstances debarred me from taking hold of my husband's case. He declared himself perfectly capable of carrying himself through, and I was so entirely absorbed in business that I permitted him to try, and when I awakened to the danger it was too late. I have cured worse cases before, but took hold of them in time. I don't think that Dr. Carpenter had anything to do with my husband's death, but I do believe it was the rejected students—students who were turned away from our college because of their unworthiness and immorality. To-day I sent for one of the students whom my husband had helped liberally, and given money, not knowing how unworthy he was. I wished him to come, that I might prove to him how, by metaphysics, I could show the cause of my husband's death. He was as pale as a ghost when he came to the door, and refused to enter, or to believe that I knew what caused his death. Within half an hour after he left, I felt the same attack that my husband felt—the same that caused his death. I instantly gave myself the same treatment that I would use in a case of arsenical poisoning, and so I recovered, just the same as I could have caused my husband to recover had I taken the case in time.

After a certain amount of mesmeric poison has been administered it cannot be averted. No power of mind can resist it. It must be met with resistive action of the mind at the start, which will counteract it. We all know that disease of any kind cannot reach the body except through the mind, and that if the mind is cured the disease is soon relieved. Only a few days ago I disposed of a tumour in twenty-four hours that the doctors had said must be removed by the knife. I changed the course of the mind to counteract the effect of the disease. This proves the myth of matter. Mesmerism will make an apple burn the hand so that the child will cry.

My husband never spoke of death as something we were to meet, but only as a phase of mortal belief. . . . I do believe in God's supremacy over error, and this gives me peace. I do believe, and have been told, that there is a price set upon my head. One of my students, a malpractitioner, has been heard to say that he would follow us to the grave. He has already reached my husband. While my husband and I were in Washington and Philadelphia last winter, we were obliged to guard against poison, the same symptoms apparent at my husband's death constantly attending us. And yet the one who was planning the evil against us was in Boston the whole time. To-day a lady, active in forwarding the good of our college, told me that she had been troubled almost constantly with arsenical poison symptoms, and is now treating them constantly as I directed her. Three days ago one of my patients died, and the doctor said he died from arsenic, and yet there were no material symptoms of poison. (Milmine, pp. 286–88)

For more on Doctor Noyes and the fake "Doctor" Eastman, a self-styled homeopath, see chapter 1. Eastman was dean of something called Bellevue Medical College, later closed down for fraud. "Doctor" Carpenter, whom Mary absolved as a cause of her husband's death, was a Boston hypnotist who gave public demonstrations for entertainment.

Mrs. Eddy's irrational fear of MAM continued to mount. In 1887 she started a regular department about MAM in the *Christian Science Journal.* Letters from Christian Scientists, published in the journal over a period of several years, reveal how thoroughly the fear of MAM had penetrated their minds.

In 1889 Mrs. Eddy, convinced that Boston had become too infused with MAM, abandoned her sumptuous twenty-room house on fashionable Commonwealth Avenue to live in a furnished house in Concord. She and her servants remained there for three years before she moved to a spot several miles outside Concord that she called Pleasant View. It was during her residence there that she established Mother Church in Boston and declared herself "Pastor Emeritus." All other Christian Science churches were named "branch churches" of Mother Church. Her *Church Manual,* which she wrote herself, was published in 1895. It went through numerous alterations before the final edition that still governs the church today.

By 1908 Mrs. Eddy became convinced that Pleasant View had become so infested with MAM that she moved again, this time to a thirty-four room mansion in Chestnut Hill, a Boston suburb. It was there that she finally succumbed to "error" and in 1910 died at age 87. Her son George, then a federal marshal in Lead, South Dakota, attended the funeral. Calvin Frye, her top servant, was given the honorary post of president of Mother Church.

Shortly before his mother died, her estranged son George Glover tried desperately to gain control of his mother's estate. He had become convinced, on the basis of a previous visit, that his mother was seriously ill and no longer mentally competent to govern her estate, then valued at about two-and-a-half million dollars. In his court action to obtain control he was aided by Mrs. Eddy's adopted son Ebenezer Foster, whom she had excommunicated, and one of her nephews. Court officials interviewed Mrs. Eddy at length in her home. They found her not only in full possession of her faculties, but also extremely knowledgeable about stocks and bonds, and a shrewd businesswoman. The court ruled against Glover and his friends.

Mrs. Eddy's final years at Chestnut Hill were years of intense suffering and loneliness. She attributed all of her ills to MAM sent through the air by her enemies. Here are some typical extracts from Calvin Frye's diary, as quoted in Edwin Dakin's *Mrs. Eddy* (1930), that reveal all too starkly the depths of her agony:

"Mrs. E. was suddenly attack(ed) with severe pain at 11.30 tonight and the 4 C.S.s in the house P.V. proved unable to relieve her. She sent for Rev. I. C. Tomlinson neither did he help her. She then sent for Dr. E. Morrill & he was out of town; she then sent for Dr. S. Morrill. He was sick & could not come. She then sent for Dr. Conn and he remained with her from 2.15 until 4 Monday morning. But the pain was so intense & slow to respond that he called Dr. Stillings for consultation who was there from 3 to 4." The entry for the following day continues: "After Conn left, Mrs. E. was a little relieved and at about 5 a.m. she slept for about one hour. But suffered every hour this forenoon from paroxysms of pain. . . . It was called renal calculi . . . then she called in Dr. E. Morrill & he gave her a hypodermic." (pp. 528–29)

* * *

Mrs. Eddy has had a belief of difficulty of breathing for the last two days and got only temporary relief from it, this morning at about 4 o'clock she called me to help her. I attempted (to) do so for about ten minutes when she told me I made her worse afterwards told me she could not rise from the bed to speak to me because of the suffocating sense it produced; worked for (her) faithfully last evening with little result. When we were together this morning at about 9:30 she discovered that the mesmerists were arguing to her inflamation and paralysis of spinal nerve to produce paralysis of muscles of lungs and heart so as to prevent breathing & heart disease with soreness (?) between the shoulder blades.

She experienced the greatest relief when she and I took up Kennedy & Arens to break their attempt to make her suffer from aforementioned beliefs, and she said "I have not breathed so easy for two days." (p. 527)

* * *

Mrs. Eddy a terrible night last night fear & fever and poisoned to death in belief. After I had attempted to mentally & audibly help & comfort her without success she said "Now stop entirely and go to sleep turn y(ou)r mind entirely away from me. If I don't speak to you again on earth, Goodbye darling." (p. 528)

* * *

Mrs. Eddy had a severe experience all day yesterday being tormented with a sense of evil all day long. She found Clara told dressmakers wrong and thereby had her dress skirt made 1½ in. too short in back

& spoiled. Laura & I both caused her trouble thro stupidity & sin so that she declared I was the cause of influencing others to abuse her. While driving she was confronted by question of membership from Mother Church to—Church & jealousy. An atmosphere & hate & revenge from testimony being taken in Montreal on W suit &c &c Stewart case. (p. 528)

*   *   *

Last evening, under the influence of MAM Mr. Tomlinson told Mrs. Eddy she was ungrateful and a tyrant. (p. 529)

*   *   *

Monday night at about 10 oclk Mrs. Eddy awoke in a severe belief and called for help but all seemed so dazed they were unsuccessful. She was surprised & declared we wanted her to die & did not love. When I told her I love her more than any other person on earth she said *"You lie!"* This morning I received a bitter letter from Geo. W. Baker which he wrote Aug. 9th. (p. 529)

*   *   *

Mr. Adam H. Dickey last night told Mrs. Eddy, that she shall not have any more morphine! She had for several days been suffering from renal calculi and had voided stones in the urine but yesterday the water seemed normal and so having had hyperdermic injections twice within a few days he believed she did not need it but that it was the old morphine habit reasserting itself and would not allow her to have it. (p. 530)

*   *   *

Mrs. Eddy called I. C. T., A. H. D., W. R. R., E. S. Rathvon, L. E. Sargent & C. A. F. and demanded of us to heal her, for she was tired of going on in this way confined to her bunk &c &c; she added that she would give any one of us $1000. to heal her.

A. H. D. said he would give $1,000. to be able to heal her &c. so said the others in substance. I did not reply for some time for I felt quite confused & discouraged, but finally said "Well all we can do is to keep up our courage and work on up to our highest understanding." She replied "Has it come to this!" She afterward said "If you all feel like that turn your (mi)nds away from me & know that I am well." (p. 530)

Calvin Frye's diary, the most valuable of all references on Mrs. Eddy's elderly years, is in the possession of Mother Church. Hopefully, it someday will be published. Edwin Dakin was allowed access to the diary, from which he quotes liberally in Appendix A, titled "The Frye Diaries," in the revised edition (1930) of *Mrs. Eddy*. It is from this appendix that I selected the above extracts.

So great was the fame of Mrs. Eddy that a year after her death the church published a 132-page volume titled *Editorial Comments on the Life and Work of Mary Baker Eddy* (1911). It reprints more than 150 laudatory obituaries from American newspapers and magazines, as well as tributes from publications in Canada, China, England, Hawaii, Mexico, and Puerto Rico. One can only marvel at the fact that two frail, uneducated women—Ellen White (of Seventh-day Adventism) and Mary Baker Eddy—could establish and during their life totally control new religions that would spread around the world and acquire millions of devoted followers. It would be interesting to know how many biographies of Mrs. Eddy have been written, most of them authorized by the church and containing nothing derogatory about the leader. There is even a profusely illustrated *Child's Life of Mrs. Eddy* by Ella Hay, published by the church in 1942.

Rumors persisted among the faithful that Mrs. Eddy would rise from the dead. A myth arose that a telephone was placed in her coffin just in case. The evangelist Billy Sunday declared: "If old Mother Eddy rises from the dead I'll eat polecat for breakfast and wash it down with booze."

Like Oral Roberts and so many of today's Bible pounding Pentecostal evangelists, Mrs. Eddy was always hearing God tell her something. If it turned out to be wrong, she decided it was not God after all but the MAM of an enemy. Here is a typical instance. In 1889 she declared that God had "just told me who to recommend" for the editor of the *Christian Science Journal.* A few days later she changed her mind. "I regret having named the one I did for Editor," she wrote. "It is a mistake, he is not fit. It was not God evidently that suggested that thought but the person who suggests many things mentally, but I have before been able to discriminate. I wrote too soon after it came to my thought" (Snowden, p. 54). Because Mrs. Eddy could not say that the inner voice came from Satan, who does not exist, she had to blame it on the MAM of a detractor! As Fleta Springer so perceptively puts it in her biography of Mrs. Eddy, "The Satan who had so terrified her childhood had reappeared" though no longer with a forked tail and cloven hoof.

Here is how James Snowden, in *The Truth About Christian Science* (1920), described the paranoia of Mrs. Eddy's later years:

> This demon proved all its powers of ubiquitous presence and evil influence and malignant destructiveness in her own household. It bedeviled her printers, froze her water pipes, and made the boiler leak. It got into her household furniture and kitchen utensils, her coal and blankets and feather pillows and silver spoons and caused them to disappear as if by some magician's wand. She accused nearly all her servants of stealing and charged their perversity to "MAM." She would send servants to outlying towns to mail letters and dispatch telegrams so that they would not pass through Boston where the mail clerks and telegraph operators were supposed to be "mesmerized" and could

poison the messages with their evil power. A long succession of tenants and housekeepers went wrong under the same evil influence. Any personal annoyance or irritation that she experienced was instantly charged to this devil. Friend after friend fell under this accusation and was forthwith excommunicated. No language could be bitter enough, no punishment could be dire enough to express her sense of the horror of this evil thing. (p. 43)

Today's Christian Scientists, certainly the faith's "liberal" members, no longer take MAM seriously. Indeed, many Christian Scientists, in spite of the chapter about it in *Science and Health,* have not even heard of it. As late as 1930, however, when Ms. Springer wrote her biography, the faithful were haunted by MAM. Springer has this to say in a footnote:

The discovery of the prevalence of the belief in and fear of "MAM" has been one of the strangest fruits of this research. The author has listened to many scarcely believable stories of this fear; some tragic, and many ludicrous. Christian Scientists suspect each other of it; and they even suspect themselves. "Handling MAM" is one of the strongest duties of every member of the Church. To MAM is attributed every thing from sickness and disaster to the slightest mishap and annoyance of daily life. The Christian Scientists' world is far more dangerous than a simple world of germs and accident. (p. 419)

The greatest of all difficulties for any theist is how a good and all-powerful God can permit evil and suffering. Mrs. Eddy's answer was that God didn't permit it at all because sin, sickness, and death are illusions, false beliefs, errors of thought that have no reality. If all is God and all is good, and evil does not exist, then the question at once arises: Why does God permit so much false belief in evil? Mrs. Eddy never answered this question.

7

Memoirs of Adam Dickey

Adam Herbert Dickey, described by someone as "built like a prize-fighter," was Mrs. Eddy's private secretary from 1908 until her death in 1910. His main job was to handle correspondence. Before he died in 1925 he wrote down his memories of three years as a faithful servant to his leader. These memoirs were not published until after his death. In 1927 his widow, Lillian S. Dickey, issued the manuscript as *Memoirs of Mary Baker Eddy*. No book by a true believer in Christian Science has been more damaging to the faith.

Church officials did not dare impugn the book's accuracy. After all, Dickey was not only Mrs. Eddy's trusted servant but he was also, at the time of his death, chairman of Mother Church's board of directors. The reason they gave for withdrawing the book from the market was that outsiders would misunderstand it. Mrs. Dickey, then a Christian Science practitioner and member of Mother Church, obeyed the decision. All copies of the book and its plates were destroyed. Copies of the original book are now as rare as copies of the first and second editions of *Science and Health*. In 1985 a paperback reprint was issued by Pasadena Press; the following year Butter Field Books, in London, printed a hardcover edition.

Born in Toronto in 1864, Dickey converted early in life from Methodism to Christian Science. In 1908 he and his wife were Christian Science practitioners in Kansas City, Missouri, where Dickey was First Reader in the city's First Church of Christian Science. When Mrs. Eddy ordered him to join her household in 1908, he considered it such an honor that he instantly abandoned his career and headed for Boston. His wife remained behind to shift for herself.

To Dickey, Mrs. Eddy could do no wrong. Her decisions were as infallible as the pope's decisions are to many Roman Catholics. Here is how he expressed this trust in his *Memoirs:*

> She seemed rarely to weigh in her thought what the consequence of her action might be. Her sole desire was to get the Divine leading and follow that unhesitatingly. Often the reasons for which our Leader took action in certain directions were not clear to the workers about her. It would seem as if the reason advanced by her was a poor one and not worthy of the action she was taking. This, of course was mortal mind's analysis of her work, and if she were acting from a spiritual impulse, it is not at all surprising that her reasons would not appeal to the judgement of onlookers. It always turned out, however, that her action was right, regardless of the reason assigned, which convinced those who were familiar with her work that her judgement was unerring in every detail and that in following the direction of Divine Wisdom, she never made a mistake. Often I heard her say with great impressiveness that in over forty years of church leadership, she had not made a mistake, a record that is most truly remarkable. (p. 42)

It was Mrs. Eddy's unerring judgment that Dickey thought explained her total control of the movement:

Mrs. Eddy's ideas of church government differed greatly from those of the general run of mankind. She knew that her Church, established as it was under Divine direction, would incur the hatred and opposition of every known form of religion, which has been evolved according to the wisdom of man. In order to be perpetuated her Church must necessarily follow Divine inspiration and not be the product of legal enactments or worldlywise evolutions. She told me that every government, every organization, every institution of whatever kind or nature, to be successful, must have one responsible head.

This is why she placed herself at the head of her own Church, because mortal mind could not be trusted to conduct it. This is why she did away with First Members, and later Executive Members, for to place enactments of holy inspiration in the hands of groups of individuals was to incur the possibility of the Divine idea being lost sight of, and human wisdom taking its place. This is also why she reduced the authority of the conduct of The Mother Church into the narrowest possible compass. Indeed, she told me, with pathos and earnestness, that if she could find one individual, who was spiritually equipped, she would immediately place him at the head of her church government. Asking me to take pencil she slowly dictated the following, as I wrote it down, "I prayed God day and night to show me how to form my Church, and how to go on with it. I understand that He showed me just as I understand He showed me Christian Science, and no human being ever showed me Christian Science. Then I have no right or desire to change what God had directed me to do, and it remains for the Church to obey it. What has prospered this Church for thirty years will continue to keep it." (pp. 42–43)

Dickey's admiration for Mrs. Eddy extended even to her decisions as to where every piece of furniture and every object on a table or mantel should be placed. She was quick to complain if after a room cleaning a piece of furniture or an object had not been replaced precisely where it was before. Dickey solved the furniture problem by driving tiny brass tacks through carpets and into the floor to mark the exact spots of each leg:

> In an earlier chapter I referred to the fact that I learned much while arranging the furniture, pictures, and ornaments under Mrs. Eddy's personal direction. It was not like arranging the furniture of an ordinary room. Here was where the most wonderful woman that the world has ever produced was to spend her time and thought in the direction and government of the greatest Christian Movement that was ever known. I could see clearly the working of divine Principle, even in the arrangement of the ornaments on her mantel. There was a reason for everything, and it was all worked out so beautifully and harmoniously that the experience was most uplifting to me, while at the same time it gave me the opportunity of getting closer in thought to our revered Leader than I had done before. (p. 44)

Until Dickey joined the household at Chestnut Hill, he had no inkling of how much MAM dominated Mrs. Eddy's life and thoughts. It was everywhere. To counteract it, Mrs. Eddy reinstituted her earlier practice of having students serve on regular "watches" to counteract MAM. The students, known as "mental workers," were brought to the house, and each given a large room and bath. They were, in effect, Mrs. Eddy's mental bodyguards, there to defend her against periodic attacks by enemies at remote localities. Whenever she felt the need for counterattack, she would write down instructions which Dickey would type and deliver to the mental workers' rooms. Here are some of Dickey's memories of the extent to which MAM pervaded the mansion.

> At this time there were four mental workers in the house, in addition to Mr. Frye, and the hours of the night were divided into four separate watches, so called. The first watch was from 9:00 to 11:00 P.M.; the next from 11:00 to 1:00 A.M.; the next from 1:00 to 3:00; and then from 3:00 until 5:00 in the morning. These watches were assigned

to different mental workers and their task was to counteract the malicious evil influence of mortal mind directed against our Leader and her establishment during their two hours. When a watch was kept, or in other words, when the mental worker was successful in freeing our Leader from attacks during that time, she always knew it and the one keeping his watch was commended the next day. (p. 45)

*   *   *

On many occasions all the workers were called in and admonished because of their seeming inability to meet the prevailing conditions. It was our Leader's custom when she went to her study in the morning to first open the Bible and read whatever appeared on the page before her. This was apparently done at random and yet she seemed directed in this work so that the reference on most occasions was particularly fitting to the subject under discussion. One passage especially seemed to thrust itself forward on these occasions. It was Matthew 24:43: "But know this, that if the goodman of the house had known in what watch the thief would come, he would have watched, and would not have suffered his house to be broken up." (p. 46)

*   *   *

Again during the course of the talk, she said, "If you will keep your watch, I shall be a well woman. If you stay here until you learn to handle animal magnetism, I will make healers out of you; I had to do it, and did it for forty years, and you must do it. You must rise to the point where you can destroy the belief in mesmerism, or you will have no Cause. It tried to overcome me for forty years and I withstood it all. Now it has gotten to the point where the students must take up this work and meet animal magnetism. I cannot do it for you. You must do it for yourselves, and unless it is done, the Cause will perish and we will go along another 1900 years with the world sunk into the blackest night. Now will you rouse yourselves?

You have all the power of God with you to conquer this lie of mesmerism. The workers in the field are not healing because they are not meeting animal magnetism which says they cannot heal." Then she turned to each one and said, "Will you keep your watch?" They all answered "Yes." She turned to me and said, "Mr. Dickey, will you keep your watch?" "Yes, Mother I will." She leaned forward in her chair and took my hand in hers, and I knew from the pressure, as well as the look she gave, she knew I would keep my watch. In explanation she said, "To keep your watch doesn't only mean to be awake at that hour and be working mentally. It means to do the work and succeed in breaking the mesmerism for the two hours assigned. If you don't succeed, you haven't kept your watch."

At another time she said, "There is a new form of sin or malpractice that has been revealed to me that nobody has ever discovered before, and that is that evil is trying to produce sudden death in sleep. The serpent typifies evil and the moccasin snake will lie right beside a person who is awake, and never touch him, but as soon as he falls asleep, he will attack." (p. 47)

Nothing more conveys the intensity of Mrs. Eddy's delusions of persecution and grandeur than this passage:

It was at this time that she said to us, "You don't any of you realize what is going on. This is a dark hour for the Cause and you do not seem to be awake to it." She said, "I am now working on a plane what would mean instantaneous death to any of you." (p. 17)

It is not easy to believe, but Mrs. Eddy became convinced that her mental workers could even control local weather!

The subjects covered by these "watches" were endless in their variety. One thing in particular that our Leader requested her workers to care for was the weather, and this was done in addition to the work of a committee in Boston appointed for that special purpose. During some of the severe New England winters when a greater amount of snow than usual was falling, our Leader would instruct her workers that they must put a stop to what seemed to be the steadily increasing fall of snow which she looked upon as a manifestation of error. She had an aversion to an excessive fall of snow. She considered it as an agent of destruction, and interference with the natural and normal trend of business. We are quick to recognize the fact that an unusually heavy fall of snow in any community is a disastrous thing. It clogs the wheels of commerce, interferes with traffic, interrupts the regular routine of business affairs, and breaks in upon the harmony and continuity of man's peaceful existence. Millions of dollars are spent annually in many places to remove the effects of heavy snowfalls, and so this was one of the points that was covered by Mrs. Eddy's mental workers. One of the "watches" issued January 15, 1910, requested her mental workers to "Make a law that there shall be no more snow this season."

When our Leader first came to live at Chestnut Hill in the spring and summer of 1908, thunder storms and electric disturbances seemed to be unusually prevalent. This was another form of error which our Leader disliked very much. A gentle rainfall was a delight to her, but a destructive, electrical storm she abhorred. She evidently looked upon it as a manifestation of evil and a destructive agency of mortal mind. Mrs. Sargent was the one to whom was especially assigned the work of watching the weather and bringing it into accord with normal conditions. For the three years during our Leader's stay in Chestnut Hill, and for several years thereafter, the recollection of the writer is that there were fewer and fewer thunder storms until they almost ceased to be. (p. 18)

It was God, of course, who altered the weather, not the mental workers. Their duty, she said, was merely to "destroy the operations of mortal mind and leave the question of regulating the weather to God."

I have heard our Leader describe in a number of instances how she
has dissipated a thunder cloud by simply looking upon it and bringing
to bear upon mortal mind's concept of this manifestation of discord
what God really has prepared for us, and she illustrated this by a
wave of her hand indicating the total disappearance of the thunder
cloud and its accompanying threat. (p. 19)

So boundless was Dickey's worship of Mrs. Eddy that he likened
her sufferings from MAM to agonies Jesus suffered from the MAM of
his enemies:

She was willing to endure the sufferings mortal mind imposed upon
her, for thereby she was enabled to take some action that would be
helpful to her Cause. How much we all owe to this dear soul, who
thus offered herself as a perpetual sacrifice for the good of humanity,
we may never know. "But he was wounded for our transgressions,
he was bruised for our iniquities; the chastisement of our peace was
upon him; and with his stripes we are healed" (Isaiah 51:5). (p. 44)

Now comes the saddest part of our bizarre saga. We have already
observed that by invoking MAM Mrs. Eddy was able to rationalize the
fact that she was growing old and feeble, suffering from various ailments,
her thin hands shaking with palsy. All her teeth had been replaced with
dentures. Her snow-white hair was starting to fall out. Unable to admit
that she lacked sufficient faith to control her false beliefs that created
the illusions of old age, she blamed it all on psychic forces coming
from afar. Although she had made a will, she still clung to the belief
that if it were not for the terrible MAM of her enemies, she could live
on for many more decades. Here is Mr. Dickey's account:

On Tuesday, August 25, 1908, my bell rang, calling me to Mrs. Eddy's
apartment. When I entered her study she was lying on the lounge
where she usually took her rest. Requesting Mrs. Sargent, Mr. Frye,

and a third student to leave the room, she beckoned me to approach. She extended her hand to me, took mine in both of hers, and asked in a deep, earnest voice, "Mr. Dickey, I want you to promise me something, will you?"

I said, "Yes, Mother, I certainly will."

"Well," she continued, "if I should ever leave here—do you know what I mean by that?"

"Yes, Mother."

"If I should leave here," she repeated, "will you promise me that you will write a history of what has transpired in your experiences with me, and say that I was mentally murdered?"

I answered, "Yes, Mother, I will."

"Now, Mr. Dickey, do not let anything interfere with your keeping this promise. Will you swear to me before God that you will not fail to carry out my wish?"

I raised my right hand and said, "Mother, I swear before God that I will do what you request of me, namely, write a history of what I have seen, and heard from your lips, concerning your life."

"That will do, dear. I know now that you will not fail me."

Her whole demeanor was one of solemn intensity, and there was an eagerness in her voice and manner such as I seldom saw.

I returned to my room and pondered deeply over what she had said. In a few minutes one of the workers and Mrs. Sargent brought me a sealed envelope. In it was a pencilled note reiterating the statement that she had made in our conversation of a short time before. (p. xiv)

Mrs. Eddy died believing it was not the normal aging of her body or the will of God that killed her. In her crazy metaphysics, her body was made of matter and therefore did not exist. Because God was good, he could not have desired her death. Moreover, it could not have been her own errors of belief that felled her. She was too good a Christian Scientist for that. In her curious mind there was only one possibility. She had not been strong enough to withstand murder!

8

Science and Health

The first edition of *Science and Health* (1875), a book of 456 pages, was printed for Mrs. Eddy by the Boston firm of W. F. Brown. A thousand copies came off the press. The cloth cover was light green. On page 23 the term "Christian Science" occurs for the first time in Mrs. Eddy's writings. The printing cost Mrs. Eddy $2,285.35. Nobody proofed the pages. Mrs. Eddy counted 490 typographical errors, not to mention bad punctuation, grammatical errors, and misplaced paragraphs. Only a few hundred copies were sold. It now is one of the rarest of all American first editions, worth thousands of dollars if you happen across one, which is extremely unlikely.

The second edition (1877) was supposed to be in two volumes, but the first volume had so many mistakes that almost all copies were destroyed. Only five hundred copies of the second volume (167 pages) were printed, with an inserted page citing printer's errors. The printing firm, again paid by Mrs. Eddy, was Rand, Very and Company, Boston. Because the green cloth cover had a picture of Noah's Ark in gold lines, collectors like to call it the "Noah's Ark edition." The spine bears the name Glover, and on the title page it is Mary Glover Eddy. Norman Beasley, in his favorable history of Christian Science, *The Cross and the Crown*, quotes a bizarre bit of doggerel by Mrs. Eddy that appeared on the book's flyleaf:

> I, I, I, I, itself, I
> The inside and outside, the what and the why,
> The when and the where, the low and the high,
> All I, I, I, I, itself, I.

The poem's "I" is not Mrs. Eddy, Beasley explains, but God, who for Mrs. Eddy is everything that is.

The two-volume third edition (1881) had 754 pages bound in purple cloth. It, too, was financed by Mrs. Eddy, using the University Press, John Wilson & Son, Cambridge. On the book's cover for the first time, as on all subsequent covers, is the familiar gold printing of a cross inside a crown, circled by the quotation from Matthew 10:8: "Heal the sick, cleanse the lepers, raise the dead, cast out devils."

It was not until the two-volume sixth edition (1883) that Mrs. Eddy added the section titled *Key to the Scriptures*. The number of pages then was 476. In 1902 numbers for lines were added to the margin, along with a section of healing testimonies titled "Fruitage." After Mrs. Eddy's death in 1910, the text was frozen in its present form.

Central to all editions is the notion, which lies at the heart of Christian Science, that the material world is *maya*, an illusion of mortal mind. This extreme form of idealism is defended today by a few eccentric New Age physicists and science journalists who are into Eastern mysticism and have only a poor grasp of quantum mechanics. In one of her many autobiographies Shirley MacLaine recalls how she once startled a group of party guests by arguing that maybe all of them, as well as the entire universe, were mere figments of her imagination. Did Shirley ever wonder, I wonder, why so few philosophers are solipsists?

Quimby's writings, which Mrs. Eddy thought would clear her of the charge of stealing from him, were finally published. *The Quimby Papers* (1921) were edited by New Thought leader Horatio W. Dresser, son of Julius Dresser who had earlier accused Mrs. Eddy of basing her teachings on the views of Quimby. New Thought, a flourishing movement in the years before and after 1900, also owed a great debt to Quimby. (We will cover New Thought in our final chapter.) Like many of today's New Agers who have revived all the basic elements of New Thought, the leaders of New Thought shared many of Mrs. Eddy's opinions, but refused to go along with her radical denial that matter existed, as well as her extreme opposition to surgery and drugs. A 1961 paperback reprint of *The Quimby Papers* has a new introduction by New Thought leader Ervin Seale. The papers in this book leave no shadow of doubt that Quimby did indeed anticipate the fundamental aspects of Christian Science.

Reams of books and articles have debated the extent of Mrs. Eddy's debt to Quimby. Christian Science leaders naturally struggle to minimize it. Books and articles by skeptics of course maximize it. Nothing makes Christian Scientists more furious than to suggest that their faith was not a new revelation from God to Mrs. Eddy, but had its origin in the mind of a medical quack named Quimby.

Few Christian Scientists today, like Seventh-day Adventists, go to the trouble of learning much about the life and character of the woman who founded their faith. Almost no Christian Scientists, outside church officials, have seen an 1875 edition of *Science and Health,* the only edition written by Mrs. Eddy with no assistance from others. It would be difficult for them to see this edition because the church has done everything in its power to forestall a reprinting.

In 1971, when the renewed copyright on the first edition expired, the church was powerful enough to persuade Congress to pass a special law—the only one if its kind—extending the book's copyright another seventy-five years. The bill was strongly supported by President Richard

Nixon's two top aides, H. R. Haldeman and John D. Ehrlichman, both Christian Scientists. Without White House support, this shameful bill surely would not have gone through. Happily, it was overturned as unconstitutional by a lower court of appeals, and in 1987 the U.S. Court of Appeals upheld the decision. I am amazed that no publisher has had the courage to reprint the 1875 edition.

Why has the church tried so hard to suppress this edition? The answer is that it swarms with evidence of Mrs. Eddy's near illiteracy: grammatical mistakes, misspelled words, weird punctuation, incoherent sentences, awkward writing, incessant repetition of ideas, internal contradictions, and faulty references. In her self-confident narcissism it never occurred to Mrs. Eddy that her great revelation from God needed editing by someone capable of writing good English, or to have her manuscript professionally proofed in galley form.

Even today, in its heavily revised authorized edition, the book is as disarranged as the Old Testament. It is a weird patchwork of notions derived from Quimby, and from random reading and private thinking, jotted down by an uneducated woman who did not know the most elementary rules for clear writing. It jumps from thought to thought with as little transition as a comic monologue by Henny Youngman, but totally without his humor. You can read even the current edition of *Science and Health* by starting anywhere and stopping anywhere.

Stefan Zweig, the noted Austrian writer, in the section on Mrs. Eddy in *Mental Healers* (English translation 1932) described *Science and Health* as follows:

> It is, therefore, in its first and primitive form that *Science and Health* is so remarkable an essay in private theology, one of those meteoric books which seem to rush from far distant skies into that of the time to which they technically belong. Bearing unmistakable marks of genius and at the same time absurd in its fierce disregard of all the accepted canons of knowledge, at once ludicrously childish and illogical, amaz-

ing, quasi-maniacal, simple and direct, this codex has a thoroughly medieval flavour, breathing as it does the religious fanaticism characteristic of all the theological outsiders, such as Agrippa of Nettesheim and Jakob Böhme. The fraudulent and the creative succeed one another in fantastic arabesques; the most contradictory trends intermingle in wild confusion; Swedenborg's astral mysticism is criss-crossed with trivial popularized science snatched from cheap handbooks; side by side with texts from the Bible are extracts from the New York daily papers, and side by side with dazzling metaphors are the most inconceivably preposterous assertions: and yet, taking it all in all, this mass of whirling words is alive through and through, glowing and bubbling over with spiritual passion, so that our eyes begin to burn as we look into the boiling crucible of molten metal. Our sober senses become obscured. We fancy ourselves in Faust's laboratory, and believe, like him, that we hear "a hundred thousand fools" speaking all together. But the circling chaos continues to revolve round a single point. Again and again, Mary Baker hammers her one and only idea into our brains, until, deafened rather than convinced, we are forced to capitulate. Or if not that, at least we are powerfully impressed by the magnificence of the achievement, by the masterly way in which this uneducated and illogical woman is able, under stress of her obsession, to make sun, moon, and stars, an entire universe, gyrate perpetually round one fundamentally absurd idea. (pp. 165–66)

Louis Rose, discussing Christian Science in his excellent book *Faith Healing* (Penguin edition, 1968), said it this way:

The often-revised *Science and Health* remains an egotistical and at times paranoid and demonic book, alternating between the repetitive and the self-contradictory. Familiar words are used in a Pickwickian sense which a glossary does little to elucidate, and idiosyncratic and *ex cathedra* pronouncements of doctrines contrary to all experience are more frequently found than logical arguments. (p. 64)

*   *   *

In summary, "Christian Science" appeals to no reason and to only one authority, that of its founder. Its services lack the attraction of either Protestant rhetoric or Catholic ritual. Its philosophy is in essence simple to the point of banality: as developed it is incomprehensible to the simple-minded and ridiculous to the sophisticated. It is without the glamour of occult oriental theosophies or the easy comfort of the offer of an automatic life after death. Above all, it flatly contradicts our most intense everyday experience: for most of us do not need to "sit on a pin, when it punctures our skin, to dislike what we fancy we feel" in order to reject its Berkeleyan idealism. (p. 68)

The *Key to the Scriptures,* which Mrs. Eddy added to *Science and Health,* opens with a weird commentary on the Bible's first book, Genesis, followed by an even stranger commentary on Revelation, the Bible's last book. Thousands of erudite commentaries on John's vision have been written, but not until Mrs. Eddy interpreted it was it revealed to be what she called the "acme" of Christian Science!

"We take the inspired Word of the Bible as our sufficient guide to eternal Life," Mrs. Eddy wrote in *Science and Health* (p. 497), but she also believed that she was the first to understand the true meaning of God's Word. Although she accepted the historical reality of some of the Bible's miracles—the Virgin Birth, the reviving of Lazarus, the Resurrection of Jesus—she rebelled against assuming that every event in the Bible had actually taken place. However, because the Bible was in her eyes the divine word of God, she believed that every event had a metaphorical, spiritual significance, and that she had been chosen by the Lord to provide these accurate interpretations. In most cases her interpretations departed wildly from traditional Christian doctrines.

Today's authorized edition of *Science and Health* has biblical quotations on almost every page as well as at the tops of chapters, but Mrs. Eddy had strange ways of interpreting what the passages actually meant. For instance, when Jesus said that God would send to earth another "Comforter," all biblical scholars agree that by "Comforter" the word refers to the Holy Spirit. Indeed, on page 497 Mrs. Eddy writes: "We acknowledge and adore one supreme and infinite God. We acknowledge His Son, one Christ; the Holy Ghost or divine Comforter; and man in God's image and likeness." All this sounds very orthodox. But when you discover what Mrs. Eddy takes the word "Comforter" to mean, it becomes almost blasphemous.

On page 55 Mrs. Eddy lets us in on the secret: "In the words of St. John: 'He shall give you another Comforter, that he may abide with you *forever*.' This Comforter I understand to be Divine Science." That Mrs. Eddy equated Christian Science with the Holy Spirit is evident from other passages in *Science and Health*. On pages 331–32, for example, she defines the trinity as: "God the Father-Mother; Christ the spiritual idea of sonship; Divine Science or the Holy Comforter. These three express in Divine Science the threefold, essential nature of the infinite." In the book's glossary, the Holy Ghost is defined as "Divine Science; the development of eternal Life, Truth, and Love" (p. 588).

Mrs. Eddy's glossary, in which she reveals the hidden, secret meanings of key biblical words, is surely the most peculiar chapter of *Science and Health*. The true metaphysical meaning of Adam, for example, is "Error; a falsity; the belief in 'original sin,' sickness, and death; evil; the opposite of good," and so on for twenty-eight more ludicrous lines. Mrs. Eddy had a low opinion of Adam. On page 338 she degrades him with a crude pun: "Divide the name Adam into two syllables, and it reads *a dam,* or obstruction." Mrs. Eddy enjoyed this kind of punning analysis of biblical terms. The atonement, she writes in three places (pp. 19, 21, 48), doesn't mean what Christians have always taken it to mean: a blood sacrifice to save sinners from hell. To Mrs. Eddy it means "at-one-ment" with God, the Divine Principle. The same pun was repeated again and again by New Thought leaders, and is still being repeated by many New Agers.

Eve gets less space in the glossary than Adam. To Mrs. Eddy, her name symbolizes "A beginning; morality; that which does not last forever; a finite belief concerning life, substance, and intelligence in matter; error; the belief that the human race originated materially instead of spiritually,—that man started first from dust, second from a rib, and third from an egg."

Abel, for Mrs. Eddy, symbolizes watchfulness. Dove refers to Christian Science. Other terms signifying Christian Science include Gad, Elias, New Jerusalem, and the rivers Euphrates and Hiddekel. Ham, Noah's son, is corporeal belief. Jacob's son Dan is animal magnetism. What is a miracle? It is "that which is divinely natural, but must be learned humanly; a phenomenon of [Christian] Science." Angels are "God's thoughts." And so on ad absurdum.

Where did Mrs. Eddy get the idea for her Pickwickian glossary? It came from *A Dictionary of Correspondences,* a book of definitions based on the writings of the Swedish spiritualist Emmanuel Swedenborg. This dictionary was published in Boston in 1847 and went through many reprintings at a time when Swedenborg's mad doctrines were taken seriously by tens of thousands of Americans, including the father of William James. In the days when Mrs. Eddy was a practicing medium and a dispenser of homeopathic drugs, she was much taken by the writings of Swedenborg and his New England disciple, the seer Andrew Jackson Davis. Many of the biblical words she chose to interpret are taken straight out of the Swedenborg dictionary, including such peculiar words as "IN."

Here are a few instances of how the Swedenborg dictionary is echoed in Mrs. Eddy's glossary. For Swedenborg the true meaning of "Ark" is "combat and temptation." For Mrs. Eddy it means "temptation overcome and followed by exaltation." "Fan" in the Swedenborg dictionary "signifies separation of the false from the good." To Mrs. Eddy it is "Separator of fable from fact." For more examples, see the appendix

MONUMENT AT BIRTHPLACE OF MARY BAKER EDDY, BOW, N.H.

Picture postcard of the granite memorial marking the birthplace of Mary Baker Eddy in Bow, N.H., printed circa 1919. An exact replica of the Great Pyramid of Egypt, the monument was dynamited in 1962 by person(s) unknown. Reprinted by permission.

Left: Daniel Patterson, Mrs. Eddy's second husband, was a dentist who practiced homeopathy. The marriage ended in divorce in 1873. From Georgine Milmine, *The Life of Mary Baker G. Eddy and the History of Christian Science* (1909).
Right: Asa Gilbert Eddy was Mrs. Eddy's third husband and the first authorized Christian Science practitioner. Although his death in 1882 was attributed to a heart attack, Mrs. Eddy claimed it was due to "malicious animal magnetism." From Milmine (1909).

Phineas Parkhurst Quimby was a faith healer and the mentor of Mary Baker
Eddy. Although unacknowledged by Mrs. Eddy, his beliefs formed the basis
of Christian Science. From Milmine (1909).

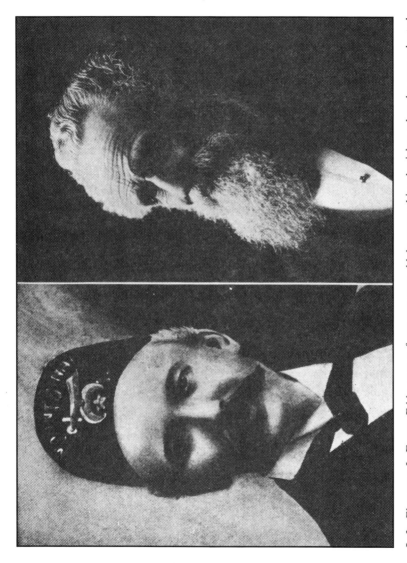

Left: Ebenezer J. Foster Eddy was a forty-one-year-old homeopathic physician when he was adopted by Mrs. Eddy. Serving as Mrs. Eddy's publisher, he would later be excommunicated for falsifying account books and having an affair with a married woman. From Milmine (1909).
Right: George Washington Glover, Mrs. Eddy's child by her first husband, and her only child, was estranged from his mother for most of his life. From Milmine (1909).

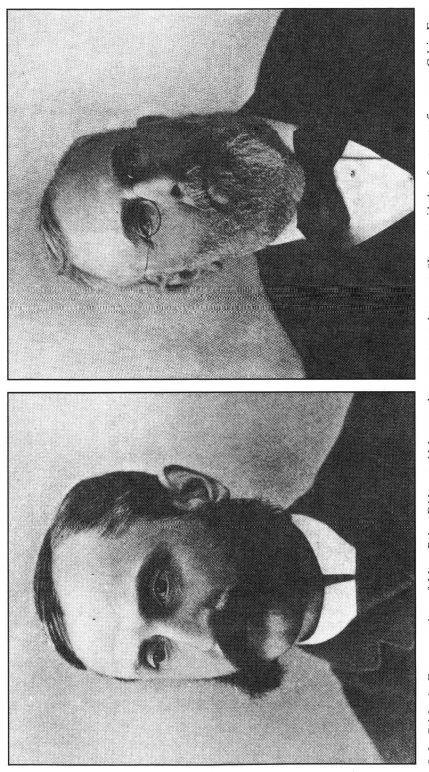

Left: Calvin A. Frye, a student of Mary Baker Eddy, would become her most trusted servant. "It was said that for twenty-five years Calvin Frye had never been outside the call of Mrs. Eddy's voice" (Springer 1930). From Milmine (1909).

Right: James Henry Wiggin worked for four years as Mrs. Eddy's "paid polisher." Well educated and a skilled editor, he regarded *Science and Health* to be "balderdash." From Milmine (1909).

A Christian Scientists' picnic, taken July 16, 1885. Mrs. Josephine Curtis Woodbury is at the right of the top row, and Mrs. Augusta E. Stetson is the third figure from the left in the third row. From Milmine (1909).

One of the controversial illustrations from Mary Baker Eddy's *Christ and Christmas* (1883). The storm of protest aroused by James F. Gilman's art was so great that Mrs. Eddy was forced to issue a disclaimer.

Ella Wheeler Wilcox, the noted New Thought poet whose writings were precursors of the New Age movement. From Ella Wheeler Wilcox, *The Worlds and I* (1918).

on Mrs. Eddy's glossary in *Mrs. Eddy Purloins from Hegel* (1936) by Walter M. Haushalter. The appendix is based in turn on Hermann S. Fricke's paper, "The Sources of *Science and Health*," in *Bibliotheca Sacra* (October 1928).

James Snowden, in *The Truth About Christian Science,* accurately described Mrs. Eddy's glossary as follows:

> All these "metaphysical interpretations" are seriously given as the "original meaning" of these terms. This egregious "Glossary" may be viewed as a literary curiosity and monstrosity, or as a pitiful display of ignorant conceit, or as a painful exhibition of sacrilegious trifling with Scripture, or as a symptom of incipient egotistic insanity, a kind of lexical madhouse; but it may be summed up by saying that it is a conglomeration of arrant nonsense and fatuous folly without a rival, so far as is known, in the English or any other language. (p. 144)

It is difficult to believe, but when Bronson Alcott, distinguished friend of Emerson and the father of Louisa May Alcott who wrote *Little Women,* read the 1875 edition of *Science and Health* he was bowled over with admiration.

"The profound truths which you announce," he said in a letter to Mrs. Eddy, "sustained by facts of the immortal life, give to your work the seal of inspiration—reaffirm in modern phrase the Christian revelation. In times like these, so sunk in sensualism, I hail with joy your voice, speaking an assured word for God and immortality, and my joy is heightened that these words are woman's divinings."

Alcott added his desire to know "more of you personally," and asked if he could propose a date for a visit. Mrs. Eddy was receptive, and a few days later the two got together in Lynn. Alcott sent a second letter recalling his host's grace and charm, and expressing a wish for a "more intimate fellowship." In a still later letter he passed along Emerson's desire to meet her.

Emerson was less effusive in his praise for *Science and Health,* but, like Alcott, he recognized it as in the tradition of their transcendentalism. In an essay on Emerson in the first series of Paul Elmer More's *Shelbourne Essays* (1904), More expressed Mrs. Eddy's debt to transcendentalism in strong terms:

> There is a mysterious faith abroad in the land, which, however we grudge to say it, is the most serious manifestation of religion discoverable in these days. We call it Christian Science, or faith healing, or what not—the gospel of a certain Mrs. Baker-Eddy; but in reality it does not owe its strength to the teaching of an ignorant woman in New Hampshire. It is a diluted and stale product of Emersonianism, and the parentage, I think, is not difficult to discern. To Emerson, as to Mrs. Baker-Eddy, sin and suffering had no real existence; a man need only open his breast to the random influences of heaven to lead the purely spiritual life. (p. 79)

Science and Health went through endless revisions. Large portions were removed, new material added, chapters shifted about, and hundreds of sentences revised. Church members were urged to buy each newly revised printing. This of course greatly augmented the revenues to Mother Church.

The most significant editing was done by a peculiar individual named James Henry Wiggin (1836–1900). He was a huge man with a boisterous laugh and a sly sense of humor. A retired Unitarian minister, he was well educated and a skilled proofreader and copyeditor. Although he never believed in Christian Science, for four years he was Mrs. Eddy's "paid polisher." He even helped edit the *Christian Science Journal,* contributing tongue-in-cheek articles under the whimsical pseudonym of Phare Pleigh. The same pseudonym was used on a pamphlet he wrote titled *Christian Science and the Bible.* He also wrote some of Mrs. Eddy's sermons. The 1886 edition of *Science and Health* was the one he most heavily altered, though he continued making changes through 1891.

There is little doubt that many literary and philosophical references that appeared for the first time in the 1886 edition were put there by Wiggin. He was also responsible for deleting scores of Mrs. Eddy's more preposterous passages. As Wiggin later said, his main job was "to keep her [Mrs. Eddy] from making herself ridiculous." As we saw earlier, he persuaded her to drop long sections in which she attacked former students for harming her with MAM, passages Wiggin rightly believed to be libelous.

In place of Mrs. Eddy's wild chapter on demonology, Wiggin substituted a sermon he himself had written. As a chapter titled "Wayside Hints," it appeared in many editions of *Science and Health* until one day Mrs. Eddy asked him if he considered the chapter his own. "Why, Mrs. Eddy, it is unquestionably my chapter," Wiggin replied. "It consists of my own words from start to finish. It is most assuredly my chapter." Mrs. Eddy removed it from all later editions, although, as Dakin remarks in his biography, remnants of it can still be found on page 575.

In addition to his labors on *Science and Health,* Wiggin also edited parts of *Retrospection and Introspection,* Mrs. Eddy's autobiography, as well as portions of *Miscellaneous Writings,* and pamphlets such as her *Unity of Good* and *No and Yes.* He even tinkered with some of her poems:

> "I know," he said, "that a deal of sport has been made over her poems, attention having been drawn with some interest and amusement to the prosody and rhyming. I planed off a good many of her poems and if they lack, after going through my hands, something in measure and comprehensibility, I surely don't know what the literary critics would have thought of the originals as they came to me."

Wiggin was the first to prepare an index to *Science and Health*. It was added to the twenty-eighth edition (1887), but later replaced by a separate *Concordance*.

The church has always kept up the pretence, which it knows to be untrue, that it was Mrs. Eddy who made all the numerous changes in *Science and Health* as it went through its many reprintings. In 1886 church officials had the audacity to announce in the *Christian Science Journal* that the new edition had been carefully revised and parts rewritten by Mrs. Eddy. No mention was made of Mr. Wiggin. Here is a typical paragraph from the *Journal* (March 1902) about the 1902 revision. I quote from Mark Twain's book on Christian Science—a book that will be the topic of chapter 11:

> Throughout the entire book the verbal changes are so numerous as to indicate the vast amount of time and labor Mrs. Eddy has devoted to this revision. The time and labor thus bestowed is relatively as great as that of the committee who revised the Bible. . . . Thus we have additional evidence of the herculean efforts our beloved Leader has made and is constantly making for the promulgation of Truth and the furtherance of her divinely bestowed mission. (p. 136)

Not until the fiftieth edition were the marginal notes added, and biblical quotations substituted for each chapter's former epigraphs of poetry and prose by famous authors. In fairness it should be said that Mrs. Eddy instructed Wiggin only to clarify, not alter, the meanings of her sentences, and of course she had final approval of all his changes.

Wiggin's sense of fun and his joking criticisms of Mrs. Eddy, who had only a marginal sense of humor, finally did him in. True to her paranoia, Mrs. Eddy eventually decided that he, too, was secretly attacking her with MAM. She charged him with "shocking flippancy" in the notes he liked to scribble on galley proofs of her writings. "This is MAM," she wrote in a letter to the printers in 1890, "and it governs

Wiggin as it has done once before to prevent the publishing of my work. . . . I will take the proof-reading out of Wiggin's hands." This she did, and we hear no more from her about Mr. Wiggin.

After being fired by Mrs. Eddy, Wiggin had this to say in a letter dated December 14, 1889, to a college friend that I take from Milmine's biography of Mrs. Eddy. She rightly calls it "probably the most trenchant and suggestive sketch of Mrs. Eddy that will ever be written."

> Christian Science, on its theological side, is an ignorant revival of one form of ancient gnosticism, that Jesus is to be distinguished from the Christ, and that his earthly appearance was phantasmal, not real and fleshy.
>
> On its moral side, it involves what must follow from the doctrine that reality is a dream, and that if a thing is right in thought, why right it is, and that sin is non-existent, because God can *behold* no evil. Not that Christian Science believers generally see this, or practise evil, but the virus is within.
>
> Religiously, Christian Science is a revolt from orthodoxy, but unphilosophically conducted, endeavouring to ride two horses.
>
> Physically, it leads people to trust all to nature, the great healer, and so does some good. Great virtue in imagination! . . . Where there is disease which time will not reach, Christian Science is useless.
>
> As for the High Priestess of it, . . . she is—well I could *tell* you, but not write. An awfully (I use the word advisedly) smart woman, acute, shrewd, but not well read, nor in any way learned. What she has, as documents clearly show, she got from P. P. Quimby of Portland, Maine, whom she eulogised after death as the great leader and her special teacher. . . . She tried to answer the charge of the adoption of Quimby's ideas, and called me in to counsel her about it; but her only answer (in print!) was that if she said such things twenty years ago, she must have been under the influence of *animal magnetism,* which is *her* devil. No church can long get on without a devil, you know. Much more I could say if you were here. . . .

People beset with this delusion are thoroughly irrational. Take an instance. Dr. R——— of Roxbury is not a believer. His wife *is*. One evening I met her at a friendly house. Knowing her belief, I ventured only a mild and wary dissent, saying that I saw too much of it to feel satisfied, etc. In fact, the Doctor said the same and told me more in private. Yet, later, I learned that this slight discussion made her *ill,* nervous, and had a bad effect.

One of Mrs. Eddy's followers went so far as to say that if she *saw* Mrs. Eddy commit a crime she should believe her own sight at fault, *not* Mrs. Eddy's conduct. An intelligent man told me in reference to lies he *knew* about, that the wrong was in *us*. "Was not Jesus accused of wrong-doing, yet guiltless?"

Only experience can teach these fanatics, *i.e.,* the real believers, not the charlatans who go into it for money. . . . As for the book, if you have any edition since December, 1885, it had my supervision. Though now she is getting out an entirely new edition, with which I had nothing to do, and occasionally she has made changes whereof I did not know. The chapter B——— told you of is rather fanciful, though, to use Mrs. Eddy's language in her last note, her "friends think it a gem." It is the one called "Wayside Hints," and was added after the work was not only in type, but cast, because she wished to take out some twenty pages of diatribe on her dissenters. . . . I do not think it will greatly edify you, the chapter. As for clearness, many Christian Science people thought her early editions much better, because they sounded more *like* Mrs. Eddy. The truth is, she does not care to have her paragraphs clear, and delights in so expressing herself that her words may have various readings and meanings. Really, that is one of the tricks of the trade. You know sibyls have always been thus oracular, to "keep the word of promise to the ear, and break it to the hope."

There is nothing really to understand in "Science and Health" except that *God is all,* and yet there is no God in matter! What they fail to explain is, the origin of the *idea* of matter, or sin. They say it comes from *mortal mind,* and that mortal mind is not divinely created, in fact, has no existence; in fact, that nothing comes of nothing, and that matter and disease are like dreams, having no existence. Quimby had definite ideas, but Mrs. Eddy has not understood them.

When I first knew Christian Science, I wrote a defensive pamphlet called "Christian Science and the Bible" (though I did not believe the doctrine). . . . I found fair game in the assaults of orthodoxy upon Mrs. Eddy, and support in the supernaturalism of the Bible; but I did not pretend to give an exposition of Christian Science, and I did not know the old lady as well as I do now.

No, Swedenborg, and all other such writers, are sealed books to her. She cannot understand such utterances, and never could, but dollars and cents she understands thoroughly.

Her influence is wonderful. Mrs. R———'s husband is anxious *not* to have her undeceived, though her tenth cancer is forming, lest she sink under the change of faith, and I can quite see that the loss of such a faith, like loss of faith in a physician, might be injurious. . . . In the summer of 1888, some thirty of her best people left Mrs. Eddy, including her *leading* people, too, her association and church officers. . . . They still believe nominally in Christian Science, yet several of them . . . are studying medicine at the College of Physicians and Surgeons, Boston; and she gave consent for at least *one* of them to study at this allopathic school. These students I often see, and *they* say the professors are coming over to *their* way of belief, which means simply that they hear the trustworthiness of the laws of nature proclaimed. As in her book, and in her class (which I went through), she says, "Call a surgeon in surgical cases."

"What if I find a breech presentation in childbirth?" asked a pupil.

"You will *not,* if you are in Christian Science," replied Mrs. Eddy.

"But if I *do?*"

"Then send for the nearest regular practitioner!"

You see, Mrs. Eddy is nobody's fool. (pp. 337–39)

After Wiggin died, a manuscript about his relationship with Mrs. Eddy was found among his papers. It consisted of recollections that

Wiggin had told to someone named Livingston Wright. The entire manuscript was published in the *New York World* (November 6, 1906) and was later issued as a booklet titled *How Rev. Wiggin Rewrote Mrs. Eddy's Book.* Mrs. Eddy's reply to Wright in the *New York American* (November 22, 1906) was reprinted in the *Christian Science Sentinel* (December 1, 1906).

What follows is from Dakin's biography. Christian Science loyalists have a point in saying that we have no way of knowing how reliable these recollections are, but they tend to ring true. Here is what Wiggin had to say:

> She was a person of great, stately mien, perfectly self-possessed and disposed to be somewhat overbearing and impressive in manner. She had a huge package of manuscript which I learned was designed to serve as the material for a forthcoming edition of *Science and Health,* with *Key to the Scriptures.*
>
> We talked over the matter of recompense and those details and she seemed satisfied with my terms, was very direct and businesslike; and we entered into arrangements, whereby I was to undertake the revision of the manuscript, although she was careful to give me to understand that she regarded herself as having already gotten the manuscript in approximately the proper shape for the printer. But there were, she confessed, "doubtless a few things here and there, that would require the assistance of a fresh mind." I did not then give the package more than a mere passing glance.
>
> I was intending to go up to the mountains with my wife, on a few days' vacation, and I put the package away in my satchel, thinking that when I got up in the hills, I would set about the revision, which I supposed could be completed in a reasonably short time. Some days later I opened the package and began a scrutiny of the manuscript. Well I was staggered!
>
> Of all the dissertations a literary helper ever inspected, I do not believe one ever saw a treatise to surpass this. The misspelling, capi-

talization and punctuation were dreadful, but those were not things that feazed me. It was the thought and the general elemental arrangement of the work. There were passages that flatly and absolutely contradicted things that had preceded, and scattered all through were incorrect references to historical and philosophical matters.

The thing that troubled me was: How could I attempt to dress up the manuscript by dealing only with the spelling and punctuation? There would be left a mass of material that would reflect on me as a professional literary aid, were my name to be in any way associated with the enterprise. I was convinced that the only way in which I could undertake the requested revision would be to begin absolutely at the first page and re-write the whole thing!

I tossed the package back into the satchel and did nothing more until I returned to Boston. I then had an interview with Mrs. Eddy and explained as kindly and gently as I could the situation as I found it. I told her I would have to rewrite the manuscript. I had rather expected something of a scene and was ready to tell her, as I had occasion to tell one or two others in times past, that if I undertook the revision, I must do so conscientiously, and that I could not be placed in a position where I might be censured for a showing that was not my own. But instead of any hesitation or hint of annoyance, Mrs. Eddy in a calm, easy, thoroughly stately manner agreed to my declaration about the matter of a re-write, acceded to my terms of recompense, and it began to slowly dawn upon me that perhaps this thing of a revision "from the ground up" as it were, was the very thing she had intended that I should do in the first place.

In the course of our conversation, I reiterated to her that she must understand, of course, that I was not a Christian Scientist, did not hold views according to her own, and did not ever expect to become a Christian Scientist. I wished this point to be thoroughly understood at the beginning, as I meant that literary revision and my own religious and ethical connections should have no affiliation, one with the other.

However, to all this Mrs. Eddy would respond in the blandest of manner, "Oh, we know you are not a believer now, Mr. Wiggin, but we hope that you may come to unite with us." And this continued to be her stereotyped comment, whenever the question of my attitude toward Christian Science came up. (pp. 225–26)

On page 19 of her autobiography, Mrs. Eddy said that her favorite studies were natural philosophy, logic, and moral science, and that her brother gave her lessons in Hebrew, Latin, and Greek. Wiggin could not believe this:

The evidence of lack of education and of ignorance concerning the writings and teachings of the famous philosophers was so overwhelming that I could not trust her references, but had to look up everything for myself, to be sure, and to feel that I was doing work that was commendable to my own standard and just to her while I remained her literary aid and counsel.

It has been many times claimed for Mrs. Eddy, and she has claimed it herself, that she knew something of the ancient languages and literature. I can positively assure you that Mrs. Eddy knew nothing whatever of the ancient languages. She could not translate a page of Latin, Greek, or Sanskrit or give a synopsis of the teaching of the great philosophers of the ancients were it to have saved her life. . . .

Thus it was that I tried to examine every sentence and to cut out whenever she would permit; for understand, there were many occasions when she insisted on using her particular words or expressions even though I had positively assured her that they had best be changed or taken from the context. So, of course, in they went! I hunted up texts and mottoes with which to head the various chapters and adorn or illustrate the reading matter. All of this was a bagatelle, however, compared to the maddening task of straightening out her weird English and bolstering up her lack of learning, to use the mildest term.

Another thing that I shall never forget was a chapter in which Mrs. Eddy had proceeded to arraign a group of physicians because her husband while under their treatment had died. Mrs. Eddy accused these men of causing the death of Asa G. Eddy by—to use her exact phrase—"arsenical poison mentally administered."

She scored the doctors dreadfully in this essay of hers, and as there was nothing whatever—an autopsy having been performed upon the deceased—to show any unprofessional, much less criminal, conduct on the part of the attending physicians who were of well known high-class reputations in their professions, I knew, of course, that the publication of any such charges as these would immediately bring her into serious trouble.

I remonstrated with Mrs. Eddy about this chapter, but she seemed determined, at first, to have one chapter go in. I urged her to think well before she made any such preposterous charges as those in print. "You'll be arrested and convicted for criminal libel as surely as you print that accusation against those doctors," I declared. Mrs. Eddy replied that she "would think it over." I came later to learn that that was her way of preparing for assent to a point that she felt could not be safely carried. A few days later she asked me if I felt the same way about that chapter. "I certainly do," I answered. "Very well," she responded. Several days passed when she once more asked me if I was still of the same opinion. I said, "Yes."

After the lapse of a few more days she said to me, "Mr. Wiggin, I have decided to leave out that chapter." I felt relieved, as may be imagined, but was surprised to hear her next statement, as she said most impressively and with peculiar suavity of mien: "Mr. Wiggin, I often feel as if the Lord spoke to me through you!" (pp. 227–28)

In the first edition of *Science and Health* Mrs. Eddy made no claims that this book was a revelation from God, but in later years, in spite of heavy revisions by Wiggin, she repeatedly made just such claims. Here is what she had to say in *The First Church of Christ, Scientist, and Miscellany:*

My first writings on Christian Science began with notes on the Scriptures. I consulted no other authors and read no other book but the Bible for about three years. What I wrote had a strange coincidence or relationship with the light of revelation and solar light. I could not write these notes after sunset. All thoughts in the line of Scriptural interpretation would leave me until the rising of the sun. Then the influx of divine interpretation would pour in upon my spiritual sense as gloriously as the sunlight on the material senses. It was not myself, but the divine power of Truth and Love, infinitely above me, which dictated *Science and Health with Key to the Scriptures.* I have been learning the higher meaning of this book since writing it.

Is it too much to say that this book is leavening the whole lump of human thought? You can trace its teachings in each step of mental and spiritual progress, from pulpit and press, in religion and ethics, and find these progressive steps either written or indicated in the book. It has mounted thought on the swift and mighty chariot of divine Love, which to-day is circling the whole world.

I should blush to write of *Science and Health with Key to the Scriptures* as I have, were it of human origin, and were I, apart from God, its author. But, as I was only a scribe echoing the harmonies of heaven in divine metaphysics, I cannot be super-modest in my estimate of the Christian Science textbook. (pp. 114–15)

I have no doubt that devout Christian Scientists look upon *Science and Health* exactly as Mrs. Eddy did. To an outsider, however, the book, in spite of Wiggin's heroic efforts to improve it, is still one of the most haphazardly written works ever to lay claim to being divinely inspired. James Snowden, in *The Truth About Christian Science,* sums it up this way:

It is difficult to give a condensed summary of the contents of *Science and Health,* because of the lack of order and system in its arrangement and in its ideas. The chapters themselves have several times been shifted around in a different order, and they might be shuffled again without any loss of logic. The very titles of the chapters sometimes have little aptness as designations of their contents. The order of the paragraphs in the chapters also follows no inherent plan and progress and frequently baffles the reader to find and follow any thread of connection. There are only a few fundamental ideas in the book, and these are endlessly iterated and reiterated until one's sense of interest and attention is dulled into drowsiness: reading the book is like listening to a player on a violin who keeps sawing on one string and making few variations on that. One really has to maintain a firm grip on his attention to keep from falling into a stupor while perusing these monotonous pages. The style is trying enough because of its peculiar lingo and its frequent obscurity, although there are passages of clear English and here and there a purple patch of fine writing, some of these patches, however, being affected and stilted to a degree. Of course, also, there is much truth in the book, even fundamental truth and wholesome teaching, wheat in its chaff, grains of gold in its sand. (p. 102)

9

Plagiarism

Ellen Gould White, the leader of Seventh-day Adventism who claimed direct contact with God and angels, was as poorly educated (she never went beyond third grade) as Mrs. Eddy and just as bad a writer. Her early scribblings, before her works were carefully edited and polished by others, were almost as crude as the 1875 edition of *Science and Health*. It has long been known that books bearing Mrs. White's name contain hundreds of plagiarisms, often word for word, from books by other writers. It is not yet known to what extent she deliberately copied, or whether it was done by her assistants and she failed to realize it. In either case, it casts serious doubts on her claim that her books were divinely inspired. Moreover, the Adventist church's effort to suppress information about Mrs. White's literary stealing casts serious doubts on the church's honesty.

Few Christian Scientists realize that Mrs. Eddy's writings, like Mrs. White's, also bristle with plagiarisms. Quite aside from what she stole from Quimby's papers, and from early books on mind healing, she copied shamelessly, often word for word, from John Ruskin, Thomas Carlyle, Charles Kingsley, Swiss critic Henri Amiel, and from other authors. Like Mrs. White, not once did she credit her sources or even suggest to readers that she was cribbing.

It was typical of Mrs. Eddy not to bother to look up original works by the authors she took from, but to pilfer their words from anthologies. Someone gave her a copy of a small book titled *Philosophic Nuggets: Bits of Ore from Rich Mines* (1899), edited by Joanne Pennington. From it Mrs. Eddy extracted scores of nuggets by the first four authors named above. Some of the stolen sentences remain even today in the authorized version of *Science and Health*. For example, in *Philosophic Nuggets* Carlyle is quoted: "it was the unseen and spiritual in them that determined the outward and actual." On page 254 of *Science and Health* we find: "To work out the spiritual which determines the outward and actual." Dozens of similar passages in Mrs. Eddy's writings after 1899 are partially copied from the nuggets in Pennington's anthology. Here are some of them, citing the original first, followed by a passage on the right by Mrs. Eddy:

Carlyle wrote about a "time-world" that "only flutters as an unreal shadow."	"This time-world flutters in my thought as an unreal shadow." (*Miscellany,* p. 268)
Carlyle wrote that the center of things is "not a madness and nothing, but a sanity and something."	"not a madness and nothing, but a sanity and something." (*Miscellany,* p. 14)
"a little group of wise hearts is better than a wilderness full of fools." (Ruskin)	"A small group of wise thinkers is better than a wilderness of dullards." (*Miscellany,* p. 162)

"We are all of us willing enough to accept dead truths, or blunt ones; which can be . . . shrouded and coffined at once out of the way . . . but a sapling truth, with earth at its root and blossom on its branches; or a trenchant truth that can cut its way through bars and sods; most men dislike the sight or entertainment of, if . . . such . . . may be avoided." (Ruskin)

"Most of us willingly accept dead truisms which can be buried at will; but a live truth, even though it be a sapling within rich soil and with blossoms on its branches, frightens people. The trenchant truth that cuts its way through iron and sod, most men avoid until compelled to glance at it" (*Miscellany*, p. 160)

"The ten dumb centuries continued voiceless . . . had no Divina Commedia to hear." (Carlyle)

"I am as silent as the dumb centuries without a Divina." (*Miscellany*, p. 268)

"the deadliest sin . . . that some supercilious consciousness of no sin." (Carlyle)

"a supercilious consciousness that saith 'there is no sin.' " (*Message to the Mother Church, 1900*, p. 15)

"Of all acts is not for a man, repentance the most divine?" (Carlyle)

"sea of repentance—which of all human experience is the most divine." (*Message to the Mother Church, 1900*, p. 15)

"quackery gives birth to nothing; gives death to all things." (Carlyle)

"quacks, giving birth to nothing and death to all" (*Message to the Mother Church, 1901*, p. 30)

"As the thing is good or bad, so is the maker of it." (Ruskin)

"As the thing made is good or bad, so is its maker." (*Miscellany*, p. 205)

"him who is seen toiling for the spiritually indispensible." (Carlyle)	"he that toiled for the spiritually indispensible." (*Message to the Mother Church, 1900*, p. 14)
"The redeemed are happier than the elect." (Amiel)	"The redeemed should be happier than the elect." (*Miscellany*, p. 229)
"to live, so as to keep this consciousness of ours in perpetual relation with the eternal." (Amiel)	"To live so as to keep human consciousness in constant relation with the divine." (*Miscellany*, p. 160)

The charge that Mrs. Eddy copied from a paper on "The Metaphysical Religion of Hegel" by Francis Lieber was first made by Episcopalian rector Walter M. Haushalter in his explosive book *Mrs. Eddy Purloins from Hegel: Newly Discovered Source Reveals Amazing Plagiarisms in Science and Health* (1936). I will cite only a few typical examples, first a passage from Lieber, followed by a passage from the first (1875) edition of *Science and Health:*

"To conclude that Life, Love and Truth are attributes of a personal Deity implies there is something in Person superior to Principle. What, then, is the person of God? Hegel makes clear that He has no personality as we narrowly view personality for this would imply Intelligence in matter. The body of God is the Idea given of Him in the harmonious order of the universe and in man (male and female) formed by Him." (Lieber, p. 82)	"To conclude Life, Love, and Truth are attributes of a personal Deity, implies there is something in person superior to Principle." . . . "What is the person of God? He has no personality, for this would imply Intelligence in matter; the body of God is the idea given of Him in the harmonious universe, and the male and female formed by Him." (pp. 44, 221, 222)

"Beauty is also eternal. The beauty of matter passes away fading at length into decay and ugliness. But beauty itself is a thing of Life exempt from age or decay and to be this it must be a thing of Spirit." (pp. 83–84)	"Beauty is eternal; but the beauty of matter passes away, fading at length into decay and ugliness. . . . But beauty is a thing of Life, exempt from age or decay, and to be this it must be a thing of Spirit." (p. 212)
"Hegel's science brings to light Truth and its supremacy, universal harmony, God's entirety, and matter's nothingness." (p. 85)	"Science brings to light Truth, and its supremacy, universal harmony, God's entirety, and matter's nothingness." (p. 28)
"As music is harmoniously controlled by its Principle, so man governed by His Principle of Being, by Soul and not sense, is harmonious, sinless, and immortal." (p. 91)	"As music is harmonious controlled by its Principle, so man governed by his Principle of being, by Soul and not sense, is harmonious, sinless and immortal." (p. 117)
"These Ideas of God never amalgamate but retain their distinct identities, and are controlled only by the principle that evoked them. The mineral, vegetable, and animal kingdoms have their distinct identities, wherein one does not create or control the other but all are created and controlled by God, Spirit." (p. 76)	"The ideas of God never amalgamate, but retain their distinct identities and are controlled only by the Principle that evoked them. The mineral, vegetable and animal kingdoms have their distinct identities, wherein one creates not or controls the other, all are created and controlled by God. (p. 71)

"The efficacy of the crucifixion of Jesus is the truth it demonstrated of the power of Spirit over matter, sin, and death." (p. 105)

"The efficacy of the crucifixion of Jesus is the practical Truth it demonstrated for our understanding, and that ultimately will deliver mankind from sickness, sin and death." (p. 310)

Haushalter gives fourteen other examples like those above. He points out that no concordance to the first edition of *Science and Health* is available, and that the parallel passages he found were the result of only a "limited search."

Although many of the claimed Lieber plagiarisms were later removed from *Science and Health,* many still remain in the current authorized edition. Here are some instances, with the Lieber quote first, followed by the passage from *Science and Health:*

"Hegel's science brings to light Truth and its supremacy, universal harmony, God's entirety, and matter's nothingness." (p. 85)

"Christian Science brings to light Truth and its supremacy, universal harmony, the entireness of God, good, and the nothingness of evil." (p. 293)

"Embryology affords no instance of one species producing another, of a serpent germinating a bird, or a lion a lamb." (p. 85)

"Embryology supplies no instance of one species producing its opposite. A serpent never begets a bird, nor does a lion bring forth a lamb." (p. 550)

"The science of Being reverses every belief of the senses. Socrates understood this when pledging the superiority of Spirit over matter in a cup of hemlock poison, refusing to care about the mortal body. The malice of that age killed the venerable philosopher because of his high regard of spiritual things." (p. 86)

"Science reverses the evidence of material sense. . . . Because he understood the superiority and immortality of good, Socrates feared not the hemlock poison. Even the faith of his philosophy spurned physical timidity. . . . The ignorance and malice of the age would have killed the venerable philosopher because of his faith in Soul and his indifference to the body." (pp. 215–16)

"Thus the noble Kant has charted the path for the entire German metaphysics of religion. The Ptolemaic system of error regarding the heavenly bodies could not affect the vital interests of man like the error of materialism relating to the body. Materialism reverses the order of science and assigns to matter the prerogative of Spirit, making man the most inharmonious phenomenon of the universe." (p. 71)

"The Ptolemaic blunder could not affect the harmony of being as does the error relating to soul and body, which reverses the order of Science and assigns to matter the power and prerogative of Spirit, so that man becomes the most absolutely weak and inharmonious creature in the universe." (p. 123)

"The barometer, that little prophet of storm and sunshine, declares it fair when personal sense sees nothing but murky clouds and drenching rain." (p. 102)

"The barometer—that little prophet of storm and sunshine, denying the testimony of the senses—points to fair weather in the midst of murky clouds and drenching rain." (p. 122)

"Though the grass seems to wither and the flowers to fade they reappear. Erase the figures that express number, shut out the tones of music, give to the worms the body called man; yet the Principle of these survives despite the so-called laws of matter and holds its Ideas immortal." (p. 102)

"Though the grass seemeth to wither and the flower to fade, they reappear. Erase the figures which express number, silence the tones of music, give to the worms the body called man, and yet the producing, governing, divine Principle lives on . . ." (p. 81)

Many of the above passages from the current edition of *Science and Health* are more extensive in the first edition, usually copying Lieber word for word. Haushalter quotes a passage from Lieber that is followed for sixteen lines on pages 33, 37, 52, 53, and 195 without any changes except that Hegel's name is omitted.

Lieber was a professor at Columbia University. His article on Hegel was handwritten. The fact that passages in *Science and Health*, taken from this manuscript, were omitted from later editions suggests that they had, in fact, been copied. However, the Christian Science board of directors investigated the case, shortly after Haushalter's book appeared, and concluded that the Lieber manuscript was an outright forgery. The same conclusion was reached by Henry Moehlman in his book *Ordeal by Concordance* (1955). In brief, both he and the church claim the manuscript was a plagiarism of passages from *Science and Health*, not the other way around. (For details about this controversy, see Appendix D in the first volume of Robert Peel's trilogy *Mary Baker Eddy* [1966], published by the church.)

No one has yet made a thorough study of Mrs. Eddy's numerous plagiarisms, but one of the longest and most flagrant instance involves *The English Reader: Or Prose and Verse from the Best Writers* (1798; fourth edition, 1823), edited by Lindley Murray. One of its selections was a sermon by the Scottish minister Hugh Blair, titled (ironically)

"The Man of Integrity." In Mrs. Eddy's "Message to the First Members," an 1895 paper reprinted in *Miscellaneous Writings* (pages 147–48), are two paragraphs taken in part almost word for word from Blair's sermon.

"It will not take much time to delineate the character of the man of integrity, as by its nature it is a plain one, and easily understood. He is one who makes it his constant rule to follow the road of duty according as the word of God, and the voice of his conscience, point it out to him. He is not guided merely by affections, which may sometimes give the colour of virtue to a loose and unstable character.

"2 The upright man is guided by a fixed principle of mind which determines him to esteem nothing but what is honourable; and to abhor whatever is base or unworthy, in moral conduct. Hence we find him ever the same; at all times, the trusty friend, the affectionate relation, the conscientious man of business, the pious worshipper, the public spirited citizen.

"3 He assumes no borrowed appearance. He seeks no mask to cover him; for he acts no studied part; but he is indeed what he appears to be, full of truth, can-

"My Beloved Students: Another year has rolled on, another annual meeting has convened, another space of time has been given us, and has another duty been done and another victory won for time and eternity? Do you meet in unity, preferring one another, and demonstrating the divine Principle of Christian Science? Have you improved past hours, and ladened them with records worthy to be borne homeward? Have you learned that sin is inadmissible, and indicates a small mind? Do you manifest love for those that hate you and despisefully use you?

"The man of integrity is one who makes it his constant rule to follow the road of duty, according as Truth and the voice of his conscience point it out to him. He is not guided merely by affections which may sometime give the color of virtue to a loose and unstable character.

"The upright man is guided by a fixed Principle, which destines

dour, and humanity. In all his pursuits, he knows no path but the fair and direct one; and would much rather fail of success, than attain it by reproachful means.

"4 He never shows us a smiling countenance, while he meditates evil against us in his heart. He never praises us amongst our friends; and then joins in traducing us among our enemies. We shall never find one part of his character at variance with another. In his manners he is simple and unaffected; in all his proceedings, open and consistent." (Blair)

him to do nothing but what is honorable, and to abhor whatever is base or unworthy; hence we find him ever the same—at all times the trusty friend, the affectionate relative, the conscientious man of business, the pious worker, the public-spirited citizen.

"He assumes no borrowed appearance. He seeks no mask to cover him, for he acts no studied part; but he is indeed what he appears to be—full of truth, candor and humanity. In all his pursuits, he knows no path but the fair, open, and direct one, and would much rather fail of success than attain it by reproachable means. He never shows us a smiling countenance while he meditates evil against us in his heart. We shall never find one part of his character at variance with another.

Lovingly yours,
Mary Baker Eddy"

Another shameful instance of the copying of entire paragraphs virtually word for word is the section in *Miscellaneous Writings* titled "Taking Offense" (pp. 223–24). As Robert Peel discloses in *Mary Baker Eddy: The Years of Trial* (1971), this is a reprinting of an anonymous article that appeared in *Godey's Lady's Book*. It had been printed twice in the *Christian Science Journal* with no credit as to its source. Peel has no explanation of how or why it turned up in *Miscellaneous Writings* as having been written by Mrs. Eddy.

It was characteristic of Mrs. Eddy, who frequently plagiarized, to devote a chapter in her autobiography, *Retrospection and Introspection,* to condemning others for copying from her own writings. Indeed, she was quick to threaten lawsuits against anyone who dared do this. Over and over again she denounced literary piracy as a grave offense. In her *Message to the Mother Church, 1900* she wrote: "A wicked man has little real intelligence; he may steal other people's good thoughts, and wear the purloined garment as his own, till God's discipline takes it off for his poverty to appear" (p. 8).

Mark Twain's famous attack on Mrs. Eddy (the topic of chapter 12) was a book put together mostly from magazine articles. One article created such a stir that Mrs. Eddy felt obliged to reply in a letter to the *New York Herald* (January 17, 1903). As Twain was delighted to point out, even Mrs. Eddy's letter contained a passage she took without credit from Carlyle.

One of the earliest disclosures of the extent to which Mrs. Eddy plagiarized was in a book titled *Christian Science versus Plagiarism* (1929) by Mrs. Annie Cecelia Bill, a British Christian Scientist. She began as a devoted follower of Mrs. Eddy. Her 413-page book *Message of Life, Liberty, and Happiness* (1926) was filled with praise for Mrs. Eddy's *Science and Health* and *Church Manual.* Believing herself to be Mrs. Eddy's successor, she established in London what she called the Christian Science Parent Church of the New Generation. Her discovery of Mrs. Eddy's plagiarisms was such a shock that it turned her into an implacable foe of the American movement. In 1930 she published her own textbook, *The Science of Reality,* in which she recommended that her followers cooperate with medical doctors. To distinguish her movement from Christian Science in America, she renamed her church the Church of Universal Design. The heretical movement grew rapidly during the 1920s and early 1930s to more than forty branch churches in England

and America. They all evaporated soon after Mrs. Bill's death. Details about her life and opinions are given in Charles Braden's *Christian Science Today* (1958) and Altman K. Swithart's *Since Mrs. Eddy* (1931).

Ann Lee, founder of the Shakers, may have contributed to Mrs. Eddy's terminology and doctrines, as Mrs. Milmine suggests in Appendix C of her biography of Mrs. Eddy. Both women were called "Mother" by their devotees. Each identified herself with the woman described in Revelation 12:1, "And there appeared a great wonder in heaven; a woman clothed with the sun, and the moon under her feet, and upon her head a crown of twelve stars." This crown of stars, linked to a cross, form the official emblem of the Christian Science Church. In Boston's Mother Church, a stained-glass window depicts the woman of the Apocalypse, with the book *Science and Health* above her. Revelation 10:2 speaks of another angel bearing a "little book open," which Mrs. Eddy identified with her textbook. Both Ann Lee and Mrs. Eddy practiced divine healing.

Both Ann Lee and Mrs. Eddy called their first edifice Mother Church. Lee began the Shaker version of the Lord's Prayer with "Our Father and Mother which art in Heaven." Mrs. Eddy also liked to refer to God as mother as well as father, even though Jesus never suggested it. Her interpretation of the Lord's Prayer, given at the close of the first chapter of *Science and Health,* begins: "Our Father which art in heaven," followed in italics by "Our Father-Mother God, all harmonious." (Versions in earlier editions were slightly different.)

Ann Lee forbade audible prayer. Mrs. Eddy also discouraged it. Ann Lee recommended celibacy. Mrs. Eddy, too, considered celibacy a more spiritual state than marriage, but taught that at this stage of history marriage was more expedient than a celibate life. As Saint Paul had said, "It is better to marry than to burn."

Mrs. Eddy also provided her own version of the Twenty-third Psalm in *Science and Health*, chapter 16. Instead of the masculine term "Lord," she substituted the word "Love."

[DIVINE LOVE] is my shepherd; I shall not want.

[LOVE] maketh me to lie down in green pastures. [LOVE] leadeth me beside the still waters.

[LOVE] restoreth my soul [spiritual sense]: [LOVE] leadeth me in the paths of righteousness for His name's sake.

Yea, though I walk through the valley of the shadow of death, I will fear no evil: for [LOVE] is with me; [LOVE'S] rod and [LOVE'S] staff they comfort me.

[LOVE] prepareth a table before me in the presence of mine enemies: [LOVE] anointeth my head with oil; my cup runneth over.

Surely goodness and mercy shall follow me all the days of my life; and I will dwell in the house [the consciousness] of [LOVE] for ever. (p. 578)

Mrs. Eddy kept a scrapbook of newspaper clippings that included columns headed "Gems of Truth" and "Dewdrops of Wisdom." Phrases and sometimes entire sentences were taken from these clippings and used by Mrs. Eddy without quotation marks or any indication that the words were not her own. Here is how Robert Peel, in *Mary Baker Eddy: The Years of Trial* (1971), describes these borrowings:

When in need of extra material to fill the earliest issues of the *Journal,* she sometimes turned to the books she had known in her young womanhood, and especially to the scrapbooks she had kept and treasured through her years of invalidism in the 1850s. Aphorisms and anecdotes from this scrapbook studded the pages of the *Journal* and found their way into her own writings, sometimes undergoing minor surgery *en route.* Verbal echoes from Pope's "Essay on Man" and Young's "Night Thoughts" rubbed elbows with phrases from the yellowed pages of forgotten New Hampshire newspapers in a style which ended up being unmistakably Mrs. Eddy's own. (p. 185)

Although Peel is convinced that Lieber's manuscript on Hegel is a forgery, he cannot dismiss the plagiarized section from Blair's sermon or the article from *Godey's Lady's Book*. He is surprised that they turn up in *Miscellaneous Writings* without quotation marks, but he offers no explanations. As for Mrs. Eddy's borrowings from her scrapbook and from *Philosophic Nuggets,* he justifies them this way: "These shorter borrowings represent the fairly normal and probably unconscious process of assimilation and adaptation to be traced in many reputable writers." He then devotes two pages to examples of similar "unconscious" borrowings by James Russell Lowell and other writers, as if that justified the practice.

It would be worthwhile if some day an interested historian of Christian Science and the life of Mrs. Eddy would make a careful, exhaustive study of all the stolen sentences in her writings. Walter Rea, a disenchanted Seventh-day Adventist minister, has done this for the stolen portions of the works of that church's prophetess, Ellen Gould White, in his book *The White Lie* (1982). As far as I know, nothing comparable has been done on Mrs. Eddy's plagiarisms.

One can only be appalled by the vehemence with which Mrs. Eddy attacked anyone who dared to take anything from *her* own writings, even when the debt was fully acknowledged, or when only thoughts were copied and not actual words. The paragraphs from Blair's sermon and the article from *Godey's Lady's Book* remain today in Mrs. Eddy's *Miscellaneous Writings* with no quotation marks or any indication that they are not her own. One would think that a church claiming its doctrines are based on God's Word, which includes the commandment "Thou shalt not steal," would at least have the grace to add a footnote acknowledging the source of these pilfered paragraphs.

10

Mrs. Woodbury and Her Prince of Peace

Mary Baker Eddy's wrath knew no bounds whenever one of her followers dared to write a favorable book about Christian Science. She regularly denounced such works, and on one occasion ordered all Christian Scientists to "burn every scrap of Christian Science literature" except *Science and Health* and the church's official publications. Students were forbidden to read any of the many books on New Thought and Mind Cure that were being published in great profusion.

In 1884 one of her disciples in Chicago, Mrs. Ursula Gestefeld, published a book titled *A Statement of Christian Science: An Explanation of Science and Health.* Mrs. Eddy was furious. The book's metaphysics, her *Journal* reported, "crawls on its belly instead of soaring in the upper air." Mrs. Gestefeld was accused of practicing MAM and expelled from the Chicago branch church. She retaliated by writing a pamphlet titled *Jesuitism in Christian Science.* It was not long until she vanished from the scene.

The most hilarious episode in the history of Christian Science involved a Boston socialite named Mrs. Josephine Curtis Woodbury. Much prettier and much better educated than Mrs. Eddy, Mrs. Woodbury was one of the church's most energetic leaders and a close associate of Mother. To the vast dismay of Mrs. Eddy and almost everyone else among the faithful, Mrs. Woodbury and her friends became firmly persuaded that if a woman were sufficiently spiritual she could conceive a child without having sex! They rested this belief on numerous ambiguous passages in Mrs. Eddy's own writings. She had clearly taught that in the far future, after Christian Science had conquered the world, marriage would become obsolete. "Until it is learned that generation rests on no sexual basis," Mrs. Eddy wrote in the 1903 edition of *Science and Health,* "let marriage continue" (p. 274). In the 1909 edition she changed this to "Until it is learned that God is the Father of all, marriage will continue." A chapter on "Wedlock" in *Miscellaneous Writings* contains this astonishing passage:

> Until time matures human growth, marriage and progeny will continue unprohibited in Christian Science. We look to future generations for ability to comply with absolute Science, when marriage shall be found to be man's oneness with God—the unity of eternal Love. At present, more spiritual conception and education of children will serve to illustrate the superiority of spiritual power over sensuous, and usher in the dawn of God's creation, wherein they neither marry nor are given in marriage, but are as the angels. To abolish marriage at this period, and maintain morality and generation, would put ingenuity to ludicrous shifts; yet this is possible in *Science,* although it is to-day problematic. (p. 286)

Here is how she puts it in the current edition of *Science and Health:*

> Speaking of the origin of mortals, a famous naturalist says: "It is very possible that many general statements now current, about birth and generation, will be changed with the progress of information." Had the naturalist, through his tireless researches, gained the diviner side in Christian Science—so far apart from his material sense of animal growth and organization—he would have blessed the human race more abundantly.

Natural history is richly endowed by the labors and genius of great men. Modern discoveries have brought to light important facts in regard to so-called embryonic life. Agassiz declares ("Methods of Study in Natural History," page 275): "Certain animals, besides the ordinary process of generation, also increase their numbers naturally and constantly by self-division." This discovery is corroborative of the Science of Mind, for this discovery shows that the multiplication of certain animals takes place apart from sexual conditions. The supposition that life germinates in eggs and must decay after it has grown to maturity, if not before, is shown by divine metaphysics to be a mistake—a blunder which will finally give place to higher theories and demonstrations. (pp. 548–49)

In light of such pronouncements from their leader, it was not far-fetched for Mrs. Woodbury and her friends to suppose that maybe even now a few individuals of high spirituality and firm mastery of Christian Science might be able to conceive without the aid of a man. In 1890 Mrs. Woodbury startled all of Boston by announcing that she had done just that. Without having had sexual intercourse with her husband, or anyone else, she had given birth to a boy. Indeed, she claimed, she did not even know she was pregnant until she heard the baby's birth cries. True, her stomach had been bulging, but she thought it was caused by a "fungoid formation." Being a good Christian Scientist, naturally she refused to consult a physician.*

---

*For all the hilarious and crazy details about Mrs. Woodbury's pregnancy and her eventual battle against Mrs. Eddy, see volumes 2 and 3 of Robert Peel's *Mary Baker Eddy*. He identifies the father of the Prince of Peace as a married student of Christian Science, in Montreal, who was seduced by Mrs. Woodbury. She had not slept with her husband for many years. To avoid telling him about her infidelity, or revealing it to her students and Mrs. Eddy, she concocted her preposterous tale about an "Immaculate Conception." Peel quotes from documents in which she freely admitted her affair. She turned bitterly against the Canadian, calling him the person "through whom she entered hell."

The miracle baby was baptized with much fanfare by three immersions in a salt pool on Mrs. Woodbury's large estate at Ocean Point, Maine. She called the pool Bethesda, and christened the boy Prince of Peace. The child was, she intimated, some kind of second Jesus. She called his birth an "Immaculate Conception," confusing the term with the Virgin Birth. This is a mistake often made by non-Catholics, unaware that the doctrine of Mary's Immaculate Conception refers not to the birth of Jesus, but to Mary having been born without sin. Mrs. Woodbury was convinced that her Prince of Peace was destined to "redeem the world." Suspecting that the child had the power to raise the dead, she once put him in a room with a corpse to test her conjecture. The corpse failed to revive.

When her child was baptized, Mrs. Woodbury wrote, his body was three times entirely under water and "his baby eyes were open, and smiling upward." She surely was recalling the infamous passage in *Science and Health,* quoted earlier, about the father who trained his baby to live under water for twenty minutes. In the original 1875 edition the passage was even more bizarre:

> Adam being created before Eve, proves the maternal egg never propagated him, and Eve being formed of Adam's rib, shows her origin was not that; "knowledge" defined man falsely then, even as at present, although physiology has since been grafted onto the forbidden "tree." An infant a few hours old was said to be immersed in water, to test the possibility of making him amphibious; and this daily ablution continued until the infant could remain under water, and the ordinary functions of lungs be suspended twenty minutes at one time, playing the while and enjoying the bath. (p. 279)

In the 1886 edition of *Science and Health* Mrs. Eddy had written:

The propagation of their species without the male element, by butterfly, bee, and moth is a discovery corroborative of the Science of Mind, because it shows that the origin and continuance of these insects rest on Principle, apart from material conditions. An egg never was the origin of a man, and no seed ever produced a plant. . . . The belief that life can be in matter, or soul in body, and that man springs from dust or from an egg, is the brief record of mortal error. . . . The plant grows not because of seed or soil. (p. 472)

This passage was later removed from *Science and Health* because Mrs. Eddy did not know at the time that butterflies, bees, and moths all require "the male element." In an article in the *Arena* (May 1899) Mrs. Woodbury quoted the original passage and argued as follows:

To what diabolical conclusions do such deductions lead? One may well hesitate to touch this delicate topic in print, yet only thus can the immoral possibilities and the utter lack of Divine inspiration in "Christian Science" be shown.

The substance of certain instructions given by Mrs. Eddy in private is as follows:

If Jesus was divinely conceived by the Holy Ghost or Spirit, without a human father, Mary not having known her husband—then women may become mothers by a supreme effort of their own minds, or through the influence upon them of an Unholy Ghost, a malign spirit. Women of unquestioned integrity, who have been Mrs. Eddy's students, testify that she has so taught, and that by this teaching families have been broken up; that thus maidens have been terrified out of their wits, and stimulated into a frenzy resembling that of deluded French nuns, who believed themselves brought into marital relations with the glorified Jesus, as veritably the bridegroom of his church. Whatever her denials may be, such was Mrs. Eddy's teaching while in her college; to which she added the oracular declaration that it lay within her power to dissolve such motherhood by a wave of her celestial rod.

The selfish celibacy of nuns and clergy, Christian or heathen, with consequent ecclesiastical interference in family life, have been, and are, mischief-breeding blunders, fatal alike to morals and health. One result of this interference on the part of Mrs. Eddy is that Christian Science families are notably childless.

Very tenacious is she of the paradoxical title carved on her Boston church, "The Discoverer and Founder of Christian Science." Surely a "Discoverer" cannot be the "Founder" of that which he has been under the necessity of discovering; while a "Founder" would have no need of discovering her own foundation. What she has really "discovered" are ways and means of perverting and prostituting the science of healing to her own ecclesiastical aggrandisement and to the moral and physical depravity of her dupes. As she received this science from Dr. Quimby it meant simply the healing of bodily ills through a lively reliance on the wholeness and order of the Infinite Mind, as clearly perceived and practically demonstrated by a simple and modest love of one's kind. What she has "founded" is a commercial system, monumental in its proportions, but already tottering to its fall. (Milmine, pp. 438–39)

We are getting ahead of our story. When Mrs. Woodbury announced her "Immaculate Conception," the Boston newspapers went to town. Greatly embarrassed, Mrs. Eddy was obliged to say that although she believed in the Virgin Birth of Jesus, and that such births might become possible at some future time, she did not expect such a miracle to be duplicated now. In a later edition of *Science and Health* she laid the matter permanently to rest by writing: "The perpetuation of the floral species by bud or cell-division is evident [no more butterflies, bees, and moths—M.G.], but I discredit the belief that agamogenesis applies to the human species" (p. 68). Note how Mrs. Eddy goes out of her way to make her sentence sound scientific. It would have been clearer had she written: "Flowers obviously perpetuate themselves by budding, but such nonsexual reproduction does not apply to humans."

In the same paragraph Mrs. Eddy has a cryptic statement: "I never knew more than one individual who believed in agamogenesis; she was unmarried, a lovely character, was suffering from incipient insanity, and a Christian Scientist cured her." Was this intended as a cruel reference to Mrs. Woodbury? If not, then to whom?

Mrs. Eddy never got along with female leaders of the church as soon as they began to encroach upon her authority. For years her relationship with Mrs. Woodbury, once a much beloved disciple, had been deteriorating. The birth of the Prince of Peace was a golden opportunity to get rid of her. She was excommunicated.

That was not the end of Mrs. Woodbury. In 1895 Mrs. Eddy made the mistake of allowing her back into the fold. Woodbury began threatening her students with death if they defied her. One disobedient student actually did drop dead, an incident that made students fear her even more. In 1896 she became embroiled in two nasty lawsuits. Fred C. Chamberlain charged her with turning his wife against him. Evelyn I. Rowe, suing her husband for non-support, accused Mrs. Woodbury of an affair with her husband Robert Rowe, of Augusta, Maine. He had been squandering all his wealth on supporting and educating the little Prince. After the *Boston Traveler* published a lurid account of this case, Mrs. Woodbury sued the paper for libel. All three lawsuits went nowhere, but the publicity was too much for Mother. This time, in 1896, Mrs. Woodbury was "forever excommunicated."

An angry Mrs. Woodbury tried to establish a rival church by preaching with her daughter in a Boston hall, but her following was meager. In 1897 she published a weird booklet titled *War in Heaven: Sixteen Years' Experience in Christian Science Mind Healing.* We earlier quoted from her article that ran in the May 1899 issue of the *Arena,* a New Thought periodical. In this article Mrs. Eddy is lambasted for her childish writing, her refusal to credit Quimby with the origin of Christian Science, her unwillingness to admit she once had been a spiritualist medium, her "demonophobia," her love of money, her constant lying about her sensational cases of healing, her forbidding followers to read anything except the Bible and *Science and Health,* her autocratic control of the church, and in general for "perverting and prostituting" the true healing faith! She accused Mrs. Eddy of lying when she said that she could have saved President Garfield's life after he was shot, but her enemies used MAM to prevent this great demonstration of her power.

Mrs. Eddy exploded in anger. Speaking from the pulpit of Mother Church on June 4, 1899, she blasted her rival, without mentioning her name, as the whore of Babylon in the Bible's Book of Revelation. Here is a portion of what she said, as it appears in *The First Church of Christ, Scientist, and Miscellany* (chapter 4):

The doom of the Babylonish woman, referred to in Revelation, is being fulfilled. This woman, "drunken with the blood of the saints, and with the blood of the martyrs of Jesus," "drunk with the wine of her fornication," would enter even the church—the body of Christ, Truth; and, retaining the heart of the harlot and the purpose of the destroying angel, would pour wormwood into the waters—the disturbed human mind—to drown the strong swimmer struggling for the shore— aiming for Truth—and if possible, to poison such as drink of the living water. But the recording angel, standing with "right foot upon the sea, and his left foot on the earth," has in his hand a book open (ready to be read), which uncovers and kills this mystery of iniquity and interprets the mystery of godliness—how the first is finished and the second is no longer a mystery or a miracle, but a marvel, casting out evil and healing the sick. And a voice was heard, saying, "Come out of her, my people" (hearken not to her lies), "that ye receive not of her plagues. For her sins have reached unto heaven, and God hath remembered her iniquities . . . double unto her double according to her works: in the cup which she hath filled fill to her double . . . for she saith in her heart, I . . . am no widow, . . . Therefore shall her plagues come in one day, death, and mourning, and famine; . . . for strong is the Lord God who judgeth her." That which the Revelator saw in spiritual vision will be accomplished. The Babylonish woman is fallen, and who should mourn over the widowhood of lust, of her that "is become the habitation of devils, and the hold of every foul spirit, and a cage of every unclean . . . bird"? (pp. 125–26)

So much for Mrs. Eddy's image among the faithful as a sweet-tempered, gentle, turn-the-other-cheek Christian!

The address was reprinted in the *Christian Science Sentinel* and the *Boston Herald.* Mrs. Woodbury sued the Boston paper for libel. Everybody knew that the Babylonian harlot was Mrs. Woodbury, an identification confirmed under oath by William Nixon, Mrs. Eddy's former publisher. However, Mrs. Eddy and her friends managed to convince the court that she was speaking of a type, not Mrs. Woodbury personally. The case was dismissed. Mrs. Woodbury blamed her loss on MAM generated by Mrs. Eddy and her friends.

Mrs. Woodbury eventually faded away, but not until she published in 1909 a book titled *Quimbyism: Or the Paternity of Christian Science.* Did her husband Frank Woodbury, who had been one of Mrs. Eddy's devoted students, ever suspect, like the Virgin Mary's husband Joseph, that his wife had been unfaithful? We may never know. He died a few months before Mrs. Eddy's address about the whore of Babylon, which made her speech unusually cruel in its reference to the whore's "widowhood." Mrs. Woodbury had accused Mrs. Eddy of murdering her husband by MAM.

When the Prince of Peace tried to attend a Christian Science Sunday School, he was bodily tossed out. No one seems to know what happened to him; the rest of his life is unknown. Mrs. Woodbury lived to be more than eighty years old, dying in Nice, France, in 1930.

Throughout its entire history the Christian Science movement has been wracked by dissension, resignations, excommunications, and outright rebellions, especially in Mrs. Eddy's later years when her control over the church became iron-fisted. An incredible number of imitators established rival "Christian Science" churches, colleges, and periodicals.

Although Mrs. Bill in England was for a short time her most annoying opponent, there were endless other apostates who either broke away from Mrs. Eddy or were booted out of the fold.

The major heretics seemed compelled to imitate their former leader by writing inspirational verse. Mrs. Woodbury, for instance, in 1898 published a book of forgettable poems titled *Echoes*. None other than James Wiggin, Mrs. Eddy's ex-polisher, provided its enthusiastic introduction. He called it a "lovely volume" that had dropped "from the press 'adorned as a bride for her husband,' to show the writer's fine manner and lofty ideals" (Beasley, *The Cross and the Crown,* p. 353). Wiggin greatly admired Mrs. Woodbury's intellect. They had become good friends when she assisted him during the period when he was editor of the *Christian Science Journal.* Did Wiggin really believe his high praise for the book's verse, or was he sarcastically striking another blow at his former boss?

11

Augusta Stetson and Other Heretics

Two of Mrs. Eddy's early rebels were Mrs. Mary H. Plunkett, and her associate, Mrs. Emma Curtis Hopkins. Hopkins was an assistant editor of the *Christian Science Journal* until Mrs. Eddy excommunicated her in 1885. (In chapter 14 we will see how her opinions led to the founding of the Unity cult.) A few years later the two women established two organizations, with Plunkett in New York City and Hopkins in Chicago. Plunkett's official magazine was called *Truth: A Magazine of Christian Science,* later changed to the *International Magazine of Christian Science.* Edited by the two women, it called itself the organ of the International Christian Science Association. Mrs. Eddy was not pleased when it recommended some fifty books on mental healing not written by her.

Colleges teaching Christian Science were set up by Hopkins in several large cities. In Chicago a Hopkins Theological Seminary trained students to become ministers. To oversimplify, the seminary taught Christian Science without the doctrine of MAM. In New York City Mrs. Plunkett founded the National School of Christian Science. Followers of the two ladies began two new publications, *Messenger of Truth* and *Mental Healing Monthly*. Both periodicals later merged with Plunkett's *International Magazine of Christian Science*. "Christian Science restrooms" appeared in New York, Chicago, and other big cities, forerunners of Mrs. Eddy's reading rooms.

In 1889 Mrs. Plunkett and her husband, J. T. Plunkett, declared their marriage "null and void." A few months later Mrs. Plunkett announced a "spiritual union" to A. Bentley Worthington, her magazine's treasurer. Because there were no legal divorce or marriage, newspapers had a romp with charges of free love in the Plunkett ranks. The press soon discovered that Worthington had been married several times before, had not bothered to divorce his previous wife, and was wanted by the police on an old charge of embezzlement. The unworthy Worthington vanished with nary a plunk. Mrs. Plunkett's magazine disappeared that same year, along with her National School of Christian Science. More details about Plunkett and Hopkins can be found in Norman Beasley's history, *The Cross and the Crown,* along with lesser apostates who tried to establish rival Christian Science organizations after being expelled by Mrs. Eddy.

A character named A. J. Swartz is worth a paragraph. He appeared on the scene in 1884, claiming he had practiced Christian Science long before Mrs. Eddy said she had discovered it. His magazine *Mind Cure and Science of Life* achieved a circulation larger than the *Christian Science Journal.* Swartz tried to persuade Mrs. Eddy to join forces with him, but of course she refused. According to Beasley, there were more than twenty periodicals in the 1880s devoted to versions of Christian Science that departed in various respects from Mrs. Eddy's doctrines.

In the United States Mrs. Eddy's most dramatic battle against heresy was fought with Mrs. Augusta E. Stetson. Although not as good looking as Mrs. Woodbury, and much heavier, she resembled Woodbury in being better educated than Mrs. Eddy, and a more spellbinding speaker. Like Woodbury, she began her career as a young, passionate Christian

Scientist. Soon her preaching skill—she was a product of Boston's Blish School of Oratory—and the fame aroused by her spectacular healings began to arouse Mrs. Eddy's envy.

Mrs. Stetson had no trouble raising more than a million dollars to construct a huge marble temple in New York, at Riverside Drive and Ninety-sixth Street. When this church, called The First Church of Christ Science in New York City, was finally built, it was even grander than Boston's Mother Church. An angry Mrs. Eddy began issuing a series of orders designed to weaken her rival's rapidly growing popularity. Mrs. Stetson had made herself the new church's pastor. Mrs. Eddy abolished the role of pastors in all branch churches.

To this day no Christian Science church has a minister. It has only two "readers," one a man, the other a woman. The Sunday morning service consists mainly of a reading from the Bible, followed by the reading of an interpretive passage from *Science and Health.* Identical selections from the two books are read every Sunday in every Christian Science church around the world. There are no rituals and no sermon. There is no choir, although there may be a solo, and Christian Science hymns are sung. A period of silent prayer (Mrs. Eddy disliked audible praying) is followed by a recitation of the Lord's Prayer with Mrs. Eddy's interpolations, and a collection of money. The only pastor, Mrs. Eddy wrote in *Miscellaneous Writings,* "is the Bible and my book" (p. 383). Church meetings on Wednesday evenings are devoted to testimonies about healings.

Mrs. Stetson, to Mrs. Eddy's frustration, faithfully obeyed every roadblock Mrs. Eddy placed in her path. She constantly showered Mother with expensive gifts that included clothing (gowns, bonnets, hoods, an ermine cape) and jewelry such as a diamond cross and a diamond brooch in the shape of a crown. She once tried to give Mrs. Eddy a marble statue of a woman to be placed in Mother Church, but this gift Mother refused. Mrs. Eddy's thank-you letters for these gifts always bubbled with gratitude. "Your wonderful gift of warmth and beauty, the ermine cape, is most acceptable, needful, and received with more gratitude than pen or lips can tell," she wrote in 1900. Another note read: "God *bless* my dear precious student who helps me to clothes while I am helping to clothe her with righteousness, the robes of heaven here and now." As Dakin discloses in his biography, Mrs. Eddy never hesitated to ask Mrs. Stetson for gifts that, as Dakin puts it, began to multiply like the loaves and fishes. For example:

> I am in great need of summer suits of clothing, will you send me samples of these? Oh how good you are to me: What can I do to pay you, tell me, dearest one? You are all the student that I can depend upon to clothe me, and inasmuch as you have done it unto me, ye have done it unto the Father. (p. 347)

By quoting the words of Jesus, Mrs. Eddy clearly implies that she herself is to be treated like the Master.

Mrs. Stetson's letters to Mrs. Eddy were always addressed to "My Precious Leader" and signed "Your loving child." As late as 1909 Augusta wrote to her leader:

> You asked me years ago this question, "Augusta, lovest thou me?" I answered, "Yes, beloved Leader, I love you." Again you repeated the query, "Lovest thou me?" and again I replied, "Yes, I love you, my Leader, Teacher and Guide to eternal Life." Then you said, "Feed my sheep." I have earnestly and prayerfully endeavored to do this. These are thine, Holy One; I trust they are all strong in Christ. . . . May none fall away! They desire to honor you, our great forever Leader; they have come up out of great tribulation, and have washed their robes. . . . Precious Leader, my love for you is inexpressible. God grant my constant prayer that I may be worthy to be called Your faithful, obedient, loving child. (Dakin, p. 482)

Although tension between Stetson and Eddy was steadily mounting, Mrs. Eddy's letters were equally affectionate. Salutations included "Augusta darling," "my precious child," "my beloved student," "my darling student," "my precious student," and so on. Her letters closed with such phrases as "lovingly your teacher and Leader"; "Ever tenderly, lovingly thine"; "With great love for you, ever thine"; "With oceans of love"; "Again darling, I say mother loves you"; "Oh dearest, precious child, how much you have done and will yet do for our cause, none knows but me"; "Darling, *rise* each hour. Now is the resurrection morn and I want Augusta to be my Mary. Lovingly ever thine"; and (thanking Augusta for a gift), "More precious than silver or gold is your love. Accept mine in big gross tons."

Note that Mrs. Eddy, asking Augusta to be her Mary, is again likening herself to Jesus. Were it not for the fact that both women were deeply religious, using the word "love" in a spiritual sense, one might suspect from these letters that they were being exchanged between two lesbians.

While Mrs. Eddy's letters to Mrs. Stetson were all sweetness and light, in letters to others she expressed great hostility toward Mrs. Stetson. Bliss Knapp, in *The Destiny of the Mother Church* (1991), quotes from an 1888 letter in which Mrs. Eddy warns a student against Mrs. Stetson. She will, wrote Mrs. Eddy, use you "only so long as you subserve her personal purpose to rule, then cast you off and herself string the fish you have caught. Beware! never come under *her influence.* She is as far from your former teacher [Mrs. Eddy] as the sky from dust."

Throughout all their excessive flattery and expressions of love, the two women were in bitter conflict. In July 1909 the church's board of directors brought charges against Mrs. Stetson for insubordination. The charges were dismissed, but revived in September. After a farcical trial by a kangaroo court, Mrs. Stetson was accused, among other things, of practicing MAM against one of Mrs. Eddy's students.

On October 16, 1909, a letter from Mrs. Eddy to Mrs. Stetson appeared in the *Christian Science Sentinel:*

My Dear Student:—Awake and arise from this temptation produced
by animal magnetism upon yourself, allowing your students to deify
you and me. Treat yourself for it and get your students to help you
rise out of it. It will be your destruction if you do not do this. Answer
this letter immediately. (Augusta Stetson, *Vital Issues in Christian
Science,* p. 159)

It was the last of a series of cold, formal letters from Mrs. Eddy
that signified the ending of their friendship. Mrs. Stetson's long, puzzled
reply takes up four pages in her book *Vital Issues in Christian Science:
With Facsimile Letters of Mary Baker Eddy* (1914). It is addressed as
always to "My precious Leader" and signed "Your loving child." Not
a line in it is critical of Mrs. Eddy. But the break was final. Mrs. Eddy
had made up her mind to get rid of Mrs. Stetson whom she feared
as a rival more than any other woman. In November 1909 Mrs. Stetson
was "forever excommunicated."

Augusta was as strong-willed and eccentric as Mrs. Woodbury. She
agreed with Woodbury that conception was possible without sex. She
increasingly assured her flock that they should never be ashamed of
having costly homes, clothes, and jewelry. She adorned herself with
diamonds. WHAP, a radio station she established in New York City,
became notorious for its whaps on Catholics and Jews.

When Mrs. Stetson took into her home a young man named Carol
Norton as her "spiritually" adopted son, Mrs. Eddy saw it as an attempt
to copy her legal adoption of "Benny" Foster. In the next edition of
her *Church Manual* she inserted a new bylaw, Article VIII, "Guidance
of Members":

No person shall be an officer or a member of this Church, who claims
a spiritually adopted child; or a spiritually adopted husband, or wife;
except they have been legally adopted, or legally married, and can
verify this according to the laws of our land.

Any member who is found living with a child improperly, or claiming a child not legally adopted, or claiming, or living with a husband, or a wife, to whom they have not been legally married, shall immediately be excommunicated, on the grounds of moral unfitness to be a teacher of Christian Science, or a member of this Church. (Springer, p. 365)

In her biography of Mrs. Eddy, Fleta Springer comments on this bylaw:

There are so many things for which a Christian Scientist may be excommunicated that it is surprising that the Church has any membership. Yet when all is said, the Manual demanded only unquestioning obedience and an undivided allegiance to Mrs. Eddy and her cause. And these her followers freely granted her—out of love, expediency, or fear. If so much as suspicion of disloyalty fell upon a member, and no by-law could be made to cover his case, the suspect suffered dismissal from the church under the by-law providing for the excommunication of mesmerists or mental malpractitioners. The proof of the malpractice was Mrs. Eddy's word. "If the author of *Science and Health* shall bear witness to the offense of mental malpractice, it shall be considered sufficient evidence thereof."

By-laws springing "from the logic of events" between editions of the Manual were published in the *Journal* to take immediate effect. Unless a close watch was kept upon the *Journal,* a member often found himself acting in violation of a by-law of which he was unaware. The merest "request" or "it is suggested" or "the Mother wishes you" in the *Journal* had the effect of a command.

A Christian Scientist may read no books on metaphysics except *Science and Health* and the Bible. He may not write books on mental healing or metaphysics. He may not speak publicly upon the subject of Christian Science without permission of the Church. He may, in short, neither think, read, speak, nor act in any way that could be construed as inimical to the Church. (pp. 365–66)

Like Mrs. Eddy and Mrs. Woodbury, Mrs. Stetson fancied herself a poet. Her *Poems: Written on the Journey from Sense to Soul* contains verse as worthless as Mrs. Eddy's. After her leader died in 1910, Mrs. Stetson defended her side of the conflict with Mrs. Eddy in numerous books, always insisting that her "Precious Leader" had no hand in her excommunication by the church's board of directors. It was an incredibly naive notion because Mrs. Eddy's control over the board was total, but it shows how deeply felt was Augusta's love and respect for Mrs. Eddy even after Mrs. Eddy abandoned her.

Here is a partial list of Mrs. Stetson's books: *Give God the Glory, Vital Issues in Christian Science, Sermons and Other Writings, My Spiritual Aeroplane, Greetings and Messages to the Dear Children,* and *Sermons Which Spiritually Interpret the Scriptures.* Her anthology *Reminiscences, Sermons, and Correspondence, Proving Adherence to the Principle of Christian Science as Taught by Mary Baker Eddy* has over 1,200 pages.

After her excommunication, and with it the loss of her Manhattan church, Mrs. Stetson continued her religious activities as the principal of what she called the New York City Christian Science Institute. She told her followers that she was immortal and would never die, but the grim reaper paid no attention, and she followed her leader to the grave in 1928. None of the entries on her in *Who's Who in America* give the date of her birth in Waldboro, Maine.

Mrs. Eddy could not bear to have Mrs. Stetson's Riverside Avenue church outshine the splendor of Mother Church in Boston. In 1902, seven years before Mrs. Stetson was kicked out of her edifice, Mrs. Eddy's board of directors raised two million dollars to enlarge Mother Church. The old church had the form of a cross. The new temple, completed in 1904, has a huge dome to represent the crown that along with the cross forms the logo of Christian Science. This huge gleaming white building stands in Boston today as a perpetual monument to the single-minded resolution of a poor country girl who first convinced herself, then millions of others, that God had selected her to revive the true Christianity of Jesus that the world had forgotten for almost two thousand years.

12

The Rage of Mark Twain

The rapid growth of Christian Science in the 1890s so aroused the ire of Mark Twain that he wrote several articles about Mrs. Eddy that ran in *Cosmopolitan Magazine* and the *North American Review*. Few writers before or since have attacked Mrs. Eddy with such vehemence. In 1903 Twain revised his articles, correcting some errors pointed out by readers, and added new chapters not previously in print to make a book. Much to Twain's annoyance, his publisher, Harper's, refused to accept the book. Not until 1907 was it finally published. After being out of print for more than half a century, thanks mainly to successful efforts by the church to suppress it, Prometheus Books had the courage to reprint it in 1986.

The administrators of Mother Church in Boston have always done their best to keep books unsympathetic to Christian Science out of libraries and bookstores. This was especially the case with Twain's *Christian Science,* and *Mrs. Eddy: The Biography of a Virginal Mind* by Edwin Franden Dakin (1929). When Dakin's book was published by Scribner's, Christian Scientists visited bookstores and libraries throughout the nation, urging them not to buy or sell the book, and threatening boycotts if they did. Thousands of angry letters were fired off to Scribner's and to stores and libraries. It is said that 70 percent of the nation's bookstores stopped selling Dakin's book.

Scribner's felt obliged to say in an advertisement:

> The result is a situation almost incredible in a free country. You may find that your bookseller either will regret his inability to sell you this biography, universally endorsed by the press of the country, or he may produce a copy hidden away under the counter. Some booksellers actually have the courage to display the book. We hope your bookseller is one of these. Throughout some eighty-five years of publishing, we have been able to say of our books "on sale at all booksellers." We regret that in this one instance we must qualify that statement.

When the enlarged second edition of Dakin's book was published, Scribner's added in front a note describing what it called a "virulent campaign of suppression":

> The publication of this popular edition of *Mrs. Eddy* marks the failure of an organized Minority to accomplish the suppression of opinions not to its liking.
>
> We published the book on its merits—one of which was its presentation of a highly interesting and significant character, about whom people were entitled to know, in a conscientious and impartial manner. And since a publisher, whatever his personal views of the subject, is required by his profession to publish material of such interest and value, we could not properly have done otherwise.
>
> The book appeared on August 16, 1929. In the ensuing weeks it was reviewed by a score of men of character and of knowledge of the subject, outside the organized Minority, in complete confirmation of our opinion of its importance and fairness.

This enthusiastic reception accorded by non-partisans was accompanied by so virulent a campaign for suppression that if the issue had been only a commercial one, it might well have seemed the part of practical wisdom to withdraw the book.

But the issue now was that of freedom of speech: if this interested Minority could force the suppression of this book, so could any strongly organized minority force the suppression of any book of which its members did not approve. The situation required us to fight it out and take the consequences.

For many weeks it seemed as if the sale of *Mrs. Eddy* might actually be so reduced that the book could not be kept on the market. Many stores were forced by threats to renounce its sale, and many to conceal it. Others openly defied those who came to threaten boycott, and in all but a few cities the book could always be bought somewhere. The American book trade recognized the principle at issue, and the moment it gained public support—as it did when the public became aware of the attempt at suppression—it so valiantly rallied against this tyranny that the sale of *Mrs. Eddy* rapidly increased.

Except for the indignant resistance of booksellers and public to the arrogant assumption of a Minority that it had the right to dictate the sources of information on a given subject, a precedent extremely dangerous to freedom of the mind would surely have been established. (p. vi)

Dakin's book, currently unavailable, was the strongest attack on Mrs. Eddy written since Mrs. Milmine's book, also now long out of print. Both books are larger, more detailed, and better organized than Twain's hastily written book, which is rambling and disconnected. Moreover, it was written before much information had come to light about Mrs. Eddy's life and character. It is still, however, worth reading for its humor, irony, biting sarcasm, and undiluted venom.

Twain was never able to obtain a copy of the original 1875 edition of *Science and Health,* which the church kept tightly under wraps, the only edition written by Mrs. Eddy without help. He knew nothing about the later reworking of the text by James Henry Wiggin, but he recognized at once the marked difference in style between the relatively smooth lines of the edition then current, and lines written by Mrs. Eddy that lacked polishing by others. He found her writings particularly amateurish in the first third of her so-called autobiography *Retrospection and Introspection,* in the prefaces to her other books, and in unedited articles that she wrote for the *Christian Science Journal.* In *Miscellaneous Writings,* a book of 554 pages, he detected only one page of the "Prospectus" and fifteen pages here and there that he believed were written by Mrs. Eddy without assistance. The rest of the pages, he maintained, showed the hand of a skilled polisher. Some of the funniest passages in Twain's book are quotations from what he called Mrs. Eddy's "bastard English," "squalid writing," and "lumbering elusiveness."

Here is how Twain summarized the characteristics of Mrs. Eddy's undoctored prose:

> Desert vacancy, as regards thought.
> Self-complacency.
> Puerility.
> Sentimentality.
> Affectations of scholarly learning.
> Lust after eloquent and flowery expression.
> Repetition of pet poetic picturesqueness.
> Confused and wandering statement.
> Metaphor gone insane.
> Meaningless words, used because they are pretty, or showy, or unusual.
> Sorrowful attempts at the epigrammatic.
> Destitution of originality. (pp. 74–75)

Why Mrs. Eddy's prefaces were never revised by someone who could write well struck Mark as particularly puzzling:

It is evident that whenever, under the inspiration of the Deity, she turns out a book, she is always allowed to do some of the preface. I wonder why that is? It always mars the work. I think it is done in humorous malice. I think the clerks like to see her give herself away. They know she will, her stock of usable materials being limited and her procedure in employing them always the same, substantially. They know that when the initiated come upon her first erudite allusion, or upon any one of her other stage-properties, they can shut their eyes and tell what will follow. She usually throws off an easy remark all sodden with Greek or Hebrew or Latin learning; she usually has a person watching for a star—she can seldom get away from that poetic idea—sometimes it is a Chaldee, sometimes a Walking Delegate, sometimes an entire stranger, but be he what he may, he is generally there when the train is ready to move, and has his pass in his hat-band; she generally has a Being with a Dome on him, or some other cover that is unusual and out of the fashion; she likes to fire off a Scripture-verse where it will make the handsomest noise and come nearest to breaking the connection; she often throws out a Forefelt, or a Foresplendor, or a Foreslander where it will have a fine nautical foreto'gallant sound and make the sentence sing; after which she is nearly sure to throw discretion away and take to her deadly passion, intoxicated Metaphor. At such a time the Mrs. Eddy that does not hesitate is lost. (p. 75)

Later in his book Twain said it this way:

The known and undisputed products of her pen are a formidable witness against her. They do seem to me to prove, quite clearly and conclusively, that writing, upon even simple subjects, is a difficult labor for her; that she has never been able to write anything above third-rate English; that she is weak in the matter of grammar; that she has but a rude and dull sense of the values of words; that she so lacks in the matter of literary precision that she can seldom put a thought into words that express it lucidly to the reader and leave no doubts in his mind as to whether he has rightly understood or not; that she cannot even draught a Preface that a person can fully comprehend, nor one which can by any art be translated *into* a fully understandable form, that she can seldom inject into a Preface even single sentences whose meaning is uncompromisingly clear—yet Prefaces are her specialty, if she has one.

Mrs. Eddy's known and undisputed writings are very limited in bulk; they exhibit no depth, no analytical quality, no thought above school-composition size, and but juvenile ability in handling thoughts of even that modest magnitude. She has a fine commercial ability, and could govern a vast railway system in great style; she could draught a set of rules that Satan himself would say could not be improved on—for devilish effectiveness—by his staff; but we know, by our excursions among the Mother-Church's By-laws, that their English would discredit the deputy baggage-smasher. I am quite sure that Mrs. Eddy cannot write well upon any subject, even a commercial one.

In the very first revision of *Science and Health* (1883), Mrs. Eddy wrote a Preface which is an unimpeachable witness that the rest of the book was written by somebody else. I have put it in the Appendix along with a page or two taken from the body of the book, and will ask the reader to compare the labored and lumbering and confused gropings of this Preface with the easy and flowing and direct English of the other exhibit, and see if he can believe that the one hand and brain produced both.

And let him take the Preface apart, sentence by sentence, and searchingly examine each sentence word by word, and see if he can find half a dozen sentences whose meanings he is so sure of that he can rephrase them—in words of his own—and reproduce what he takes to be those meanings. Money can be lost on this game. I know, for I am the one that lost it.

Now let the reader turn to the excerpt which I have made from the chapter on "Prayer" (last year's edition of *Science and Health*), and compare that wise and sane and elevated and lucid and compact piece of work with the aforesaid Preface, and with Mrs. Eddy's poetry concerning the gymnastic trees, and Minerva's not yet effete sandals, and the wreaths imported from Erudition's bower for the decoration of Plymouth Rock, and the Plague-spot and Bacilli, and my other exhibits (turn back to my Chapters I and II) from the *Autobiography* and finally with the late Communication concerning me, and see if he thinks anybody's affirmation, or anybody's sworn testimony, or any other testimony of any imaginable kind would ever be likely to convince him that Mrs. Eddy wrote that chapter on Prayer. (pp. 157–58)

Twain, of course, went too far. That Mrs. Eddy, who once wrote that after discovering Christian Science she forgot everything she learned in grade school, was unable to write clearly, there is no doubt. On the other hand, the basic ideas of *Science and Health* clearly were her own. The fact that her lines were polished by Wiggin and others led Twain to believe that the entire book was somehow ghost-written:

I think that if anything in the world stands proven, and well and solidly proven, by unimpeachable testimony—the treacherous testimony of her own pen in her known and undisputed literary productions— it is that Mrs. Eddy is not capable of thinking upon high planes, nor of reasoning clearly nor writing intelligently upon low ones.

Inasmuch as—in my belief—the very first editions of the book *Science and Health* were far above the reach of Mrs. Eddy's mental and literary abilities, I think she has from the very beginning been claiming as her own another person's book, and wearing as her own property laurels rightfully belonging to that person—the *real* author of *Science and Health*. And I think the reason—and the only reason— that he has not protested is because his work was not exposed to print until after he was safely dead.

That with an eye to business, and by grace of her business talent, she has restored to the world neglected and abandoned features of the Christian religion which her thousands of followers find gracious and blessed and contenting. I recognize and confess; but I am convinced that every single detail of the work except just that one —the delivery of the product to the world—was conceived and performed by another. (p. 159)

After Twain began the magazine articles that later became part of his book, he received two letters of praise from a blind and dying Wiggin. He was the person Mark had called Mrs. Eddy's "paid polisher," Wiggin wrote, adding that many Christian Scientists were pleased when later editions of *Science and Health* had less "Wiggin" in them.

Mrs. Eddy was particularly incensed by Twain's contention that in allowing herself to be called Mother, she implied that she was some kind of second Mary. In a letter to the *New York Herald*, reprinted in *The First Church of Christ, Scientist, and Miscellany*, she defended the charge as follows:

In view of the circulation of certain criticisms from the pen of Mark Twain, I submit the following statement: It is a fact, well understood, that I begged the students who first gave me the endearing appellative "Mother" not to name me thus. But, without my consent, that word spread like wildfire. I still must think the name is not applicable to me. I stand in relation to this century as a Christian discoverer, founder, and leader. I regard self-deification as blasphemous; I may be more loved, but I am less lauded, pampered, provided for, and cheered than others before me—and wherefore? Because Christian Science is not yet popular, and I refuse adulation. . . . I believe in but one incarnation, one Mother Mary, and I know I am not that one, and never claimed to be. (pp. 302–303)

Mark was quick to point out, when his articles appeared in the book, the many passages in which Mrs. Eddy not only claimed divine inspiration for *Science and Health*, but also expressed satisfaction in being called Mother:

It is hard to locate her, she shifts about so much. She is a shining drop of quicksilver which you put your finger on and it isn't there. There is a paragraph in the *Autobiography* (page 96) which places in seemingly darkly significant procession three Personages:

1. The Virgin Mary.
2. Jesus of Nazareth.
3. Mrs. Eddy.

This is the paragraph referred to:

"No person can take the individual place of the Virgin Mary. No person can compass or fulfil the individual mission of Jesus of Nazareth. No person can take the place of the author of *Science and Health,* the discoverer and founder of Christian Science. Each individual must fill his own niche in time and eternity."

I have read it many times, but I still cannot be sure that I rightly understand it. If the Saviour's name had been placed first and the Virgin Mary's second and Mrs. Eddy's third, I should draw the inference that a descending scale from First Importance to Second Importance and then to Small Importance was indicated; but to place the Virgin first, the Saviour second, and Mrs. Eddy third, seems to turn the scale the other way and make it an ascending scale of Importances, with Mrs. Eddy ranking the other two and holding first place.

I think that this was perhaps the intention, but none but a seasoned Christian Scientist can examine a literary animal of Mrs. Eddy's creation and tell which end of it the tail is on. She is easily the most baffling and bewildering writer in the literary trade. (pp. 83–84)

As early as 1890, Twain tells his readers, Mrs. Eddy sent the following telegram to a session of the National Christian Science Association held in New York City: "All hail! He hath filled the hungry with good things and the sick hath He not sent empty away.—Mother Mary."

As Twain points out, the title "Mother" was not given to Mrs. Eddy until five years later. In his opening address to the 1890 session, the president stated: "There is but one Moses, one Jesus, and there is but one Mary." He meant Mary Baker Eddy. Jesus' mother seems to have evaporated. How much better it would have been, Twain writes, and more modest, if Mrs. Eddy had signed her telegram "Mother Baker." He also observes that in her telegram Mrs. Eddy changed a significant word in the sentence she quoted from Luke 1:53. Luke did not speak of sending the "sick" away; he spoke of sending away the "rich."

In her reply to Mark, Mrs. Eddy professed to be unhappy with being called Mother. "Her memory is at fault here," Twain wrote, pointing out that in the bylaws of her *Church Manual* (Article 22, Section 1) she had written:

The Title Mother. In the year 1895 loyal Christian Scientists had given to the author of their textbook, the Founder of Christian Science, the individual, endearing term of Mother. Therefore, if a student of Christian Science shall apply this title, either to herself or to others, except as the term for kinship according to the flesh, it shall be regarded by the Church as an indication of disrespect for their Pastor-Emeritus, and unfitness to be a member of The Mother Church.

As a result of Twain's criticism, in the next edition of the *Church Manual* she revised the bylaw:

The Title of Mother Changed. In the year eighteen hundred and ninety-five, loyal Christian Scientists had given to the author of their textbook, the Founder of Christian Science, the individual, endearing term of Mother. At first Mrs. Eddy objected to being called thus, but afterward consented on the ground that this appellative in the church meant nothing more than a tender term such as sister or brother. In the year nineteen hundred and three and after, owing to the public misunderstanding of this name, it is the duty of Christian Scientists to drop this word "mother" and to substitute "Leader," already used in our periodicals.

Twain relished another bylaw in which Mrs. Eddy, after mentioning *Science and Health,* added "the Bible and the above named book, with other works by the same author. . . ." Mrs. Eddy clearly meant other books by herself, but the sentence was so carelessly worded that it seems to say that both the Bible and *Science and Health* are by the same author.

Twain doesn't mention it, but Mrs. Eddy once asked a disciple to do genealogical research that would trace her ancestry back to the Virgin Mary. When the research failed to find a connection, Mrs. Eddy blamed the failure on MAM.

Mary Baker Eddy was an extraordinary woman, but she was far from the saint portrayed in authorized biographies. The truth is that she was self-centered, egotistical, credulous, shrewd, domineering, and devoid of any understanding of science. In her elderly years, as we have seen, she suffered from delusions of both grandeur and persecution. "Oh, the marvel of my life!" she exclaimed in an 1891 letter to Augusta Stetson. "What would be thought of it, if it was known in a millionth of its detail? But this cannot be now. It will take centuries for this." (The letter is reprinted in Stetson's *Sermons and Other Writings,* p. 31.) Of course it hasn't taken centuries. The details, alas, are only too well known. Throughout her entire life Mrs. Eddy was embroiled in bitter quarrels with relatives and friends, and with endless court litigations. There is not the slightest doubt that she was a chronic liar, especially in her vehement denials of any debt to Quimby.

Many pages in Twain's book show how cleverly Mrs. Eddy managed to elevate herself to a position of absolute power over her church, increasing her wealth and at the same time rising in the reverence and love of her flock. She personally selected the board of directors as well as readers in the branch churches. We find in the bylaws of an early edition of the *Church Manual:*

The Pastor Emeritus of the Mother Church shall have the right (through a *letter* addressed to the individual of the Church of which he is the Reader) to remove a Reader from this office in any Church of Christ, Scientist, both in America and in foreign nations; or to appoint the Reader to fill any office belonging to the Christian Science denomination. (*Church Manual,* Article II, section 2)

Twain comments:

The belated By-law has a sufficiently quiet look, but it has a ton of dynamite in it. *It makes all the Christian Science Church Readers on the globe the personal chattels of Mrs. Eddy.* Whenever she chooses, she can stretch her long arm around the world's fat belly and flirt a Reader out of his pulpit, though he be tucked away in seeming safety and obscurity in a lost village in the middle of China.
. . . That By-law puts into Mrs. Eddy's hands *absolute command* over the most formidable force and influence existent in the Christian Science kingdom outside of herself, and it does this *unconditionally* and (by auxiliary force of Laws already quoted) *irrevocably.* Still, she is not quite satisfied. Something might happen, she doesn't know what. Therefore she drives in one more nail, to make sure, and drives it deep:

"This By-law can neither be amended nor annulled, except by consent of the Pastor Emeritus."

Let some one with a wild and delirious fancy try and see if he can imagine her furnishing that consent. (pp. 103–104)

The Christian Science church, Twain believed, had become a "sovereignty more absolute than the Roman Papacy," with Mrs. Eddy as its pope—a tyrant with power so total that church officials had turned into her "personal chattels":

With her own untaught and untrained mind, and without outside help, she has erected upon a firm and lasting foundation the most minutely perfect, and wonderful, and smoothly and exactly working, and best safe-guarded system of government that has yet been devised in the world, as I believe, and as I am sure I could prove if I had room for my documentary evidences here.

It is a despotism (on this democratic soil); a sovereignty more absolute than the Roman Papacy, more absolute than the Russian Czarship; it has not a single power, not a shred of authority, legislative or executive, which is not lodged solely in the sovereign; all its dreams, its functions, its energies, have a single object, a single reason for existing, and only the one—to build to the sky the glory of the sovereign, and keep it bright to the end of time.

Mrs. Eddy is the sovereign; she devised that great place for herself, she occupies that throne.

In 1895, she wrote a little primer, a little body of autocratic laws, called the *Manual of The First Church of Christ, Scientist,* and put those laws in force, in permanence. Her government is all there; all in that deceptively innocent-looking little book, that cunning little devilish book, that slumbering little brown volcano, with hell in its bowels. In that book she has planned out her system, and classified and defined its purposes and powers. (p. 186)

Elsewhere in his book Twain puts it this way:

I think that any one who will carefully examine the By-laws (I have placed all of the important ones before the reader), will arrive at the conclusion that of late years the master-passion in Mrs. Eddy's heart is a hunger for power and glory; and that while her hunger for money still remains, she wants it now for the expansion and extension it can furnish to that power and glory, rather than what it can do for her towards satisfying minor and meaner ambitions.

I wish to enlarge a little upon this matter. I think it is quite clear that the reason why Mrs. Eddy has concentrated in herself all powers, all distinctions, all revenues that are within the command of the Christian Science Church Universal is that she desires and intends to devote them to the purpose just suggested—the upbuilding of her personal glory—hers, and no one else's; that, and the continuing of her name's glory after she shall have passed away. *If she has overlooked a single power, howsoever minute, I cannot discover it. If she has found one, large or small, which she has not seized and made her own, there is no record of it, no trace of it.* In her foragings and depredations she usually puts forward the Mother-Church—a lay figure—and hides behind it. Whereas, she is in manifest reality the Mother-Church herself. It has an impressive array of officials, and committees, and Boards of Direction, of Education, of Lectureship, and so on—geldings, every one, shadows, spectres, apparitions, wax-figures: she is supreme over them all, she can abolish them when she will; blow them out as she would a candle. She is herself the Mother-Church. (p. 125)

Let me digress for a moment from Mark Twain to speak of the *Christian Science Hymnal.* The first edition (1892) contained lyrics by Mrs. Eddy for two hymns. A third hymn by her was added in 1903, a fourth in 1910, and two more in 1932. The present hymnal is twice the size of the original.

Most of Mrs. Eddy's hymns are set to several tunes. The book includes a number of evangelical songs, such as "I Love to Tell the Story," and "Onward, Christian Soldiers," as well as some curiosities such as a parody of "Rock of Ages," and two melodies for "Speak Gently." The latter was a once-popular bit of doggerel that Lewis Carroll satirized in *Alice in Wonderland* as the Ugly Duchess's song "Speak Roughly." I doubt if it has ever been sung in Christian Science services for the past fifty years.

Hymnal Notes for Use with Christian Science Hymnal (1933) correctly identifies the author of "Speak Gently" as one David Bates, of Philadelphia. The note apologizes for the fact that in the 1910 edition of the *Hymnal* the lyrics were wrongly attributed to George Washington

Langford, misspelling Hangford, the man's supposed real name. Actually his real name *was* Langford. For many decades he was incorrectly identified as the author of "Speak Gently." (For a detailed account of the curious history of this poem, see my essay "Speak Roughly" in *Gardner's Whys and Wherefores*.)

Few Christian Scientists, I suspect, know that in her bylaws Mrs. Eddy decreed that one of her hymns be sung in church by a soloist at least once a month. If a soloist refuses, the law states, the singer's salary is to be discontinued.

Hymnal Notes opens with a reprint of an essay by Maria Louise Baum on Mrs. Eddy's lyrics. (The essay had first appeared in the *Christian Science Journal,* February 1914). How Twain would have guffawed had he seen Ms. Baum's raptures! Here are some of her opinions:

> To tell the beauty of these hymns is beyond the power of mere criticisms. They are their own praise, their own proof, proof of a supreme and unique literary achievement. . . . They are such deep revelings as have rarely been trusted to a printed page. Touching what must be read between the lines, the most reverent and tender words must fall silent. . . . They are on the tongue and in the ears perhaps of more people more constantly than any other hymns in the language.

Actually, unless you have attended a Christian Science service, you will not have heard any of them. The words are so uniformly banal that it is hard to decide which hymn is the worst. Here are the five stanzas of "Mother's Evening Prayer," which can be sung to six different melodies:

> O gentle presence, peace and joy and power;
>   O Life divine, that owns each waiting hour,
> Thou love that guards the nestling's faltering flight!
>   Keep thou my child on upward wing tonight.

Love is our refuge; only with mine eye
   Can I behold the snare, the pit, the fall;
His habitation high is here, and nigh,
   His arm encircles me, and mine, and all.

O make me glad for every scalding tear,
   For hope deferred, in gratitude, disdain!
Wait, and love more for every hate and fear . . .
   No ill—since God is good and loss is gain.

Beneath the shadow of His mighty wing;
   In that sweet secret of the narrow way,
Seeking and finding, with the angels sing:
   "Lo, I am with you alway"—watch and pray.

No snare, no fowler, pestilence or pain;
   No night drops down upon the troubled breast,
When heaven's aftersmile earth's tear-drops gain,
   And mother finds her home and heav'nly rest.

Back to Mark Twain. Some of the funniest pages in his book are devoted to two oil paintings that hung in the "Mother's Room" of Boston's Mother Church. This room was designed for the exclusive use of Mrs. Eddy when she was in Boston, but apparently she slept there only once. It became a shrine for visitors. They were allowed into it only four persons at a time, and permitted to stay five minutes while they listened in awed silence to a lecture about the room's expensive furnishings.

In one of the magazine articles preceding his book, Twain wrote that the room contained an oil painting of Mrs. Eddy, with perpetually burning lights in front of it. By the time he put together his book, however, he was told that no such portrait hung there. Twain says he is not sure whether it ever did or not, but upon investigation, he discovered that hanging then in the "Holy of Holies" was not a portrait of Mrs. Eddy but an oil painting of the horsehair rocking chair in which she sat while writing *Science and Health!*

> Now, then, I hope the wound is healed. I am willing to relinquish the portrait, and compromise on the Chair. At the same time, if I were going to worship either, I should not choose the Chair.
>
> As a picturesque and persistently interesting personage, there is no mate to Mrs. Eddy, the accepted Equal of the Saviour. But some of her tastes are so different from His! I find it quite impossible to imagine Him, in life, standing sponsor for that museum there, and taking pleasure in its sumptuous shows. I believe He would put that Chair in the fire, and the bell along with it; and I think He would make the show-woman go away. I think He would break those electric bulbs, and the "mantel-piece of pure onyx," and say reproachful things about the golden drain-pipes of the lavatory, and give the costly rug of duck-breasts to the poor, and sever the satin ribbon and invite the weary to rest and ease their aches in the consecrated chairs. What He would do with the painted windows we can better conjecture when we come presently to examine their peculiarities. (p. 134)

Joseph Armstrong in *The Mother Church* (1897) devotes a chapter to Mother's Room and its costly furnishings: a mantelpiece of onyx from Mexico, an eiderdown rug made by Eskimos, an Athenian hanging lamp two centuries old, antique Persian rugs, a basin of red African marble, gold-plated fixtures in the washroom, and so on. Above the entrance door, in gold letters on a white marble tablet, is the word "Love." The room's three stained-glass windows are based on three illustrations in Mrs. Eddy's book *Christ and Christmas* (1883). The window showing Mrs. Eddy in the attic of her home in Lynn, searching the Bible while light from the Star of Bethlehem shines on her head and on the Holy Book, was based on a picture in the Christmas book that obviously is a likeness of Mrs. Eddy. However, Armstrong assures his readers, "The face of the woman in the central window, 'Seeking and Finding,' is not a portrait of our teacher and mother but is a type which presents the thought of her, searching the Scripture with unalterable trust in the divine wisdom, above and beyond mortal concept" (p. 71).

Armstrong describes the huge oil painting of Mrs. Eddy's rocking chair as six by five feet. The picture, he says, was a gift from Mrs. Eddy herself! "The effect of the painting, so placed, is to enlarge as well as enrich the room for it is so realistic that, looking at it, one seems to be gazing into another apartment" (p. 73).

Twain, who never believed Mrs. Eddy when she insisted that she was uncomfortable with being called Mother, would have enjoyed knowing about the following letter from Mrs. Eddy to the church's board of directors in 1894. Armstrong quotes it in full:

> My beloved Students, Permit me to make this request relative to the Mother's Room, and if you think best grant it. On the marble floor at the entrance engrave the word, Mother; and on the arch above the word, Love.
>
> Ever affectionately yours,
MARY BAKER EDDY. (p. 70)

A year before she died, Mrs. Eddy, perhaps still stinging from Twain's sarcasm about the Mother Room, ordered it dismantled.

To her followers, Twain writes, Mrs. Eddy is:

> Patient, gentle, loving, compassionate, noble-hearted, unselfish, sinless, widely cultured, splendidly equipped mentally, a profound thinker, an able writer, a divine personage, an inspired messenger whose acts are dictated from the Throne, and whose every utterance is the Voice of God.
>
> She has delivered to them a religion which has revolutionized their lives, banished the glooms that shadowed them, and filled them and flooded them with sunshine and gladness and peace; a religion which has no hell; a religion whose heaven is not put off to another

time, with a break and a gulf between, but begins here and now, and melts into eternity as fancies of the waking day melt into the dreams of sleep.

They believe it is a Christianity that is in the New Testament; that it has always been there; that in the drift of ages it was lost through disuse and neglect, and that this benefactor has found it and given it back to men, turning the night of life into day, its terrors into myths, its lamentations into songs of emancipation and rejoicing. (p. 156)

In Twain's own opinion, Mrs. Eddy is:

Grasping, sordid, penurious, famishing for everything she sees—money, power, glory—vain, untruthful, jealous, despotic, arrogant, insolent, pitiless where thinkers and hypnotists are concerned, illiterate, shallow, incapable of reasoning outside of commercial lines, immeasurably selfish. (p. 155)

Stefan Zweig, a prolific Austrian novelist and biographer, has a long section about Mrs. Eddy in his book *Mental Healers* (English translation, 1932). His rhetoric is even harsher than that of Mark Twain. Here are some of the terms Zweig applies to her: stupid, daimonic, inane, domineering, tyrannical, mulish, absurd, preposterous, masculine, unwomanly, egocentric, self-centered, grasping, humorless, fanatical, muddle-headed, crazy, a humbug, childish, illogical, monomaniacal, not even half-educated, and "a strange mixture of genius and insanity." An often quoted sentence describes her as "scarcely more than half-witted, always ailing, and of very dubious character."

Almost all of Zweig's attack on Mrs. Eddy is based on Mrs. Milmine's book, which he calls the "black biography," and the authorized biography by Sibyl Wilbur, which he calls the "rose-colored" book that contains not a single derogatory remark. The black biography, he adds, turns Mrs. Eddy into a remarkable, fascinating woman; the rose-colored one simply makes her seem ridiculous:

She had nothing but an idea, and an extremely questionable one, but she thought of absolutely nothing else. She had only this one standpoint, but to this she clung as if her feet had been rooted to the earth. Motionless, unshakable, deaf to every objection, with her frail lever she moved the world. In twenty years out of a maze of metaphysical confusion she created a new method of healing; established a doctrine counting its adherents by the myriad, with colleges and periodicals of its own, and promulgated in textbooks credited with inspiration; established a Church and built numerous churches; appointed a sanhedrim of preachers and priests; and won for herself private wealth amounting to three million dollars. Over and above all this, by her very exaggerations she gave contemporary psychology a vigorous forward thrust, and ensured for herself a special page in the history of mental science. (p. 105)

Twain described Mrs. Eddy's writings as frantic, slipshod, incoherent, and so obscure as seemingly written in the Unknown Tongue: "The minute you think the light is bursting upon you the candle goes out and your mind begins to wander" (p. 71).

On the other hand, like Zweig, Twain had unbounded admiration for the skill in which Mrs. Eddy built up her religion, then growing so rapidly that Twain actually feared it might someday overshadow mainline Christianity. Indeed, he predicted in 1899 that there would soon be ten million Christian Scientists in the United States, three million in England, and that these ranks would be trebled by 1930!* Over and over again he praises Mrs. Eddy with a sarcasm so profound that several naive church journalists have cited these passages as proving

---

*Exaggerated predictions about the growth of Christian Science were common among skeptics in Twain's day. Elbert Hubbard, for example, in his attack on Mrs. Eddy in *Little Journeys to the Homes of Great Teachers* (1908), predicted that "Christian Science is going to sweep the earth and in twenty years will have but one competitor, the Roman Catholic faith."

that Twain greatly admired their leader. Here are some of Mark's sarcastic passages:

> In several ways she is the most interesting woman that ever lived, and the most extraordinary. (p. 60)

> *   *   *

> It is thirteen hundred years since the world had produced anyone who could reach up to Mrs. Eddy's waistbelt. (p. 61)

> *   *   *

> She is easily the most interesting person on the planet, and, in several ways, is easily the most extraordinary woman that was ever born upon it. (p. 192)

Albert Bigelow Paine, in *Mark Twain: A Biography* (1912), quotes Mark as saying:

> Christian Science is humanity's boon. Mother Eddy deserves a place in the Trinity as much as any member of it. She has organized and made available a healing principle that for two thousand years has never been employed except as the merest kind of guesswork. She is the benefactor of the age. (Vol. III, p. 1271)

Lyman Powell, in his authorized hagiography *Mary Baker Eddy: A Life Size Portrait* (1930), and Norman Beasley, in his history of Christian Science, *The Cross and the Crown* (1952), each totally missed Twain's sarcasm in the above remarks. They actually quote them as proof that Mark completely reversed his low opinion of Mrs. Eddy—a fact, Powell states, that "may come as news to many."

Twain's final opinion of Christian Science is better expressed in a letter that Robert Peel quotes in *Mary Baker Eddy: The Years of Authority:*

> My view of the matter has not changed. To-wit, that Christian Science is valuable; that it has just the same value now that it had when Mrs. Eddy stole it from Quimby; that its healing principle (its most valuable asset) possesses the same force now that it possessed a million years before Quimby was born; that Mrs. Eddy the fraud, the humbug, *organized* that force and is *entitled to high credit for that.* Then with a splendid sagacity she hitched it to the shirt-tail of a religion—the surest of all ways to secure friends for it, and support. In a fine and lofty way—figuratively speaking—it was a tramp stealing a ride on the lightning express. Ah, how did that ignorant village-born peasant woman know the human ass so well? She has no more intellect than a tadpole—until it comes to *business*—then she is a marvel! (pp. 205–206)

13

The Decline of Christian Science

As we have seen, Mrs. Eddy confidently expected Christian Science to become the dominant religion of the world. At the time this was not too far-fetched a hope. Somehow, in spite of endless apostasies, bitter personal feuds and legal battles, and vicious opposition by mainline Christians (on one occasion a town even burned her in effigy), her iron will managed to hold together her empire and to see it grow.

This growth was all the more remarkable in view of the constant turnover of leaders. Most of the editors of the *Christian Science Journal*—Mrs. Hopkins, Reverend Frank Mason, Joshua Bailey, William Nixon, and others—lasted only a few years before they left the faith or were fired. Beginning March 14, 1897, Mrs. Eddy, fearing MAM, suddenly ordered all teachings suspended for a year while instructors and students alike studied *Science and Health* and her other writings. Disobedient members were threatened with expulsion.

From 1903 to 1906 Mrs. Eddy again suspended teaching. Only "demonstrations" (healings) were allowed to continue. Yet in spite of this aberrant behavior and autocratic rule, the faith steadily prospered.

201

Churches sprang up everywhere like mushrooms. There were First Churches in almost every large city in the nation; in some of those cities even Second Churches were being built.

Fleta Springer, in her biography, quotes a touching letter that Mrs. Eddy wrote on April 7, 1890, to her son Glover. It reveals so clearly Mrs. Eddy's monumental pride in what she had accomplished, her great loneliness, and her ambivalent feeling toward her son:

> That which you cannot write I understand and will say, I am reported as dying, wholly decrepid and useless, etc. Now one of these reports is just as true as the others are. My life is as pure as that of the angels. God has lifted me up to my work, and if it was not pure it would not bring forth good fruits. The Bible says the tree is known by its fruit.
>
> But I need not say this to a Christian Scientist, who knows it. I thank you for any interest you may feel in your mother. I am alone in the world, more alone than a solitary star. Although it is duly estimated by business characters and learned scholars that I lead and am obeyed by 300,000 people at this date. The most distinguished newspapers ask me to write on the most important subjects. Lords and ladies, earls, princes and marquises and marchionesses from abroad write to me in the most complimentary manner. Hoke Smith declares I am the most illustrious woman on the continent—those are his exact words. Our senators and members of Congress call on me for counsel. But what of all this? I am not made the least bit proud by it or a particle happier for it. I am working for a higher purpose.
>
> Now what of my circumstances? I name first my home, which of all places on earth is the one in which to find peace and enjoyment. But my home is simply a house and a beautiful landscape. There is not one in it that I love only as I love everybody. I have no congeniality with my help inside of my house; they are no companions and scarcely fit to be my help.
>
> I adopted a son hoping he would take Mr. Frye's place as my

bookkeeper and man of all work that belongs to man. But my trial of him has proved another disappointment. His books could not be audited they were so incorrect, etc., etc. Mr. Frye is the most disagreeable man that can be found, but this he is, namely (if there is one on earth), an honest man, as all will tell you who deal with him. At first mesmerism swayed him, but he learned through my forbearance to govern himself. He is a man that would not steal, commit adultery, fornication, or break one of the Ten Commandments. I have now done, but I could write a volume on what I have touched upon.

One thing is the severest wound of all, namely, the want of education among those nearest to me in kin. I would gladly give every dollar I possess to have one or two and three that are nearest to me on earth possess a thorough education. If you had been educated as I intend to have you, to-day you could, would, be made President of the United States. Mary's letters to me are so misspelled that I blush to read them.

You pronounce your words so wrongly and then she spells them accordingly. I am even yet too proud to have you come among my society and alas! mispronounce your words as you do; but for this thing I should be honoured by your good manners and I love you. (pp. 396–97)

In 1908, when she was eighty-seven, Mrs. Eddy founded a daily newspaper, the *Christian Science Monitor.* The first issue appeared on November 15. By reporting objectively on current affairs without covering deaths, crimes, murders, epidemics, and sexual scandals, it has given more respectability to Christian Science than any of its other publications.

It was not until about 1960 that the church began to experience hard times, losing both members and money. There is an old joke about the Christian Scientist who said he left the faith because he was tired of being so damn happy all the time. (For a classic discussion of the role of cheerfulness and optimism in Christian Science and New Thought, see Lectures 4 and 5 on "healthy mindedness" in William James's *Varieties of Religious Experience* [1902].) Seriously, why the sudden decline?

It can be attributed in part, I suppose, to the rising tide of evangelical and fundamentalist Protestantism, especially in its Pentecostal form, and perhaps also to the surprising growth of such off-trail sects as Mormonism, Seventh-day Adventism, and Jehovah's Witnesses. The revival of New Thought in the New Age movement, with its stress on optimism, psychic healing, and alternative medicines, may be another factor. Other causes are surely the steady improvement of medical science and surgery, and the increasingly frequent reports of the tragic deaths of children whose Christian Science parents refuse to take them to a doctor for treatment of a life-threatening illness. It is not likely today that even the child's parents will attribute such a death, as in past decades, to MAM. Is it possible, one dares to think, that a growing number of Christian Scientists are becoming aware that sin, sickness, and death have a way of not vanishing when they are redefined as nonexistent?

Whatever the causes, the church today is in serious financial straits. Surprisingly, the respected *Christian Science Monitor* has been a major drain on funds. It is said to be losing millions of dollars every year. And church leaders are squabbling, more than ever before, over mismanagement of funds and who is most responsible for the losses. As early as 1931, Stefan Zweig, in his attack on Mrs. Eddy in *Mental Healers,* wrote these prophetic words:

> With the death of the great conquistador, the new religion lost its pugnacity. The Christian Science healer works peacefully side by side with the State-accredited physician. This peculiar form of religious suggestion takes its orderly place in the armamentarium of modern psychology and psychiatry. Like countless other theories that were revolutionary in their day, this one has come to terms with the powers that be. Christian Science still lives, but it has grown rigid and formal. What was molten lava when erupted from the volcanic soul of Mary Baker

Eddy, is now cold, and a tranquil fellowship of undistinguished folk
has established itself on the lower slopes of the extinct crater. (p. 246)

A major source of discontent among church leaders is their confusion
over the degree to which divinity should be assigned to their leader.
This confusion owes much to Mrs. Eddy's own ambiguous assertions.
It is true that she repeatedly denied she was divine in the sense that
Jesus was divine. On the other hand, like Mrs. White, her counterpart
in the Seventh-day Adventist movement, she firmly believed she was
God-inspired to establish on earth the one true faith that Christianity
had long ago abandoned. Even though Mrs. Eddy often objected to
being elevated to sainthood, many of her followers in the past, and
still today, did so elevate her. Devout church members continue to read
Science and Health more diligently than they read the Bible. They commit
its passages to memory. Some sleep with it beside their bed or even
under their pillow.

A notion of how difficult it has been for Christian Scientists to
pin down the exact degree of Mrs. Eddy's sainthood can be gained
by considering the furor aroused by the publication in 1883 of *Christ
and Christmas.* This was Mrs. Eddy's poem about the birth of Christ
and the coming of Christian Science. It is the only work by Mrs. Eddy
to be illustrated. Its fifteen four-line stanzas are accompanied by ten
full-page pictures in black and white, drawn by James F. Gilman, a
young Christian Science artist whose work Mrs. Eddy admired.

At the back of the book, inside a rectangular border, are the words:
"Mary Baker Eddy and James F. Gilman, Artists." Note that Mary's
name precedes Gilman's. Mrs. Eddy had no talent for sketching, but
listed herself as a co-artist because she suggested to Gilman the subject
matter of his pictures and carefully instructed him on how to draw
them. Judging from Robert Peel's account in *Mary Baker Eddy: The
Years of Authority,* their collaboration was a stormy one. Mrs. Eddy
constantly demanded changes in the art, some of which Gilman did

not like, but he always deferred to her wishes. Her moods would alternate between high praise and temperamental outbursts of anger over what she considered defects.

The illustration for the fourth quatrain—we mentioned this in the previous chapter as the model for one of Mother Church's stained-glass windows—is a picture of Mrs. Eddy in an attic, studying the Bible. A shaft of light from the Star of Bethlehem shines on her through a skylight, and there is a halo of light around her head. The picture for the tenth stanza is particularly amusing. It shows a small child, who cannot be older than four, illuminated by a similar shaft of light while she reads *Science and Health!* Can you imagine a child of four reading and understanding that book's turgid prose?

The drawing that aroused the greatest controversy was the illustration for stanza twelve. It shows Jesus holding the right hand of a woman who has the same features and hairstyle as Mrs. Eddy in the attic. She is clothed in the same white robe as Jesus. In her left hand is a scroll bearing the words "Christian Science." Shafts of supernal light from on high illumine both figures. Around the heads of both are radiating halos of equal strength.

Here are the two stanzas that accompany this picture:

> For Christian Science brings to view
>   The great I Am—
> Omniscient power—gleaming through
>   Mind, mother, man.
> As in blest Palestina's hour,
>   So in our age,
> 'Tis the same hand unfolds His power,
>   And writes the page.

"Palestina's hour" refers to the days of Jesus in Palestine. "Mother," in the last line of the first stanza, suggests Mother Eddy. The final line clearly implies that the pages of *Science and Health* were written by the same hand that wrote the Bible.

Readers were quick to note that in the picture Jesus is seated but the woman is standing. Julia Field-King, editor of the *Christian Science Journal,* wrote, "I see a greater than Jesus is here." Field-King later developed heretical views and was excommunicated in 1902.

Implications of divinity become more blasphemous in the picture that shows the same woman, bearing the same scroll, with the same burst of light around her head. She is knocking at a door. Gilman originally drew a book in her hand to represent *Science and Health,* but Mrs. Eddy thought it made the woman look too much like a door-to-door book salesman, so he changed the book to a scroll. As the book's glossary makes clear, the picture is based on Christ's declaration, "Behold, I stand at the door and knock: If any man hear my voice, and open the door, I will come in to him, and will sup with him, and he with me" (Revelation 3:20).

In Gilman's picture, however, it is not Jesus knocking at the door. It is the woman of the previous pictures—a woman who strongly resembles Mary Baker Eddy. The implication is that today it is Mrs. Eddy who knocks on your door and asks to be invited in, not Jesus.

The storm of protest aroused by Gilman's art, much of it coming from church members, was so great that Mrs. Eddy was forced to issue a disclaimer. In the *Christian Science Journal* (February 1894) she wrote:

> The illustrations in *Christ and Christmas* refer not to my personality, but rather foretell the typical appearing of the womanhood, as well as the manhood of God, our divine Father and Mother. . . . The illustrations were not intended for a golden calf, at which the sick may look and be healed. Christian Scientists should beware of unnatural snares, and adhere to the divine Principle and rules for demonstration. They must guard against the deification of finite personality.

Mrs. Eddy was not pleased to hear from mothers who said their children had been healed merely by looking at Gilman's pictures, especially at the last picture, which showed an ascending Jesus with cherubs in the clouds. After the book's second edition, Mrs. Eddy decided to kill its sales. In a letter to Ebenezer Foster in 1894 she wrote:

> I have stopped my book *Christ & Xmas* being printed! The students made a golden calf of it and therefore I pull down this dagon. Don't ever speak of it as a healer. I did in my article for our Mag. but did not know then the *modus operandi* abroad. The books heal *scientifically*. The Poem is not made the healer but the pictures are . . . and the picture-healing is made by misuse of Charm-healing such as pagans use, and mind-curers mesmerists and faith-curers adopt to save learning through *growth* out of error into Truth. (Peel, *Mary Baker Eddy: The Years of Authority*, p. 63)

Four years later Mrs. Eddy allowed the book back in print with the cherubs' faces fading away. In a later edition the entire picture was replaced by one showing a cross and a crown, the symbols of Christian Science. First and second printings of the book are, of course, extremely rare, but a current edition is readily available today through any Christian Science reading room. I am somewhat surprised that the church keeps it in print because its verse is doggerel of the lowest order and the pictures are mediocre.

When *Christ and Christmas* first appeared, believers searched it for concealed meanings. As Robert Peel says in *Mary Baker Eddy: The Years of Authority* (p. 391), this search reached bizarre heights with the appearance in 1941 of a 980-page volume titled *Angelic Overtones of Christ and Christmas*. The author, Angela L. Orgain, had been a member of Mother Church before, as Peel puts it, she "had taken off on her own." Peel calls the book an "esoteric mishmash" that "rivals in tireless ingenuity some of the more recondite studies of *Ulysses* and *Finnegans Wake*."

The latest hullabaloo over the degree of Mrs. Eddy's divinity erupted in 1991 when the Boston headquarters published *The Destiny of The Mother Church* by Bliss Knapp. It is a work that elevates Mrs. Eddy's divinity to a level considered blasphemous by mainline Christians, and which even Christian Scientists consider heretical. Why then did the church publish such a book? It is a sordid tale.

Twice the church refused to accept Knapp's manuscript—first in 1948, and again in 1956. Then, to the vast embarrassment of church officials, Knapp's widow and his sister-in-law, before they died, left a will offering the church a bequest now worth $98 million if it would print and distribute the book before May 1993. Otherwise, all the loot would go to Stanford University and to the Los Angeles County Museum of Art.

In 1991 the church published the book. Like Mrs. Eddy, its leaders fibbed about their motives. It wasn't the money, they said. No, God forbid! They just wanted the faithful to have access to an alternate point of view about their leader!

Since 1991 the church has been doing its best not to promote or distribute Knapp's unwelcome book. In November 1992 I had great difficulty obtaining a copy. A local bookstore owner was at first told the book was out of stock. After several other phone calls she finally located someone willing to send her a copy, but only after a third degree of questioning about who wanted the book and why.

Bliss Knapp, a Harvard graduate, was greatly admired by Mrs. Eddy. He lectured widely on Christian Science, practiced healing, and taught the faith. He was twice president of Mother Church, and for several years was its First Reader. His father, Ira O. Knapp, belonged to the church's original board of directors, and was an active practitioner. It was he, by the way, who was most responsible for Mrs. Eddy's sermon in which she blasted Mrs. Woodbury as the whore of Babylon. The elder Knapp's letter to Mrs. Eddy about the prostitute of the Apocalypse was published in the *Christian Science Journal* (vol. 4, p. 409) under the title "The Scarlet Woman."

As we have seen, Mrs. Eddy clearly taught that the Comforter, promised by Jesus, is Christian Science, and that the rise of Christian Science fulfilled biblical prophecies about his Second Coming. Knapp goes much further. Not only does he regard Mrs. Eddy as the second of God's great witnesses to the Truth; he maintains that it is not just the church that represents the Second Coming, but Mrs. Eddy herself. Here is how Knapp phrases it:

> Who is the personality or individuality manifesting the second-coming?
> The answer of every true Christian Scientist will be: The person or individual who has done, and is doing, the works, in a sense above and beyond that of the average of those, even, who are addressing themselves to the task of regenerating the race.
> Is there one such?
> Christian Scientists unhesitatingly answer, Yes: The Reverend Mary Baker Eddy. (p. 275)

*   *   *

> In so far as these evidences are being now brought into view through Christian Science, may it not be consistently claimed that the second-coming is here; and in so far as a single Woman has been the instrument of bringing these evidences into view, may it not be consistently claimed that she is the personal representative of that second-coming? Is there anything far-fetched or unreasonable in this? (p. 280)

There is more. Knapp was convinced that just as the first coming of Jesus was foretold in the Old Testament, so do both Testaments predict the coming of Mary Baker Eddy.

Take Daniel 12 for example. God tells Daniel (verse 4) to "shut up the words, and seal the book, even to the end of time: many shall run to and fro, and knowledge shall be increased." In Knapp's view this sealed book is none other than *Science and Health,* inspired by God and now open to aid a suffering humanity.

Jeremiah 4:31 speaks of a "woman in travail" whose "soul is wearied because of murderers." Knapp takes this to be a prophecy of Mrs. Eddy. Was she not persecuted by the malicious animal magnetism of her enemies?

Ezekiel 2:9 mentions a "roll of a book." In the next chapter Ezekiel is told to eat the book. He does so and finds that it tastes like honey. Knapp believes that this "roll of a book" is another reference to *Science and Health.*

Isaiah 53 is a chapter widely regarded by conservative Christians as a prophecy of the coming of Christ. It is followed by chapter 54, which Knapp takes to be a prophecy of the coming of Mrs. Eddy. Verse 4 speaks of the woman's widowhood. Was not Mrs. Eddy a widow? The chapter also describes the woman as "barren," never having given birth to a child. How does Knapp get around this? He reminds his readers that Mrs. Eddy's only child was "taken from her," and therefore she was "to all intents and purposes, without a child of the flesh." "No weapon that is formed against thee shall prosper," says verse 17. Did not Mrs. Eddy conquer all her foes?

Christian Scientists widely believed in Mrs. Eddy's lifetime that the book sealed with seven seals, cited in Revelation 5, and the "little book" held by the "mighty angel" in Revelation 10, are both references to *Science and Health.* John writes (12:10) that he ate the little book, finding, like Ezekiel, that it tasted like honey.

Revelation 12:1–2 describes a woman "clothed with the sun, and the moon under her feet, and upon her head a crown of twelve stars." This "woman of the Apocalypse," as we have learned, has long been regarded as another prediction of the coming of Mrs. Eddy. The "great red dragon" in verse 3 is the great enemy of Christian Science, malicious animal magnetism. Knapp buys all this. He reminds his readers that the Apocalypse is not a document written by John. It was written by God, who gave it to Jesus, who then passed it on to John.

When Jesus said, "Thou art Peter, and upon this rock I will build my church" (Matthew 16:18), was he speaking about Catholic or Protestant Christianity? Neither, according to Knapp. He was speaking of Christian Science. Did not Mrs. Eddy herself in *Miscellaneous Writings* assert:

> In 1896 it goes without saying, preeminent over ignorance or envy, that Christian Science *is founded by its discoverer,* and built upon the rock of Christ. The elements of earth beat in vain against the immortal parapets of this Science. Erect and eternal, it will go on with the ages, go down the dim posterns of time unharmed, and on every battle-field rise higher in the estimation of thinkers and in the hearts of Christians. (p. 383)

The Star of Bethlehem, Knapp is convinced, symbolized not just the birth of Jesus, but also the birth of Christian Science. He quotes from Mrs. Eddy's *Miscellaneous Writings:* "The Star of Bethlehem is the Star of Boston, high in the zenith of Truth's domain, that looketh down on the long night of human beliefs, to pierce the darkness and melt the dawn" (p. 320).

Knapp's belief in Mrs. Eddy's paranormal powers is boundless. Not only did she perform miraculous healings, she also had the ability to read minds. That Mrs. Eddy herself believed she possessed this power is evident from a letter to a judge that Knapp quotes:

> I possess a spiritual sense of what the malicious mental malpractitioner is mentally arguing which cannot be deceived. I can discern in the human mind, thoughts, motives, and purpose; and neither mental arguments nor psychic power can affect this spiritual insight. It is as impossible to prevent this native perception as to open the door of a room and then prevent a man who is not blind from looking into the room and seeing all it contains. This mind-reading is first sight; it is the gift of God. And this phenomenon appeared in my

childhood; it is associated with my earliest memories, and has increased with years. It has enabled me to heal in a marvelous manner, to be just in judgment, to learn the divine Mind—and it cannot be abused; no evil can be done by reason of it. If the human mind communicates with me in sleep, when I awake, this communication is as palpable as words audibly spoken. (pp. 42–43)

Not only did God inspire *Science and Health,* but in Knapp's opinion her *Church Manual* was also inspired. He declares, "God actually *dictated* these two books to Mary Baker Eddy" (p. 224).

Knapp retells the story, found in so many biographies of Mrs. Eddy, of the time she aroused her servant Calvin Frye from a deep stupor. To Knapp, this was a genuine "resurrection":

It is indeed heartening to know that Mrs. Eddy could raise the dead. The Bible records indicate that Elijah, Elisha, Daniel, Jesus, Peter, and Paul all overcame death through their understanding of the Fatherhood of God. Now that the Motherhood of God has been revealed to us through Christian Science, experience has proved that women as well as men can defeat the last enemy and raise the dead. (p. 120)

Knapp parades numerous quotations from Mrs. Eddy to reinforce his belief in her infallibility and psychic powers. "But for the claim of animal magnetism," she once said to a patient, "I could walk right out of the window without falling." In an 1896 letter to Knapp's mother she wrote:

No greater mistake can be made than to disobey or to delay to obey a single message of mine. *God* does speak through me to this age. This I discern more clearly each year of my sojourn with you. (p. 113)

In 1938, Knapp reminds us, the church's board of directors authorized a careful study of all of Mrs. Eddy's published and unpublished writings. Their report (published in the *Christian Science Sentinel,* June 5, 1943, and in the *Christian Science Journal,* July 1943) concluded that Mrs. Eddy did indeed assume that she was the "Woman of the Apocalypse" "who fulfilled prophecy by giving the full and final revelation of Truth; her work being complimentary to that of Christ Jesus. As Christ Jesus exemplified the fatherhood of God, she (Mrs. Eddy) revealed God's motherhood."

Although Mrs. Eddy firmly believed that *Science and Health* was divinely inspired and the first great revelation of Truth since the time of Jesus, she also occasionally voiced resentment against a deification that placed her on the same level as Jesus. There is an interesting passage in her *First Church of Christ, Scientist, and Miscellany,* which Knapp does *not* quote. Mrs. Eddy recalls being startled to hear Phineas Quimby say to her, "I see that I am John, and that you are Jesus." Here is her comment on this episode:

> At that date I was a staunch orthodox, and my theological belief was offended by his saying and I entered a demurrer which rebuked him. But afterwards I concluded that he only referred to the *coming* anew of Truth, which we both desired; for in some respects he was quite a seer and understood what I said better than some others did. For one so unlearned, he was a remarkable man. Had his remark related to my personality, I should still think that it was profane. (p. 307)

Mark Twain, as we have seen, loved to bash the church for its financial greed. In his article in the *North American Review* (1902), he put it like this:

> Its God is Mrs. Eddy first, then the Dollar. Not a spiritual Dollar but a real one. From end to end of the Christian-Science literature

not a single (material) thing in the world is conceded to be real except the dollar. . . . The hunger of the Trust for the Dollar, its adoration of the Dollar, its lust after the Dollar, its ecstasy at the mere thought of the Dollar—there has been nothing like it in the world, in any age or century, nothing so coarse, nothing so ludicrous, nothing so bestial, except a French novelist's attitude towards adultery.

One could easily devote a dozen pages to the clever ways Mrs. Eddy invented for extracting money from her followers. In the *Christian Science Journal* (February 1908) she wrote:

I request Christian Scientists universally to read the paragraph beginning at line thirty of page 442 in the edition of *Science and Health*, which will be issued February 29. I consider the information there given to be of *great importance* at this stage of the workings of animal magnetism, and it will *greatly aid* the students in their individual experiences. (Snowden, p. 251)

What was this new information of such monumental importance? It consisted of two lines: "Christian Scientists, be a law to yourselves that mental malpractice cannot harm you either when asleep or when awake." By "mental malpractice" she meant, of course, MAM.

On another occasion, in the *Christian Science Journal* (February 1890), the faithful were informed:

Christian Science Spoons.—On each of these most beautiful spoons is a motto in bas-relief that every person on earth needs to hold in thought. Mother requests that Christian Scientists shall not ask to be informed what this motto is, but each Scientist shall purchase at least one spoon, and those who can afford it, one dozen spoons, that their families may read this motto at every meal and their guests be made partakers of its simple truth. Mary Baker G. Eddy.

The above-named spoons are sold by the Christian Science

Souvenir Company, Concord, N.H., and will soon be on sale at the Christian Science reading rooms throughout the country. (Snowden, p. 255)

What great motto was on these spoons? It was "Not matter but mind satisfies." Additional spoons, with other brief mottos, were offered for sale at different times. One was called the "Mother Spoon" because Mrs. Eddy's face was on it.

In her *Journal* (May 1899) Mrs. Eddy wrote:

It is with pleasure I certify that after months of incessant toil and at great expense Mr. Henry P. Moore, and Mr. J. C. Derby of Concord, N.H., have brought out a likeness of me far superior to the one they offered for sale last November. The portrait they have now perfected I cordially endorse. Also I declare their sole right to the making and exclusive sale of the duplicates of said portrait. I simply ask that those who love me purchase this portrait. Mary Baker Eddy. (Snowden, p. 256)

Four days before Christmas 1889, in the *Christian Science Sentinel,* Mrs. Eddy let her flock know what she wanted for yuletide gifts:

Beloved: I ask this favor of all Christian Scientists. Do not give me on, before, or after the forthcoming holidays, aught material except three tea jackets. All may contribute to these. One learns to value material things only as one needs them, and the costliest things are those that one needs least. Among my present needs material are these three jackets. Two of darkish heavy silk, the shade appropriate to white hair. The third of heavy satin, lighter shades but sufficiently sombre. Nos. 1 and 2 to be common-sense jackets, for Mother to work in, and not overtrimmed by any means. No. 3 for best, such as she can afford for her drawing room. Mary Baker Eddy. (Snowden, p. 253)

In 1992 there were about twenty-six hundred Christian Science churches around the globe, most of them white on the outside to symbolize the divine light of Truth. More than eighteen hundred of these churches are in the United States. The number of church members is unknown because Mrs. Eddy ordered the church to keep such statistics secret, and the church still obeys. As stated in the *Church Manual* (Article 8, Section 28): "Christian Scientists shall not report for publication the number of the members of The Mother Church, nor that of the branch churches. According to the Scripture they shall turn away from personality and numbering the people." It is estimated that about three-fourths of the church members are women, most of them elderly. A much larger fraction of women make up the practitioners.

Just as devout Catholics now practice birth control methods forbidden by the Vatican, and many even have abortions, so today's Christian Scientists allow drugs to kill illusory pain, go to dentists, and wear false teeth and spectacles as Mrs. Eddy did in her declining years. If they break a bone, they see a bone doctor. If they are going blind from cataracts, they have them removed by an ophthalmologist.

There remains, sadly, a remnant of true believers who refuse to see physicians. This has taken a grim toll. The *Journal of the American Medical Association* (September 22, 1989) reported on a study of 5,558 Christian Scientists as compared to a control group of 29,858 non-Scientists. The death rate among the Christian Scientists from cancer was double the national average, and 6 percent of them died from causes considered preventable by doctors. The non-Scientists, on the average, lived four years longer than Christian Scientists if they were women, and two years longer if they were men. Male Christian Scientists are more likely to seek medical help than female believers. Similar studies have shown that Seventh-day Adventists, on the average, live nine years longer than non-Adventists.

Ellen White, the Adventist prophetess who in so many ways resembled Mrs. Eddy, was originally opposed to mainline medicine. Over the decades, however, her followers, while retaining that church's emphasis on vegetarianism and opposition to alcohol, tobacco, tea, coffee, and spicy foods, have warmly embraced modern medicine. Some of the best hospitals in America are Adventist owned and operated. It is impossible to imagine the Christian Science church founding and operating a hospital. Even Pentecostal faith-healer Oral Roberts combined prayer with orthodox surgery and medicine in his Tulsa hospital.

When Mrs. Eddy spoke of death as not being real, she did not mean to deny that our unreal material bodies experience the illusion of death. In the far-distant future, when almost everyone is a Christian Scientist, she taught that death would be conquered along with sin and sickness, but she had no hope that this would happen soon. She put it this way in *Science and Health:*

> I have never supposed the world would immediately witness the full fruitage of Christian Science, or that sin, disease, and death would not be believed for an indefinite time; but this I do aver, that, as a result of teaching Christian Science, ethics and temperance have received an impulse, health has been restored, and longevity increased. If such are the present fruits, what will the harvest be, when this Science is more generally understood? (pp. 348–49)

As I write, Christian Science is in severe financial and bureaucratic difficulties. The furor over the Knapp book was only partly responsible for numerous resignations of top officials and editors. In 1992 the church was forced to close down Monitor Channel, its cable television network started the year before, as well as its Boston TV station, WQTV. Losses were estimated at $325 million. In May 1993 it ceased publishing *World Monitor,* a newspaper launched in 1988, after losses of more than $36 million.

The *Christian Science Monitor* is still going, although it is said to be losing $13 million annually. The church has also retained its monthly

Christian Science Journal, its weekly *Christian Science Sentinel,* and its Monitor Radio. Church leaders, repeatedly accused of financial greed and mismanagement, continue to squabble among themselves. Church membership is said to have dropped by more than half from its height in the mid-1930s, and the number of practitioners has dwindled from some 12,000 in the 1950s to less than 3,000.

As for the $98 million the church is supposed to get for publishing Knapp's book, it is possible it may never see this money. A California appellate court, after hearing complaints by Stanford University and the Los Angeles County Art Museum, has put the money on hold until more hearings are held. The will assumed that the book would be distributed to all Christian Science reading rooms, and sold widely through other channels. This has not been the case. The book is hard to obtain, and many reading rooms have refused to carry it.

The *Boston Globe* has been publishing dozens of articles on the church's decline, and the woes have been documented in such articles as "Tumult in the Reading Rooms" (*Time,* October 14, 1991), "A Church That Needs Healing" (*Newsweek,* March 23, 1992), "A House Divided" (*Chicago Tribune,* January 27, 1993), and the *New York Times* (March 12, June 8, and June 9, 1992).

In spite of past disappointments, Seventh-day Adventists still earnestly hope and believe, as Mrs. White taught, that Jesus will return bodily to earth any day now to bring to a close the great controversy between Christ and Satan. Mrs. Eddy's loyal followers, to the extent that they think on such things, believe that Jesus has already returned in the form of Christian Science, and that the world is now moving slowly toward a millennium in which will be destroyed not Satan, who doesn't exist, but all false beliefs in sin, sickness, and death, which also are not real.

Such are the sad hopes of true believers in the two greatest religious movements to have emerged in the United States from the minds and boundless energies of the two most extraordinary women to flourish on the fringes of Christianity's recent history.

14

New Thought, Unity, and Ella Wheeler Wilcox

Because I want to focus on the support given to New Thought by the poet Ella Wheeler Wilcox (1850–1919), I will make only a feeble attempt to summarize the extraordinarily complex history of the New Thought movement. As we saw in chapter 1, it was foreshadowed by the New England transcendentalists, especially by the writings of Emerson, but its more immediate debt was to the teachings of Phineas Parkhurst Quimby and Mary Baker Eddy. Hundreds of famous men and women were caught up in New Thought. Thousands of books were devoted to the movement and tens of thousands of magazine articles.*

The movement began slowly with independent local groups popping up here and there, usually organized by an energetic leader such as

---

*The best and most accurate history of New Thought is Charles S. Braden's 571-page *Spirits in Rebellion: The Rise and Development of New Thought* (Southern Methodist University Press, 1963). Its ninth printing (1987) is currently available as a paperback. In the back of his book Braden lists more than a hundred New Thought periodicals that came and went, estimating that his list comprises only about a third of the total number.

Mrs. M. E. Cramer, who formed an early group in San Francisco called the Divine Science Association. In 1890 a New Thought convention in Hartford, Connecticut, led to the founding of the first major national organization, the International New Thought Alliance (INTA).

I would have imagined, before I researched this chapter, that INTA had long since faded, but no, the organization, headquartered in Mesa, Arizona, is still very much alive. It publishes *New Thought,* a handsome quarterly that began in 1914. Blaine C. Mays is its present editor. Its 44-page Summer 1992 issue announced the Seventy-seventh INTA Congress in July at the Riviera Hotel in Las Vegas. There are ads for scores of New Thought books and tapes, and for a New Thought cruise to the Caribbean. Churches advertising in the issue have such names as the Hillside International Truth Center, Atlanta; the First Church of Religious Science, Manhattan; the First Church of Understanding, Roseville, Michigan; the Church of the Universal Christ, Baltimore; the First Church of Divine Science, Milwaukee; the Unity Church of Christianity, Houston; the Huntington Beach (California) Church of Religious Science; the Sanctuary of Truth, Alhambra, California; and the Unity Church, Hammond, Indiana. Four pages of small type list almost two hundred other New Thought churches and centers around the nation.You can even buy T-shirts with the words "Only love is real" on one side, and "Only love heals" on the other.

New Thought was at first confined mainly to a pantheistic emphasis on God as permeating all of nature and dwelling inside every person. By getting "In Tune with the Infinite" (the title of one of the earliest and certainly the most popular of all New Thought books, and written by Ralph Waldo Trine) one could not only free oneself from disease without using drugs, but one would become supremely happy and make lots of money. Although early New Thoughters shared the Christian Scientists' refusal to accept medical treatments, they soon diverged from Mrs. Eddy by recognizing the physical basis of ailments and becoming much more tolerant of doctors.

Jesus was always considered a prophet of New Thought, but the movement, like Christian Science, was essentially non-Christian in its denial of a Fall of Man, and therefore seeing no necessity for a blood atonement by Christ or for a hell of eternal punishment for the unsaved. Over and over again in New Thought literature, as in Christian Science and in today's New Age books, the word "atonement" was spelled "at-one-ment" to suggest that each of us is a part of God, united to everything else in the universe. Recall Shirley MacLaine's chant of "I am God" on the beach in a movie based on one of her many autobiographies?

Slowly during the first few decades of the twentieth century, as Charles Braden puts it, New Thought began to behave like the general who jumped on his horse and rode off in all directions. It became as hard to pin down its precise beliefs as it is hard today to say exactly what New Agers believe. It began to absorb all the occult elements that are part of today's New Age. Leaders began to import doctrines from the East, especially reincarnation. There was nothing about reincarnation in the teachings of Jesus, or in the writings of Quimby, but Charles and Myrtle Fillmore, who founded the New Thought church of Unity, enthusiastically embraced the doctrine. We shall have more to say about Unity later. Today, most members of this still flourishing cult believe in reincarnation.

New Thought also began to beat the drums for all forms of psi phenomena (ESP, PK, precognition), numerology, astrology, and (in a few cases) the wonders of the Great Pyramid. The Psychic Research Company in Chicago was one of many publishing houses specializing in New Thought books. It also founded a magazine called *New Thought* (not the later INTA publication) of which the poet Ella Wilcox was an associate editor. Like today's New Agers, New Thoughters became fascinated by such alternative medicines as osteopathy, homeopathy, and naturopathy.

Here is a typical Psychic Research Company ad for a New Thought book by William Walker Atkinson:

A wonderfully vivid book answering the questions: Can I make my life more happy and successful through mental control? How can I affect my circumstances by my mental effort? Just how shall I go about it to free myself from my depression, failure, timidity, weakness and care? How can I influence those more powerful ones from whom I desire favor? How am I to recognize the causes of my failure and thus avoid them?

Can I make my disposition into one which is active, positive, high strung and masterful? How can I draw vitality of mind and body from an invisible source? How can I directly attract friends and friendship? How can I influence other people by mental suggestion? How can I influence people at a distance by my mind alone? How can I retard old age, preserve health and good looks? How can I cure myself of illness, bad habits, nervousness, etc.? (Ella Wheeler Wilcox, *The Heart of the New Thought*, p. 94)

Another ad has this to say about a book by Sydney Flower:

Although this is the last of this series of books it is in some respects the most important of any. A life-time of study and practice will not exhaust its stores of knowledge. It deals with Psychometry, Phrenology, Palmistry, Astrology, Mediumship and Somnopathy. This last is a new word, coined by the author, Sydney Flower, to define his discovery of a new method of educating the young, i.e., during natural sleep. Of this method, a lady writing in the *Washington Post,* of recent date, said: "I never punish my little ones, I simply wait till they are asleep, and then I talk to them, not loud enough, you understand, to wake them, but in a low voice. I tell them over and over that they must be good, I suggest goodness to them, for I think the mind is just as susceptible to suggestion during the natural sleep as during the working state. I concentrate my mind on it, and I am confident that before long all mothers will adopt my method. It is the best way I know of to bring up children." This method is fully described by its discoverer in this work, and the endorsements of prominent physicians are given in full. (Ella Wheeler Wilcox, *The Heart of the New Thought,* p. 96)

It was the Psychic Research Company that published Mrs. Wilcox's first book about the movement, *The Heart of the New Thought* (1902). The copy I own is identified as a twentieth printing! She followed it with *New Thought Common Sense and What Life Means to Me* (1908), *The Art of Being Alive: Success Through New Thought* (1914), and *New Thought Pastels* (1907), a book of New Thought poetry.

Here is a typical forgettable poem from *New Thought Pastels:*

> All sin is virtue unevolved,
> Release the angel from the cloud—
> Go love thy brother up to God.
>
> Of this great trinity no part deny,
> Affirm, affirm the Great Eternal I.
>
> When the great universe was wrought,
> To might and majesty from naught,
> The all creative force was—
> > *Thought*

Mrs. Wilcox's first book about New Thought consists mainly of admonitions and platitudes. They are even duller than those in books by liberal Protestant ministers such as Norman Vincent Peale and Robert Schuller, both of whom are carrying on the New Thought tradition. "Feel good" ministers is what traditional Christians like to call them. Their messages about "the power of positive thinking" and how such thinking will make you happy and prosperous, although clothed in Christian terminology, are straight out of the New Thought movement.

Here are some of Mrs. Wilcox's gems from *The Heart of the New Thought:*

Age is all imagination. Ignore years and they will ignore you.

*   *   *

Eat moderately and bathe freely in water as cold as nature's rainfall. [Hydrotherapy, or water cure, was then popular among New Thoughters.]

*   *   *

Be alive, from crown to toe.

*   *   *

Regard any physical ailment as a passing inconvenience, no more.

*   *   *

Never for an instant believe you are permanently ill or disabled. Think of yourself as on the threshold of unparalleled success. A whole, clear, glorious year lies before you! In a year you can regain health, fortune, restfulness, happiness!

*   *   *

Push on! Achieve, achieve!

The essence of New Thought, Mrs. Wilcox tells us, is simply the "science of right thinking." By putting yourself in tune with the infinite God who is also within you, "physical pains will loosen their hold, and conditions of poverty will change to prosperity." This belief that right thinking will bring fiscal rewards runs through all New Thought literature from the beginning on to the inspirational books of Schuller and Peale. Here is "Assertion," a poem in Mrs. Wilcox's book *Poems of Power*—by "power" she meant the power of right thinking to tune in to God—that captures the heart of New Thought:

I am serenity. Though passions beat
    Like mighty billows on my helpless heart,
I know beyond them, lies the perfect sweet
    Serenity, which patience can impart.
And when wild tempests in my bosom rage,
"Peace, peace," I cry, "it is my heritage."

I am good health. Though fevers rack my brain
    And rude disorders mutilate my strength,
A perfect restoration after pain,
    I know shall be my recompense at length,
And so through grievous day and sleepless night
"Health, health," I cry, "it is my own by right."

I am success. Though hungry, cold, ill-clad,
    I wander for awhile, I smile and say,
"It is but for a time—I shall be glad
    To-morrow, for good fortune comes my way.
God is my father, He has wealth untold,
His wealth is mine, health, happiness and gold."

(p. 18)

Like all New Thoughters and New Agers, Mrs. Wilcox is down on traditional Christianity. Its emphasis on sin, hell, and redemption is seen as blaspheming the true teachings of Jesus about a loving God. Away with this old and dismal set of doctrines that came from Saint Paul, not from Jesus! "A wholesome and holy religion," Mrs. Wilcox writes in *The Heart of the New Thought,* "has taken its place with the intelligent progressive minds of the day, a religion which says: 'I am all goodness, love, truth, mercy, health. . . . I am a divine soul and only good can come through me or to me.' . . . This is the 'new' religion; yet it is older than the universe. It is God's own thought put into practical form" (p. 34).

From *Every-Day Thoughts* I take the following poem:

Let there be many windows to your soul,
That all the glory of the universe
May beautify it. Not the narrow pane
Of one poor creed can catch the radiant rays
That shine from countless sources. Tear away
The blinds of superstition; let the light
Pour through fair windows broad as truth itself
And high as God.
                              Why should the spirit peer
Through some priest-curtained orifice, and grope
Along dim corridors of doubt, when all
The splendor from unfathomed seas of space
Might bathe it with the golden waves of Love?
Sweep up the débris of decaying faiths;
Sweep down the cobwebs of worn-out beliefs,
And throw your soul wide open to the light
Of Reason and of Knowledge. Tune your ear
To all the wordless music of the stars
And to the voice of Nature, and your heart
Shall turn to truth and goodness, as the plant
Turns to the sun. A thousand unseen hands
Reach down to help you to their peace-crowned heights,
And all the forces of the firmament
Shall fortify your strength. Be not afraid
To thrust aside half-truths and grasp the whole.

(p. 101)

Like Mrs. Eddy, Mrs. Wilcox is convinced that right thinking is the best way for fat people to reduce. She recommends, however, that this be combined with eating only two meals a day, and if one's life is sedentary, one meal is enough. You must be patient. Miracles are seldom instantaneous. They take time.

Near the end of *The Heart of the New Thought* Mrs. Wilcox admits that not all misfortunes are caused by wrong thinking, or can be done away with by right thinking. She gives as an example the child who "toddles in front of a trolley car and loses a leg," or the person born deaf, blind, or deformed. To account for such evils "we must go farther back, to former lives, to find the first cause of such misfortunes" (p. 79). In her earlier book, *Every-Day Thoughts* (1901), Mrs. Wilcox was just as specific about reincarnation. "I believe the spirit of man has always existed and always will exist; that it passed through innumerable forms and phases of life, and that which it leaves undone in one incarnation must be accomplished in another."

Deep breathing exercises are recommended as valuable aids to meditation. One should perform them sitting in a chair facing east in the morning and west at night "because great magnetic forces come from the direction of the sun."

Prenatal influences on the unborn are taken for granted. Did not Napoleon's mother, Mrs. Wilcox asks, read Roman history while she was bearing him? Mrs. Wilcox deplores the ignorance of young women about the importance of having happy thoughts during pregnancy, otherwise fears and worries can damage the baby's brain. Right thinking can even "wear away the stone" of harmful genetic tendencies.

I will spare the reader quotations from Mrs. Wilcox's later books on New Thought or from the syndicated columns she contributed to William Randolph Hearst's chain of newspapers. But I cannot resist quoting in full an advertisement at the back of *The Heart of the New Thought:*

The many friends and admirers of Ella Wheeler Wilcox will be interested to learn that this gifted author and thinker has connected herself, in the capacity of associate editor, with the *New Thought* magazine,* and that hereafter her writings will appear regularly in that bright publication, of which the aim is to aid its readers in the cultivation of those powers of the mind which bring success in life. Mrs. Wilcox's writings have been the inspiration of many young men and women. Her hopeful, practical, masterful views of life give the reader new courage in the very reading, and are a wholesome spur to flagging effort. She is in perfect sympathy with the purpose of the *New Thought* magazine. The magazine is having a wonderful success, and the writings of Mrs. Wilcox for it, along the line of the new movement, are among her best. Words of truth, so vital that they live in the memory of every reader and cause him to think—to his own betterment and the lasting improvement of his own work in the world, in whatever line it lies—flow from this talented woman's pen.

The magazine is being sold on all news stands for five cents. It is the brightest, cleanest and best publication in its class, and its editors have hit the keynote of all sound success. The spirit of every bit of print from cover to cover of the magazine is the spirit of progress and upbuilding—of courage, persistence and success. Virile strength and energy, self-confidence, the mastery of self and circumstances are its life and soul, and even the casual reader feels the contagion of its vigor and its optimism.

Free.—The publishers will be pleased to send a handsome portrait of Mrs. Wilcox, with extracts from her recent writings on the New Thought, free. Address, The New Thought, 100, The Colonnades, Vincennes Ave., Chicago. (p. 93)

---

*According to Braden, the magazine *New Thought* mentioned in the ad was founded in 1902 by Sydney Flower. Originally it had been *Hypnotic* magazine. The name was changed in 1898 to *Suggestive Therapeutics.* When Ella's book was published in 1902, the magazine merged with the *Journal of Magnetism* and took the name *New Thought.* In 1910 it merged with *Health and Success* magazine, and finally expired. It should not be confused with another periodical called *New Thought,* mentioned earlier as the organ of INTA. It began publishing as *New Thought Bulletin,* later appearing under various names and finally becoming a quarterly in 1941.

Ella Wheeler was born in 1850 on a farm in Johnson Center, Wisconsin. She was a precocious, deeply religious child, believing strongly in God, prayer, and the protection of guardian angels. Her writing career began in her teens with selling essays and verse to the *New York Mercury*, and to periodicals published by the houses òf Harper and Frank Leslie.

Young Ella shuttled back and forth between the family's small farm house and nearby Milwaukee. For a short while she attended the University of Wisconsin, then called Madison University. Her first job was editor of the literary page of a Milwaukee trade magazine that folded after a few months. In addition to her steady output of verse, Ella began selling short stories here and there. Eventually she turned out some forty books, most of them collections of sentimental, moralizing verse. She also wrote a batch of romantic novels, books of essays on general topics, books promoting New Thought, and two autobiographies, *The Story of a Literary Career* (1905) and *The Worlds and I* (1918). Since she contributed regularly to Hearst newspapers and to *Cosmopolitan* magazine, there must be hundreds of magazine and newspaper articles that never appeared in book form.

Ella's first book of poems, *Drops of Water* (1872), was devoted to attacks on alcohol at a time when the temperance movement was going full blast. It was *Poems of Passion* (1883), however, that catapulted her to fame. The book was roundly condemned by shocked reviewers, which of course made it a best seller. By today's standards, it contained not a pornographic stanza, but it did have such lines as "Here is my body; bruise it if you will," and torrid passages such as:

> And on nights like this, when my blood runs riot
> With the fever of youth and its mad desires,
> When my brain in vain bids my heart be quiet,
> When my breast seems the center of lava-fires,
> Oh, then is the time when most I miss you,
> And I swear by the stars and my soul and say

That I will have you, and hold you, and kiss you,
Though the whole world stands in the way.

(pp. 14–15)

Some critics have speculated that such passionate lines, written when Ella was in her early thirties, came entirely from her imagination; that actually she was a shy, inexperienced virgin at the time. I don't believe it. Photographs of Ella, in the frontispieces of most of her books of verse, show her to be a beautiful, fine-figured woman, and her auto-biography speaks of a "kaleidoscopic panorama of romances" in her youth, including one suitor's "earnest love making."

Ella turned down several proposals of marriage before she met and fell in love with Robert Wilcox, a businessman who shared her enthu-siasms for God, prayer, and angels, as well as her forays into New Thought and occultism. For several years they lived in Meriden, Con-necticut, then moved to a Manhattan apartment where they stayed for nineteen years before settling into a Connecticut house on the Sound. Their only child, Robert M. Wilcox, Jr., died twelve hours after birth.

Ella has been called the nation's female Eddie Guest. (It is inter-esting to know that Edgar Guest [1881–1959], America's most popular versifier during the first half of this century, was a devout Christian Scientist.) This too seems to me unfair. Her verse was several cuts above Eddie's, even though none of it was great and today has been almost totally forgotten except for its continued inclusion in anthologies of popular verse. Her best remembered lines are the opening lines of "Solitude": "Laugh and the world laughs with you; / Weep, and you weep alone." The poem first appeared in the *New York Sun* (February 21, 1883), and later in *Poems of Passion*. The first two lines became so famous that today most people who recall them think they are an anonymous folk proverb. They have even been parodied: "Laugh and the world laughs with you, snore and you sleep alone."

"Solitude" became the center of one of those insane storms of controversy that frequently dog a poem so popular that it is widely reprinted in newspapers and magazines, but without a by-line. Colonel John Alexander Joyce (1840–1915) published in 1885 an autobiography titled *A Checkered Career,* which contained a poem identical to "Solitude" except for a transposition of its last two stanzas. Ten years later, in his revised autobiography *Jewels of Memory,* the colonel described how he came to write the poem in 1863 when he was attached to a Kentucky army regiment. Ella was understandably furious. She offered five thousand dollars to anyone who could produce a printed copy of the poem prior to its 1883 newspaper appearance. No copy turned up, but the colonel never ceased to claim authorship. "He is only an insect," Ella wrote in her second autobiography, "and yet his persistent buzz and sting can produce great discomfort."

Burton Stevenson, who devotes a chapter to all this in his *Famous Single Poems* (1935), reprints a paragraph from the colonel's first version of his autobiography, *A Checkered Life,* in which he admits being confined for several months to the Eastern Kentucky Lunatic Asylum in Lexington because of his "mania" for building a perpetual motion machine.

It is hard to believe, but Colonel Joyce managed to have published biographies of Edgar Allan Poe, Oliver Goldsmith, Robert Burns, and Abraham Lincoln, as well as worthless collections of prose and verse. The controversy he raised over "Solitude" might have died quickly had not Eugene Field (1850–1895), as one of his many practical jokes, kept devoting his newspaper columns to defending Mrs. Wilcox against Joyce. Ella was not amused.

Almost as well known as the opening of "Solitude" are the first four lines of "Worth While," from *Poems of Sentiment:*

It is easy enough to be pleasant,
    When life flows by like a song,
But the man worth while is one who will smile,
    When everything goes dead wrong.

It is true that the above lines sound as if Eddie Guest had penned them, but Eddie could never have written "The Winds of Fate," one of Mrs. Wilcox's most anthologized poems:

One ship drives east and another drives west
    With the selfsame winds that blow.
        'Tis the set of the sails
        And not the gales
Which tells us the way to go.

Like the winds of the sea are the ways of fate,
    As we voyage along through life:
        'Tis the set of a soul
        That decides its goal,
And not the calm or the strife.

Nor could Eddie have composed sonnets as well crafted as "Winter Rain," from *Maurine and Other Poems:*

Falling upon the frozen world last night,
    I heard the slow beat of the Winter rain—
    Poor foolish drops, down-dripping all in vain;
The ice-bound Earth but mocked their puny might,
Far better had the fixedness of white
And uncomplaining snows—which make no sign,
But coldly smile, when pitying moonbeams shine—
Concealed its sorrow from all human sight.
Long, long ago, in blurred and burdened years,
    I learned the uselessness of uttered woe.

> Though sinewy Fate deals her most skillful blow,
> I do not waste the gall now of my tears,
> But feed my pride upon its bitter, while
> I look straight in the world's bold eyes, and smile.

(p. 145)

As a good Christian Scientist, Eddie would have been incapable of poking fun, as Mrs. Wilcox did in "Illusion" (from *Poems of Power*), at Mrs. Eddy's belief that everything is *maya,* a dream, except God, the one sole reality:

> God and I in space alone
>   And nobody else in view.
> "And where are the people, O! Lord," I said,
> "The earth below, and the sky o'er head
>   And the dead whom once I knew?"
>
> "That was a dream," God smiled and said,
>   "A dream that seemed to be true.
> There were no people, living or dead,
> There was no earth, and no sky o'er head
>   There was only myself—in you."
>
> "Why do I feel no fear," I asked,
>   "Meeting you here this way,
> For I have sinned I know full well,
> And is there heaven, and is there hell,
>   And is this the judgment day?"
>
> "Nay, those were but dreams," the Great God said,
>   "Dreams, that have ceased to be.
> There are no such things as fear or sin,
> There is no you—you never have been—
>   There is nothing at all but *Me.*"

(p. 17)

Today's critics profess amazement over the once enormous popularity of Mrs. Wilcox's verse. Why, I don't know. Obviously she was not a great poet. In the prefatory poem of *Maurine* she called herself "only the singer of a little song," awed by the truly great poets of the past, and occupying only a minor place at the edge of poetry's "fair land." She was one of Longfellow's "humbler poets" whose "songs gushed from their hearts." Mediocre as most of her verse is, it is far from doggerel, and in my opinion superior to such non-poets as William Carlos Williams, so much admired by tin-eared critics who cannot abide musicality in poetry.

Mrs. Wilcox's resemblances to Shirley MacLaine are striking—one a famous promoter of New Thought, the other a famous promoter of New Age. Both were and are talented, attractive, energetic, unbelievably gullible, and totally ignorant of science. Shirley's talent is in acting, dancing, and singing. Although Ella loved to ballroom dance, to swim, and to play the harp and ukelele, her talent lay in writing poetry and prose.

So great was Mrs. Wilcox's fame that strange men were perpetually trying to meet and seduce her. "Lunatics I Have Known," a chapter in her 1918 autobiography, is devoted to such creatures, and how she had to seek police protection from some of them. The flames of their passions were fanned by totally false rumors about her many adulterous affairs and previous marriages. The truth is that she and her husband were each married only once, and throughout their lives deeply devoted to one another.

Like Mary Baker Eddy and Shirley MacLaine, Mrs. Wilcox broke away from a conventional Protestant upbringing, but retained an admiration for Jesus as an inspired teacher whose views, she believed, were mangled by followers. Her early interest in New Thought soon led to her becoming a Theosophist. She speaks in her autobiography of her first encounter with Madame Blavatsky's *Secret Doctrine,* and about her unbounded admiration for Annie Besant, the British theosophical leader. In addition to accepting the Eastern doctrines of reincarnation and karma, she also came to believe in astrology, palmistry, faith healing, astral projection (today called out-of-body experiences), the photographing of thoughts, and all forms of psychic phenomena including the ability of the dead to contact the living through voice mediums, slate writing, automatic writing, dreams, and Ouija boards.

Mrs. Wilcox's interest in spiritualism is detailed at length in *The Worlds and I.* She opens this second autobiography with a foreword that consists entirely of an editorial from a spiritualist journal, *Harbinger of Light,* and closes with a paragraph that could have been written by Miss MacLaine:

Back of all the spheres, at the center of all things, is the Solar Logos—God—from whom all the universe proceeds. In the immensity of space are vast heaven worlds, filled with spirits in various states of development from the earth-bound souls to the great archangels—all bent on returning to the source eventually and becoming "one with God." A wise teacher has said truly, "Orderly gradation is Nature's method of expression. Just as a continuous chain of life runs down from man, so also it must rise above him until it merges into the Supreme Being. Man is merely one link in the evolutionary chain." And Alfred Russel Wallace, who was called the grand old man of science, said, "I think we have got to recognize that between man and God there is an almost infinite multitude of beings, working in the universe at large at tasks as definite and important as any we have to perform. I imagine the universe is peopled with spirits, intelligent beings, with duties and powers vaster than our own. I think there is a spiritual ascent from man upward and onward."

And from this mighty storehouse we may gather wisdom and knowledge and receive light and power, as we pass through this preparatory room of earth, which is only one of the innumerable mansions in our Father's house.

Think on these things.

That last sentence repeats the last four words of Philippians 4:8, a favorite biblical verse among Christian Scientists and New Thoughters:

> Finally, brethren, whatsoever things are true, whatsoever things are honest, whatsoever things are just, whatsoever things are pure, whatsoever things are lovely, whatsoever things are of good report; if there be any virtue, and if there be any praise, think on these things.

As an illustration of Mrs. Wilcox's credulity and ignorance of science, consider the following paragraph from chapter 73 of *Every-Day Thoughts:*

> Hate is poison. I once visited the laboratory of a scientific man, where, by a peculiar combination of chemicals he was able to test the mental mood of a person who breathed into a glass cylinder. Different mental conditions produced different colors in the chemicals. Anger and resentment produced an ugly brown effect—and in the chemicals thus colored by anger, *a virulent poison* was generated.
>   This puts a scientific basis to the theory of spiritual-minded people. That hate is poison. (p. 249)

After her husband Robert died in 1916, Ella drifted into deep depression coupled with a great longing to communicate with him. He had promised that if he predeceased her he would do his utmost to reach her through the veil. Ella visited numerous mediums through whom Robert's voice seemed to come, and mediums who produced chalked messages from him on slates. Although Ella never doubted the honesty of these seers, or the paranormal phenomena they produced, she believed that evil or malicious spirits in the other world often claimed identities not their own. None of the messages she received impressed her as coming from her husband.

Finally, what she hailed with joy as authentic communications began to arrive—not through mediums, but through her own hands as she placed them, alongside the hands of friends, on a planchette. It scooted rapidly across the Ouija board to spell out messages just as vapid as those she had earlier received through mediums, but so desperate was Ella to make contact with her husband that she convinced herself the messages were genuine. Details of this sad story are in Ella's second autobiography in two chapters, "The Search of a Soul in Sorrow" and "The Keeping of the Promise."

Most voice mediums in those days spoke only with dead relatives and friends, not with entities who could describe a sitter's previous incarnations. Although Ella believed she had earlier lives, she is silent about them in her books. Had she been living today, she surely would have been as smitten by the New Age channelers as Miss MacLaine and other naive stars of stage and screen. Happily, we are spared details about Ella's former lives.

In spite of her scientific illiteracy and other limitations, Ella Wheeler Wilcox was a fascinating woman, a skillful writer of prose, and a poet of modest talents. Although not active politically or well read in economics, she held democratic socialist views that emerge in many of her essays. Her respect was low for great wealth and conspicuous waste. In *Every-Day Thoughts* she writes: "I believe in co-operative methods of business and in the public ownership of large industries. I have not the kind of brain which formulates the plans for such results, but I have the foresight to see their certain approach" (p. 7).

Mrs. Wilcox was dismayed by the horrors of war, poverty, and racial injustice, but her positive thinking made her an unbounded optimist. "Slowly but surely the world is gaining a higher moral plane; slowly, but surely, the selfish animal in man is giving way to Man the Image of Divinity. . . . The world is growing better with every whirl upon its axis" (*Every-Day Thoughts,* pp. 198–99).

New Thought optimism about the future of humanity was as irrepressible as it is in the optimism of Peale and Schuller. Here is another expression of it in one of Mrs. Wilcox's perishable poems from *Every-Day Thoughts:*

> Though the world is full of sinning,
>   Of sorrow and of woe,
> Yet the devil makes an inning
>   Every time we say it's so.
> And the way to set him scowling
>   And to put him back a pace,
> Is to stop this stupid scowling
>   And to look things in the face.
>
> If you glance at history's pages,
>   In all lands and eras known,
> You will find the vanished ages
>   Far more wicked than our own.
> As you scan each word and letter,
>   You will realize it more
> That the world to-day is better
>   Than it ever was before.
>
> And in spite of all the trouble
>   That abounds on earth to-day,
> Just remember it was double
>   In the ages passed away.
> And these wrongs shall all be righted,
>   Good shall dominate the land,
> For the darkness now is lighted
>   By the torch in Science's hand.
>
> Forth from little motes in chaos,
>   We have come to what we are,
> And no evil force can stay us—
>   We shall mount from star to star.
> We shall break away each fetter

That has bound us heretofore,
And the world to-day is better
Than it ever was before.

(pp. 192–93)

Next to Christian Science, the Unity School of Christianity is the largest and best organized of all the religions that trace back to Phineas Quimby and New Thought. Unity operates several hundred "centers" around the nation and abroad, and has a membership of millions. In today's New Age atmosphere it is growing about as fast as Christian Science is declining. Hundreds of books and pamphlets have come from its presses, of which Emilie Cady's *Lessons in Truth* (1894) has been a basic textbook and Unity's most popular work, as well as one of the classics of New Thought. Miss Cady was a homeopathic physician practicing in New York City. Her lessons had originally been published as a series in the magazine *Unity.*

Unlike Christian Science, which it strongly resembles in its pantheism and its emphasis on faith healing, Unity does not accept Mrs. Eddy's idea that sin, sickness, death, and the material world do not exist. It differs also in embracing the doctrine of reincarnation. Although it professes no dogmatic creed, its husband and wife founders, Mary Caroline (Myrtle) (1845–1931) and Charles Sherlock Fillmore (1854–1948), preached reincarnation, and most of today's Unity members share that belief.

Also unlike Christian Scientists, who have their own churches, Unity members prefer to remain inside Protestant denominations, attending churches of their choice, and at the same time seeking instruction from Unity centers and from its many books and periodicals. The three magazines with the largest circulation are *Unity, Daily Word,* and *Wee Wisdom,* the nation's oldest magazine for children. *Wee Wisdom* even has an edition in Braille.

A graduate of Oberlin College, Myrtle Fillmore began her spiritual pilgrimage as a Christian Scientist, though her contact was not through Mrs. Eddy's church but through Chicago's Christian Science Theological Seminary. This was a school founded and run by Emma Curtis Hopkins, a former editor of the *Christian Science Journal* who had been excommunicated by Mrs. Eddy for holding heretical views. After being healed of her tuberculosis by faith, Mrs. Fillmore founded her own version of Christian Science in 1889. At that time she was living in Kansas City, Missouri, with her husband Charles. He had been a wealthy real estate developer until he lost a fortune during an economic depression.

After his wife converted him to her brand of Christian Science, or perhaps New Thought is a better designation, Charles too was healed, or so he claimed, of a crooked spine, a short leg, and deafness in one ear. He had earlier developed an interest in spiritualism, theosophy, and Hindu mythology, and is said to have been responsible for introducing reincarnation (though not karma, which he rejected) into his wife's thinking. Braden, in his history of New Thought, reveals that Mr. Fillmore once told him that he (Fillmore) was the reincarnation of Saint Paul!

Unity's first magazine was called *Modern Thought*. The title was changed to *Christian Science Thought* in 1890, but when Mrs. Eddy complained and threatened legal action, the Fillmores shortened the title to *Thought*. Unity was a member of the International New Thought Alliance (INTA), until 1922, when it had grown so large that the Fillmores decided to go it alone.

Charles was so overwhelmed by the dropping of atom bombs on Japan that he wrote an article titled "The Atomic Prayer" that ran in *Unity*'s November 1945 issue. The following memorable extract will give you some notion of Fillmore's prose and scientific acumen:

> Our modern scientists say that a single drop of water contains enough
> latent energy to blow up a ten-story building. This energy, existence

of which has been discovered by modern scientists, is the same kind of spiritual energy that was known to Elijah, Elisha, and Jesus, and used by them to perform miracles.

By the power of his thought Elijah penetrated the atoms of hydrogen and oxygen and precipitated an abundance of rain. By the same law he increased the widow's oil and meal. This was not a miracle —that is, it was not a divine intervention supplanting natural law— but the exploitation of a law not ordinarily understood. Jesus used the same dynamic power of thought to break the bonds of the atoms composing the few loaves and fishes of a little lad's lunch—and five thousand people were fed.

Charles's posthumous book, *The Atom Smashing Power of Mind* (1949), is still available from Unity.

Although the Fillmores rejected Mrs. Eddy's denial that matter was real, and defended an endless series of reincarnations here on earth, in many respects they agreed with her views. Sin, sickness, and death were considered "unreal" and subject to elimination if one had the right thoughts. Like Mrs. Eddy, they took the Bible to be a revelation from God, yet a revelation that was not to be taken as historically accurate, but more like an allegory of truths. As in Christian Science, the doctrine of hell was considered blasphemous.

In his later years Charles Fillmore developed a curious aversion toward sex, regarding the act of love as robbing the body of "essential fluids" and hastening old age and bodily decay. Like Mrs. Eddy, he toyed with the notion that if one could only live up fully to the principles of Unity, the atom-smashing power of the mind might actually smash death and allow one to remain in his or her present body. When asked about this possibility, here is how he replied, as quoted in Ruth Tucker's *Another Gospel* (1989):

This question is often asked by *Unity* readers. Some of them seem to think that I am either a fanatic or a joker if I take myself seriously in the hope that I shall with Jesus attain eternal life in the body. But the fact is that I am very serious. . . .

It seems to me that someone should have initiative enough to make at least an attempt to raise his body to the Jesus Christ consciousness. Because none of the followers of Jesus has attained the victory over this terror of humanity does not prove that it cannot be done.

Like Mrs. Eddy, Charles Fillmore was inspired to write his own version of the Twenty-third Psalm. It could have been written by Norman Vincent Peale or any one of dozens of evangelists who stress the power of God to make one wealthy. Here is the psalm's amazing rewording as given by Fillmore in his book *Prosperity* (1936):

> The Lord is my banker; my credit is good
> He maketh me to lie down in the consciousness of omnipresent
>   abundance;
> He giveth me the key to His strong-box
> He restoreth my faith in His riches
> He guideth me in the paths of prosperity for His name's sake.
> Yea though I walk through the very shadow of debt
> I shall fear no evil, for Thou art with me;
>
> Thy silver and gold, they secure me,
> Thou preparest a way for me in the presence of the collector;
> Thou fillest my wallet with plenty; my measure runneth
>   over.
> Surely goodness and plenty will follow me all the days of
>   my life;
> And I shall do business in the name of the Lord forever.

                                                    (p. 60)

The Fillmores made plenty of money, all right, but like Mrs. Eddy, they lacked enough faith in God's atom-smashing power to live forever in their present bodies. After Myrtle died in 1931, Charles, then seventy-seven, married his longtime secretary Cora Dedrick in 1933. They ruled over Unity with iron fists until both passed on. When Charles died at age ninety-four, his sons took over. More can be read about Charles in Hugh D'Andrade's *Charles Fillmore: Herald of the New Age* (Harper and Row, 1974).

Now in the hands of Fillmore descendents, the cult is headquartered on a vast estate at Unity Village in Lees Summit, Missouri, a suburb of Kansas City. The village includes a large vegetarian cafeteria that is open daily to swarms of visitors, and operates a service called "Silent Unity." The service employs a large staff that is on duty twenty-four hours each day to provide free consultation by phone (of course donations are welcome) and to reply to every letter asking for guidance and help. Oral Roberts was the first Pentecostal evangelist to visit Unity headquarters and adopt just such a service for his ministry in Tulsa.

Next in size to Unity is Divine Science, founded a century ago by Nona L. Brooks and Mrs. Malinda Cramer. The Divine Light Federation in Denver sells two books by Brooks: *Mysteries* (1977) and *In the Light of Healing* (1986). Mrs. Cramer's *Divine Science and Healing* (1905) seems to be out of print. Hazel Deane's *Powerful is the Light: The Story of Nona Brooks,* published by Denver's Divine Science College in 1945, also seems to be no longer in print.

The next larger New Thought denomination big enough to support conferences and periodicals is the Church of Religious Science, founded by Ernest Shurtleff Holmes in 1927. It is still flourishing with some one hundred branches scattered around the United States. *Books in Print* (1991–92) lists more than thirty of Holmes's books and pamphlets, most of them published by Science of Mind in Los Angeles where the church is headquartered. Holmes edited a variety of periodicals, of which the monthly *Science of Mind* is still sold in New Age bookstores and even on some newsstands. Current issues stress the paranormal aspects of New Age ideas. Holmes died in Los Angeles in 1960.

Smaller church groups inspired by New Thought have risen and died over the decades with such names as the Society for the Healing Christ, Home of Truth, the Church of the Truth, Psychiana (a mail-order faith), and scores of others. It would take many pages just to cite the more influential New Thought thinkers of the past and today. Here are a few listed alphabetically with titles of their best-loved books:

- Raymond Charles Barker, *The Science of Successful Living, Spiritual Healing for Today,* and *You are Invisible;*

- Claude Bristol, *The Magic of Believing;*

- Robert Collier, *The Secret of the Ages, Prayer Works,* and *Be Rich;*

- Emmet Fox, *Power Through Constructive Thinking, The Sermon on the Mount,* and *The Lord's Prayer;*

- Ervin Seale, *Ten Words That Will Change Your Life,* and *Learn to Live;* and

- Ralph Waldo Trine, *In Tune with the Infinite.*

Other poets besides Mrs. Wilcox have been followers of New Thought, notably Edwin Markham, Victor and Angela Morgan, Don Blanding, and Margery Wilson.

Many Protestant ministers outside fundamentalist and evangelical camps have been strongly influenced by New Thought. We have already mentioned Norman Vincent Peale and Robert Schuller. Incidentally, although Peale poses as a mainline Protestant, he is on record as a firm believer in psychic phenomena of all sorts, including the reality of apparitions of the dead.

In the last few years the most surprising revival of New Thought, in a form closely related to Christian Science and Unity, is *A Course in Miracles,* said to be channeled by Jesus himself through Helen Schucman, a New York psychologist. The *Course*'s leading trumpeter is Marianne Williamson, now drawing huge crowds at her lectures in Manhattan and Los Angeles. Her 1992 book *A Return to Love* became such a hot seller that Random House gave her an advance of several million dolars for her next two books.

One of the admirable features of New Thought, at least among most of its leaders past and present, is its tolerance of beliefs other than its own. This is also true of most New Agers. Does not Shirley MacLaine, for example, frequently say that persons are free to do their own thing, to make their own space?

New Thought poet Edwin Markham expressed this tolerance well in "Outwitted," one of his most quoted poems:

> He drew a circle that shut me out—
> Heretic, rebel, a thing to flout.
> But Love and I had the wit to win:
> We drew a circle that took him in!

Ella Wheeler Wilcox shared the same sentiments. Let her have the final word. Here, from *Poems of Power,* is "The World's Need."

> So many gods, so many creeds,
>> So many paths that wind and wind,
>> While just the art of being kind,
> Is all the sad world needs.

(p. 159)

Selected Bibliography

Books Favorable to Mrs. Eddy and Christian Science

Beasley, Norman. *The Cross and the Crown*. Duell, Sloan and Pearce, 1952.

———. *Mary Baker Eddy*. Duell, Sloan and Pearce, 1963.

Carpenter, Gilbert C., Sr., and Gilbert C. Carpenter, Jr. *Mary Baker Eddy*. Pasadena Press, 1985.

Dickey, Adam. *Memoirs of Mary Baker Eddy*. Privately published, 1927. Reprinted by Butterfield Books, 1986.

Kennedy, Hugh Studdert. *Mrs. Eddy*. Privately published, circa 1940. Curiously, my copy of this well-crafted work bears neither the name of a publisher nor a date.

Knapp, Bliss. *The Destiny of Mother Church*. Christian Science Publishing Society, 1991.

Peel, Robert. *Mary Baker Eddy: The Years of Discovery*. Christian Science Publishing Society, 1966.

Peel, Robert. *Mary Baker Eddy: The Years of Trial.* Christian Science Publishing Society, 1971.

———. *Mary Baker Eddy: The Years of Authority.* Holt, Rinehart and Winston, 1977.

Powell, Lyman. *Mary Baker Eddy.* Macmillan, 1930. Reprinted by the Christian Science Publishing Society, 1950.

Siliburger, Julius. *Mary Baker Eddy: An Interpretive Biography of the Founder of Christian Science.* Little Brown, 1980. A psychoanalytic study.

Wilbur, Sibyl. *The Life of Mary Baker Eddy.* Christian Science Publishing Society, 1907. The first "official" biography.

Books Critical of Mrs. Eddy and Christian Science

Bates, Ernest Sutherland, and John Dittemore. *Mary Baker Eddy: The Truth and the Tradition.* Knopf, 1932.

Braden, Charles. *Christian Science Today.* Southern Methodist University Press, 1958.

Dakin, Edwin Franden. *Mrs. Eddy.* Scribner's, 1929. Revised edition, 1930.

Milmine, Georgine. *The Life of Mary Baker G. Eddy and the History of Christian Science.* Doubleday Page, 1909. Reprinted by Baker Book House, 1971.

Simmons, Thomas. *The Unseen Shore: Memories of a Christian Science Childhood.* Beacon, 1991.

Snowden, James E. *The Truth About Christian Science.* Westminster Press, 1920.

Springer, Fleta. *According to the Flesh: A Biography of Mary Baker Eddy.* Coward-McCann, 1930.

Twain, Mark. *Christian Science.* Harper and Brothers, 1907. Reprinted by Prometheus Books, 1986.

Zweig, Stefan. *Mental Healers.* Viking Press, 1932. Reprinted by Frederick Ungar, 1962.

Index of Names

251